Praise for the first edition:

"This volume contains some of the most intelligent writing on contemporary India that one is likely to encounter ... an engaging register of language and argument ... a unique publication."
– Burton Stein, *South Asia Research*

"... a picture of India that cannot be praised too highly ... absolutely essential reading."
– Gilbert Etienne, *Review Tiers-Monde*

"The considerable achievement of this book is to explain so much so clearly and so briefly."
– R. K. Newman, *International Affairs*

"He knows his India."
– G. P. Deshpande, *Economic and Political Weekly*

"A series of tightly constructed, closely argued essays ... a neat yet compendious volume."
– Peter Reeves, *Campus Magazine*

"... of great scope and sweep and densely packed with rich historical and contemporary data ... comprehensive and provocative ... fascinating reading ...."
– P. Radhakrishnan, *Indian Review of Books*

Changing India: Bourgeois Revolution on the Subcontinent
Second Edition

The revised edition of Robert Stern's book brings India's story up-to-date. Since its original publication in 1993, much has altered and, yet, central to the author's argument remains his belief in the remarkable continuity and vitality of India's social systems and its resilience in the face of change. This is a colourful, readable and comprehensive introduction to modern India. In a journey through its family households and villages, the author explains its long-lived and little understood caste and class systems, its venerable faiths and extraordinary ethnic diversity, its history as "the jewel in the crown" of British imperialism and its post-Independence career as a major agricultural and industrial nation. While paradoxes abound in an India that is constantly transforming, Stern demonstrates how and why it remains the largest and most enduring democracy in the developing world.

Robert W. Stern has written extensively on South Asia. His publications include *Democracy and Dictatorship in South Asia: Dominant Classes and Political Outcomes in India, Pakistan and Bangladesh* (2000).

Changing India

Bourgeois Revolution on the Subcontinent

Second Edition

Robert W. Stern

CAMBRIDGE
UNIVERSITY PRESS

PUBLISHED BY THE PRESS SYNDICATE OF THE UNIVERSITY OF CAMBRIDGE
The Pitt Building, Trumpington Street, Cambridge, United Kingdom

CAMBRIDGE UNIVERSITY PRESS
The Edinburgh Building, Cambridge CB2 2RU, UK
40 West 20th Street, New York, NY 10011–4211, USA
477 Williamstown Road, Port Melbourne, VIC 3207, Australia
Ruiz de Alarcón 13, 28014 Madrid, Spain
Dock House, The Waterfront, Cape Town 8001, South Africa

http://www.cambridge.org

First published 1993
Second edition first published 2003

Printed in China by Everbest Printing Co.

Typeface Adobe New Aster 9/12 pt.   *System* QuarkXPress® [BC]

A catalogue record for this book is available from the British Library

National Library of Australia Cataloguing in Publication data
Stern, Robert W., 1933–   .
Changing India: bourgeois revolution on the subcontinent.
2nd ed.
Includes index.
ISBN 0 521 81080 9.
ISBN 0 521 00912 X (pbk).
1. India – History – British occupation, 1765–1947.
2. India – History – 1947–   . 3. India – Social conditions.
I. Title.
954

ISBN 0 521 81080 9 hardback
ISBN 0 521 00912 X paperback

For Barbara

"See, while everything else was changing, so were we. We were changing too …"

George V. Higgins, *Bomber's Law* (New York: Henry Holt and Company, 1993), p. 39.

Contents

Maps and tables

Maps

Tables

Preface to the second edition

I posted the manuscript of *Changing India's* original edition to Cambridge in early 1992, some months before December when Hindu militants wrecked the Babri Masjid in Ayodhya. It was a major event in modern Indian history. And there have been others. The advent in New Delhi of a "Hindu nationalist" Bharatiya Janta Party-led government in 1998 was one, certainly. The on-going liberalization of the Indian economy had just begun in 1992. As had the climb to power of the Other Backward Classes that nowadays dominate Indian politics. The "Kargil War" of 1999 was a major event in India's international relations, and not only with Pakistan; as was America's "war on terrorism" in Afghanistan and the attack by *jihadis* on the Indian parliament in 2001.

In this second edition of *Changing India* I have tried to share with readers new to South Asian studies and colleagues immersed in them my observations of these and other changes over the past decade: not only in India, but in the ways in which I've come to understand it. To that end, I've done some signposting with phrases such as "since 1992," "over the past decade," and so forth. To fit it all in, I've had to edit some of my discussion of changes that took place before 1992. In some cases this wasn't at all difficult, and in others it was salutary. Hindsight gives us some perspective on the past. Still, "… what's past is prologue."* Not to everything, certainly, but to enough. And that may be particularly true of India where the past is long-lived and often disguises itself as the present. What I've particularly tried to keep is what the prologue helps us to understand of the present. Thus, for example, sacred

---

* *The Tempest*, II.i

ideologies and sacralized ways of doing business have in themselves lost currency over the decade, and even before that. But they've left their mark on the present and they help us to see how things have changed and to explain why they have remained the same. Why the Indian view of the naturalness of social inequality persists even as Indians participate as citizens in a genuine and well-established parliamentary democracy. Why that democracy is energized by the ancient and paradigmatically anti-democratic institution of caste. Paradoxes abound in changing India. The prologue links them to the present.

Glossary

ahimsa	Literally, non-violence. A concept common to Hinduism, Buddhism and Jainism; and given modern currency by Mahatma Gandhi.
Ashraf	Literally, nobility. North Indian Muslims of high social status.
Ayodhya	A temple town in Uttar Pradesh. The site of the Babri Masjid–Ram Janmabhumi Mandir imbroglio, and used as a shorthand name for it.
babu	Literally, father. A title for "white collar" bourgeois, in general, and Bengali *bhadralok* in particular. May be used descriptively or disdainfully.
baniya	A businessperson, or a member of a caste whose traditional occupation is business. May be used descriptively or disdainfully.
bhadralok	Literally, gentlefolk; specifically, members of those Bengali upper castes that cultivate the skills of literacy and numeracy and are inclined to educated employment.
bhakti	Hindu devotionalism; a medieval Hindu devotionalist movement.
Bharat	The Indian name for India: appears on currency, stamps, etc. in *devanagari* script. It may be used to describe rural India or used with folkish overtones.
bhujan	Common people, ordinary folks.
Bollywood	The Indian film industry, particularly the Hindi-language *filmi duniya* (film world) of Mumbai (Bombay).

Centre	India's national government.
crore	Ten million. A *crorepati* is a millionaire.
Dalit	Literally, the oppressed; the preferred name nowadays for groups that were referred to in the past as scheduled castes, untouchables, Harijans, ex-untouchables.
dar al-lslam	A place ruled according to the sacred laws of Islam. Its opposite is *dar al-harb*: the place of war and infidelity.
deshi	Of the countryside, local, Indian provincial. Also, *dehati*.
dharna	A traditional form of protest in which the aggrieved through self-inflicted punishment attempts to shame his or her antagonist into a negotiated settlement of their conflict.
Dilli durbar	The regime in Delhi.
durbar	The regime in a former princely state, the court. Also a public audience or reception.
garibi hatao	Literally, abolish poverty! A slogan, and no more than that, of prime minister Indira Gandhi.
gotra	An exogamous division of a caste, a clan.
gaddi	The head of government, "the throne." Literally, the cushion.
Hindutva	Literally, Hindu-ness; specifically, an ideological and programmatic commitment to "Hindu nationalism," although what exactly this would mean is unclear.
jati	Literally, breed; the village-based, face-to-face unit of caste. A quasi *jati* is a social group of non-Hindus with *jati*-like traits.
jajmani system	An asymmetric, "traditional," heritable and ritualized relationship, now largely vestigial, of goods-for-services exchange between a village *jajman* (patron) and his *kamin* (literally, lesser; client).
karkhana	A workshop, small factory.
Khilafat Movement	Between 1920 and 1922, a popular, anti-British Muslim movement in support of the Ottoman *khalifah*, and to which Mahatma Gandhi attached his Non-Cooperation Movement.
Maharaja	A Hindu client prince of the British Indian Empire. The Muslim equivalent is Nawab.
mandal	From the Second Backward Classes [Mandal] Commission Report of 1980. Used as shorthand for OBC-centered, caste politics. vb. *mandalize*.
mandir	Literally, temple. From the Babri Masjid–Ramjanmabhumi Mandir imbroglio and used as shorthand for *Hindutva*-centered politics.
mantra	A Hindu sacred formula, hymn, incantation; may be used disparagingly: a meaningless incantation.

Manuvad	Literally, Manu-ism: an ideological commitment to Brahminical Hinduism. The reference is the Code of Manu, which was probably written some time between 100–300 CE and designed to give divine sanction to a caste hierarchy in which Brahmins were on top.
masala	A mixture.
masjid	Mosque.
mullah	A Muslim cleric-cum-legist. Also, *alim* (sing.) *'ulama* (pl.).
Naxalite	Revolutionary communist militias, named for their early base of operations in the West Bengal countryside.
OBC	Other Backward Classes. The agglomeration of some thousands of castes which the Mandal Commission deemed to be "backward" and therefore entitled to reserved positions in central government employment and university enrollment.
panchayat	A customary council, of villagers or *jati* fellows, headed by a *sarpancha*.
panchayati raj	A statutory system of rural self-government instituted by Congress state governments in the late 1950s and afterwards.
pariwar	Family. See *sangh pariwar*.
purdah	Literally, curtain; the seclusion of Hindu or Muslim women, either in their homes or in public by costumes of conventional modesty.
Quaid-i-Azam	Great leader, Mohammad Ali Jinnah's title.
raj	Regime, kingdom, realm, rule, state, etc. The Raj refers to the former British government of India.
sanghathanan	Unity, specifically the unity of Hindus.
sangh pariwar	Literally, the family of organizations; that group of affiliated organizations that are ideologically and programmatically attached to *Hindutva*. The BJP is the *pariwar's* political party.
sarpancha	The head of a *panchayat*
satyagraha	Literally, truth-insistence; Mahatma Gandhi's name for his *dharna*-based strategy of non-violent conflict and conflict resolution.
shari'ah	Islamic sacred law.
shastra	A work of Hindu injunctive scripture, i.e., sacred law.
Sikhism	From the sixteenth century in Punjab, a religion largely synthesized from *bhakti* and Sufism. The Sikh faith is the *panth* (path) and the community is the *khalsa*.
Sufism	The Islamic expression of devotionalism and mysticism.

swadeshi	Reference to goods made in India, particularly in cottage and handicraft industries. The term was popularized by various nationalist movements, including the Indian National Congress's.
swaraj	Literally and vaguely, self-rule; popularized by Mahatma Gandhi.
tamasha	Show, spectacle, entertainment; may be used disparagingly: a meaningless show.
twice-born	A reference to castes of high social status, and generally accepted as belonging to the Brahmin, Kshatriya and Vaishiya *varnas*.
varna dharma	In Hinduism, a hierarchical order (*dharma*) of those categories (*varnas*) into which God divided humanity at the time He created it, viz. Brahmin (priest), Kshatriya (warrior and ruler), Vaishiya (producer of wealth), Shudra (worker).

Introduction

Change, the societies of India and Indian society

Bourgeois revolution and change

This book is about contemporary Indian society and how it is changing. More than a billion people live in India. Of every six people in the world, one is an Indian. Contemporary Indian society is heir to one of the world's great, enduring and eclectic civilizations. It permeates the entire Indian subcontinent, and its influence is manifest throughout Asia. In contemporary Indian society there are old ways that retain their vibrancy, their credibility and influence, and prevail. But, there are new ways as well: in a lively and well-established parliamentary democracy, a stable quasi-federal republic, programs of social and economic reform, modern agriculture and industry, science and technology, literature and art. In the meetings of old and new ways there are synergies no less than contradictions. Over the past decade or so, India has become an important player in the global economy. An increasingly assertive, nuclear- and missile-armed Indian Union is a major power today in Asia, the Indian Ocean and the world.

So, India is changing. Of course, it has always been changing: only the pace of change has varied from time to time, group to group and locality to locality. This insight of Hindu and Buddhist antiquity is apposite: change is the condition of everything that lives. Change is the condition of social continuity. Change may be barely perceptible even to those who experience it directly or it may be, as it is in India today, self-evident, rapid and profound. There may be ideological or pragmatic reasons for denying that change has occurred or for disguising its occurrence. But there is always change.

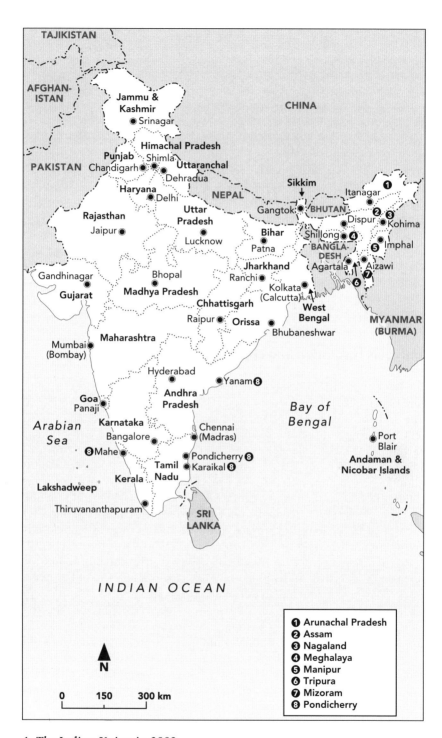

1 The Indian Union in 2002

It may, from a variety of causes, follow some dominant pattern. My argument is that nowadays the *dominant* pattern of change in India is what Barrington Moore, Jr. calls "bourgeois revolution." Moore defines his revolutions by the "broad institutional results to which they contribute."[1] Bourgeois revolution's essential institutional contribution is to the development *together* (allowing for leads and lags) of capitalism and parliamentary democracy. In my meaning, this development is synonymous with bourgeois revolution. It began in India and continues as a revolution from the top down. Increasingly as it proceeds, however, combining and incorporating elements in a society that long antedates it, it has become as well a revolution upward from expanding middle classes.

"Much of the confusion and unwillingness to use larger categories," like bourgeois revolution, Moore tells us, is because "those who provide the mass support for a revolution, those who lead it, and those who ultimately profit from it are very different sets of people." There is little confusion in India but that bourgeois revolution's leaders, families that have profited by it or even directly experienced its changes, have come largely from the middle classes. In general terms, these classes are comprised chiefly of families whose incomes are derived from employment in the educated professions (including politics, many of whose practitioners these days have been schooled at Hard Knocks), managerial and other higher salaried positions in modern industry and commerce, ownership of urban capital and of family farms that are engaged in commercial agriculture. While they have established their hegemony over most spheres of Indian public life, these classes are neither closed nor entirely self-perpetuating. Accompanying bourgeois revolution in India, and congruent with it, is substantial and accelerating embourgeoisement – the migration of new entrants into the ranks of the middle classes.

In the chapters of part I, I have focused my argument on the contributions of bourgeois revolution to changes in the basic social institutions of rural India and in the lives and fortunes of the seven out of ten Indian families that live in their country's more than 600,000 villages and country towns. More and more, villages and their villagers' institutions – families, castes and religious communities – are bringing themselves and being brought into the political and economic streams of a wider provincial and Indian society. Without replacing caste as India's customary social system, particularly of its countryside, class has increasingly impinged its secular values and considerations onto the sacred values and considerations of caste. The communitarian ties within castes and caste fragments have been strengthened by their participation as players and vote banks in provincial and national politics, and as actors in the countryside's institutions of civil society. Indian states have become at once the seats of vibrant, bare-knuckle, grass-roots democracies, and the constituent units of a stable and parliamentary democratic Indian multi-nation state.

Urban India is the focus of part II. Its chapters chart the general course in India of bourgeois revolution. Initially, its political and economic impetus was provided by the interaction between British imperialism and Indian urban elites. From the late nineteenth century, bourgeois revolution was domesticated in the subcontinent's nationalist movements: most critically, in the Indian National Congress under the leadership of Mahatma Gandhi. Since Independence in 1947, bourgeois revolution has been promoted and institutionalized by Congress Party governments and, more recently, by their successors at the Centre – the central government – in New Delhi and in the states of the Indian Union.

For my purposes, the concept of bourgeois revolution makes up for its theoretical shortcomings with its limited usefulness: its manageability and malleability. I use the concept to serve the purpose of organizational economy: the binding into one small volume of material that is virtually boundless. Arguments, it hardly needs to be said, are arguable. There are no definitive statements on the pages that follow. I use bourgeois revolution to serve the purpose of explanation. I do not imagine, however, that it explains everything. It is the *dominant* pattern of change in Indian society only in the sense that it describes the general direction of its political and economic development, and concomitant changes. There are crosscurrents and shores untouched by bourgeois revolution. It describes, in part, the recent revival of political Hinduism, for example. But changes in religious Hinduism, it hardly describes at all. It does not describe the proletarianization of small farm families, although their numbers may be no less than those of the families that have become *embourgeoisées*. The development in tandem, more or less, of capitalism and parliamentary democracy has not, or not yet, substantially effected any fundamental structural change in Indian society. Indeed, a recurring theme throughout this study is of the compatibility, adaptability and, even, functionality of long-lived Indian social structures to bourgeois revolution.

Is it really a "revolution" at all, then? My best answer is twofold. First, to concur with Moore that the "main problem, after all, is what happened and why, not the proper use of labels." We are not unused to questionable labels in Indian studies. In chapter 2, we encounter the label "sanskritization." It certainly described what *was* happening, but the label was regarded as misleading even by the distinguished anthropologist who designed it. Second, in chapters to follow, I hope this becomes clear: the development *together* in India of capitalism and parliamentary democracy has brought basic political, economic and social changes to the rapidly growing middle classes. Their families number in the hundreds of millions and they have become the directors and constituencies of political and economic change. Like any revolution, bourgeois revolution is partial in its own way.

There was and is no inevitability about bourgeois revolution in India. Capitalism and parliamentary democracy have not always developed together. They need not have in India. If, for example, from the latter decades of the nineteenth century, the British had been more successful in encouraging the collective participation in Indian politics of their client Indian princes and they, in turn, had had the foresight to participate collectively and seek the alliance of the new classes of Indian industrialists, we might now have no Indian bourgeois revolution to argue about. It is also possible that bourgeois revolution may be only a misunderstood and passing phase in India's history. Although this seems less likely today than it did in 1992. Certainly, bourgeois revolution has yet to reach more than a proportion – albeit, a substantial and growing proportion – of Indian families.

What proportion? It is accurate enough for us and convenient to follow India's National Council of Applied Economic Research and identify the Indian bourgeoisie as members of those families, rural and disproportionately urban, that constitute the rapidly growing upper income-earning half of Indian households: those designated by the NCAER as middle-middle, upper-middle and upper income groups.[2] To be sure, between the lower and upper edges of this range there are great differences in the capacity of households to purchase goods and services, and the same income buys more or less in different locations. But so it is for middle classes, however designated, in other places. Indian economic statistics, which in this case (as in most) should be understood as suggestive, indicate that this upper 50 percent of income-earning households account for about 70–75 percent of Indian household expenditure.[3] Given the prevalence within this privileged half of holdings in excess of legal land ceilings, black money and other under- and undeclared assets, its actual control of India's wealth is likely to be greater than the statistics suggest.

NCAER data indicate that the economic advantages that are enjoyed today by an upper half of Indian income-earning households were enjoyed a decade ago by about half that percentage. Statistics confirm what, I think, is self-evident to most observers: embourgeoisement in India has been rapid and profound. For those who demand statistics, embourgeoisement can be fairly well inferred from the coincident doubling over the past decade or so of household savings – a statistically understated middle-class phenomenon – and the more-than-doubling over the past decades of particularly middle-class consumption: of electricity for domestic use, for example, which trebled over the twenty years to 1990 and has trebled again since then. Or automobile (including taxi) registration, which has increased eightfold since 1970, and the registration of "two-wheelers" – the iconic vehicle of middle middle-class families – which is 50 times greater than it was 30 years ago. The production of refrigerators for domestic use is 30 times greater than it was in 1970 and the production of consumer electronics has more than doubled in the past decade.[4] Also, in the past decade, the provision of services – most of them consumed and/or attended to by middle-class families – has outstripped both agriculture and industry to become the largest sector in the Indian economy.[5]

The culmination of bourgeois revolution in India is no less likely to be a momentous event in world history than the transformation of China into a modern industrial state. Why is there so little understanding of this in the West? Three explanations, at least, come to mind: the methodology and underlying ideology of development economics, the rhetoric of Indian politics and economic planning, and our Western images of India.

Development economics tends to measure change in per capita terms. And in these terms, poverty is certainly more notable in India than is embourgeoisement. India's Planning Commission estimates that the percentage of Indians living below its poverty line has decreased from 36 percent in 1992–93 to 27 percent in 1999–2000.[6] 270 million people! To this figure we must add the tens of millions of Indians who are poor by any measure, other than that they manage to subsist above the official poverty line. India still provides the world with its largest national pool of poor people and illiterates, and the amelioration of their poverty and illiteracy over the decades has been slow. But India's development is not taking place here. It is not taking place per capita or among the poor. It is taking place in its expanding middle classes.

For development economists, the poor are the focus of change.[7] But in India they are neither the focus of change, nor the directors of change, nor their primary constituency. Nor are the poor the major participants in change, and they are certainly not its major beneficiaries. Neither are they likely to become so: not through proletarian revolution – whose occurrence becomes increasingly unlikely as bourgeois revolution proceeds – nor by "direct action" campaigns, nor by capturing the instrumentalities of parliamentary democracy, nor by dragging bourgeois revolution to a halt with the inertia of their poverty. The poor are certainly not passive. They are increasingly assertive. They affect the course of change and its pace, including the pace of embourgeoisement. They are the recipients of some varying and significant, managed and incidental trickle-down effects of bourgeois revolution. But the engine of change is in the hands of the middle classes, and they use it, not exclusively, but primarily, to serve themselves. Explicit and implicit government subsidies to the rural middle classes, for example, are far more generous than government expenditure on its various poverty alleviation programs. While the standard (Gini) index of income equality/inequality for India is much the same as it is for, say, the United States and the United Kingdom, the implications of income inequality in India are starker and bleaker. Thus, for example,

> ... in 1992–3, compared to the richest 20 percent of Indians, the poorest quintile had about 2.5 times the infant mortality and under-five mortality rates, double the fertility rate, and nearly 75 percent higher rates of child mortality ... [T]he [school] enrollment rate is 25 percentage points lower for the poorest households ... than for the richest households ... And the drop-out rate for the poorest households is about four times that of the richest ones.[8]

Sadly, this is unlikely to have changed much in a decade. So, measured in terms of the welfare of the other half of India's population, bourgeois revolution is a stunning failure. I do not want to be mistaken for one of bourgeois revolution's apologists. I do not invite development economists to be its apologists. They are doubtlessly correct in their assumption that reducing poverty is the straightest path to accelerating development. But that is not the path of bourgeois revolution in India. And it is unlikely to be made so by World Bank exhortations. Things are as they are. Development economists might be of greater assistance in describing them if, for example, they continue to turn some of their efforts in refining poverty lines to the construction of embourgeoisement thresholds and trickle-down indicators.

In India's constitution, its nine successive five-year plans, hundreds of its party manifestos, thousands of its laws and myriad speeches of its politicians, there is an ostensible commitment to a process of change whose chief beneficiaries are "the poor." "Socialism," once the talisman of economic development, even among Congressmen, has been largely abandoned, even by Communists. Indira Gandhi decorated her "emergency" of 1975–77, her assumption of dictatorial power, with the slogan, *Garibi Hatao* – abolish poverty. But it was only a slogan. Today Indian politics is befogged by assertions and counter-assertions, accusations and counter-accusations, among politicians of all parties as to why their policies and not those of their opponents are truly "pro-poor." This is not entirely the meaningless hypocrisy and meaningful fakery of politicians and their minions. It serves, for example, to give governments a legitimate purpose and the governed of the nether half legitimate demands. But it no more serves to describe the realities of change in Indian society nor the role of Indian governments in making them real than did the chimera of "socialism." Like the economists' poverty lines, the rhetoric of Indian politicians has drawn attention away from what is happening to what is not happening.

With regard to our Western images of India, this is what I wrote in the introduction to *Changing India*'s first edition:

> India is ... rather like a supermarket that specializes in exotica, that caters to our fantasies and our nightmares. We pick things off its shelves for our use, without knowing how they got there or where they came from. India supplied its poverty and super- stitions to the vocations of Christian missionaries. It supplied its spiritual insights to the enlightenment of European scholars and litterateurs. Its "underdevelopment" supplied the United States for almost two decades with a cause in Asia worthy of its surplus wheat and university graduates. Its plans for development and their implementation have supplied Western economists of all persuasions with grist for their publishers' mills, consultancies and anecdotes. For the perplexed and disillusioned among us, India supplies the dispensations of its itinerant swamis and guru- entrepreneurs. Its horror stories of bride burnings and female infanticide and human sacrifices, apparently provide for readers of our afternoon tabloids some variation from more familiar horrors and some assurance that however bad things are in New York or Northern Ireland they are worse in Calcutta and Bihar.

How much has changed in a decade? My guess is, not much. With the notable exception of Britain, where India and Indians and things Indian have established a presence, they remain very much on the periphery of our concerns. Compared to the coverage afforded to China and/or Japan by our quality media, the space allotted by them to news from India is sparse and most generous when we are part of the story or when it speaks to our interests or threatens us. The visit of an American president or an Australian cricket team is news. So is our vision of the Indian middle class as an omnivorous consumer of Western goods. India's relationship to Washington's "war on terrorism" is news, as is our worry about India's gate-crashing into our nuclear club. When the story is mostly about India, it tends to reinforce our stereotypes: naked *sadhus*, the colorful costumes of Rajasthani women, Bombay's *dhabawalas*, bandit queens and monkey men, and above all, the frenzy of religious "fundamentalism." Hindu zealots wreck a mosque in Ayodhya, and murder a Christian missionary in Orissa. Enraged Muslims incinerate a train-load of Hindu pilgrims, and a thousand people die in the aftermath of communal hatred. A couple that dared to marry across the barriers of caste are lynched by their relatives. These things, of course, have happened. But other things have happened as well, and are happening. One of them, the extraordinary emergence of India as a lively, genuine and stable parliamentary democracy is the central story of this book.

Alas, the stories of South Asia told by our university scholars have never had more than small audiences and readerships. South Asian studies have always been on the margin of our university curricula, and they have probably been further marginalized by recent inventions and reinventions of universities as service industries. Indian migrants to our silicon valleys have not come to bring us into their stories, but to make it in ours. From the spate of English-language novels set in India, the stories are mostly about the urban Indian middle classes. They are people like the novels' authors, and like us.[9] Things Indian – art and artifacts – are still largely fashion items. Exotica. And fashions change. I recall Ravi Shankar's musings in Sydney some years ago. "It's the sitar here today," he said, "tomorrow it will be the koto."

And what of the day after tomorrow? Consider. India is the second most populous country in the world. In no small measure as a consequence of governmental efforts that have succeeded in halving the general death rate and doubling the life expectancy of Indians at birth, India's population has trebled since it became an independent nation. To all but its Jeremiahs, this "population explosion" is much less worrisome now than it appeared to be in the 1960s. India's population is larger than it has ever been. But it is also healthier and more literate. It continues to grow, but at a decelerating rate. India nowadays produces more than enough food to feed itself. Once a land of famines, India is now a net exporter of food grains and famine is as unlikely there as it is in the United States. There are still hungry people in India, far too many of them; but they are a shrinking proportion of the Indian population, and their plight is a consequence not of the scarcity of food but – as is poverty in the West – of the maldistribution of income.

Increases in all food and other crops – cotton and sugarcane, for example – proceeded from land reform legislation of the 1950s and 1960s that virtually eliminated non-cultivating landlords from the business of agriculture and located agricultural production squarely in the hands of tens of millions of village households whose families own and cultivate small farms. In addition, government sponsored the consolidation of the fragmented holding of village farm families, established price and production incentives for farmers, expanded the area of cultivation, developed agricultural extension and research agencies, expanded credit and marketing facilities, facilitated a trebling of the area under irrigation and a manifold increase in the consumption of chemical fertilizers. Since the late 1960s, when the application of Green Revolution technology[10] to Indian agriculture began, the production of rice has more than doubled, the production of wheat more than trebled. Except for its cotton, jute and tea, a rural slum of the British empire before

Independence, the Indian Republic has become one of the world's two major producers of food crops.

Accompanying the post-Independence success of Indian agriculture is a social paradox. While on the one hand, India's poverty, illiteracy, its caste oppression and gender inequality, its "backwardness" is most prevalent and enduring in its countryside, on the other hand, it is there that bourgeois revolution in India has had its most critical social effect. When India became an independent republic, more than 90 percent of its population lived in villages, and village societies were overwhelmingly of peasants: of cultivators who were subject to political, economic, social and ideological direction by superordinate classes of non-cultivators – moneylenders; resident and absentee, aristocratic and capitalist landlords; imperial law-makers and bureaucrats. Here bourgeois revolution is social revolution. Nowadays, the combination of cultivator ownership, agricultural development and parliamentary democracy at state and local levels has turned that 20-to-25 percent of village households with viable holdings into families of farmers: no more subject than their counterparts in Iowa or Queensland to the direction of their non-cultivating betters.

In their economy and élan, the upper quintile-to-quartile of India's cultivating proprietors are capitalist: legally secure in their tenure, producing for an anonymous market, acquisitive, enterprising, socially mobile, exploitative of their laborers, ambitious for their children, politically assertive and *the* force to be reckoned with in local and state politics. Proper bourgeois! But, for the most part, petit bourgeois: only relatively large small-holders, rich only in comparison with the poor. Farming in India is overwhelmingly the small business of household families. Of these, fewer than 2 percent farm ten or more hectares. The annual incomes of only the richest farm households would even approximate those of successful urban professional men and women. Proper bourgeois! But not of closed middle classes. Inheritance and the market have taken their toll. Since 1970, the average size of farm holdings and the areas cultivated by large farmers have declined as percentages of the whole.

Many of the households with smaller holdings belong to families whose castes fall into the constitutional and political category of "Other Backward Classes." Typically groups of yesterday's small-holding peasants of plebian caste, today's OBCs are the New Men and Women of India. Over the past decade, the increasing power of OBC castes in caste-based or related politics at state and local levels, the crucial role of popularly elected state governments in apportioning political and economic favor, the non-existence of economies of scale in much of Green Revolution commercial agriculture and the assiduous use by small farmers of family labor: all have substantially eroded the post-Independence social and political status quo in village India. And all of this has set tens of millions of households of small-holders with middle-class aspirations on the route from peasantry to embourgeoisement. Following in the wake of OBC politics, rural India's most numerous landless underclass, known variously as scheduled castes, untouchables, Harijans (God's people), and, now, Dalits (the oppressed), have fought in the past decade as never before for political power, personal security and social honor.

Since 1970, the annual production of finished steel in India has increased more than fivefold, as has the production of commercial vehicles. The value of machine tools manufactured annually has grown from approximately the recent equivalents of less than US$10 million to more than US$400 million. Industrial production, in general, has more than doubled. Installed capacity for the generation of electricity has increased from about 16.3 million kilowatts to more than 105 million kilowatts, and the generation of electricity has increased more than eightfold to about 500 billion kilowatts. Chemical fertilizer production, which was about one million tonnes in 1970, is now about 14 million tonnes. Surfaced roads have increased in length from less than 400,000 kilometers to more than 1.5 million kilometers. Railway travel has doubled and freight-tonne kilometers have trebled. What was a fledgling motorcycle and scooter industry in 1970, is now one of the world's largest, producing more than 3 million vehicles each year. In the last decade or so, an electronics industry has sprung into being. It produces a full range of computer hardware and software, modern communications equipment and consumer electrical goods. This included about 3.5 million television sets in 1999–2000, double the number of five years earlier. Now major producers in the world of computer software, information technology companies in India have since the mid-1990s increased tenfold the value of their software production for export.

From Independence until little more than a decade ago, India's industrialization developed and languished within the confines of a planned economy, behind the barriers of an import-substitution policy, below the "commanding heights" of a dominant and uncompetitive public sector, inside a labyrinth of government rules and regulations pertaining to private sector industries and foreign participation in them. Within these confines, Indian industry and India as a great industrial nation were meant to develop. And they did. But the confines outlasted their usefulness. While much of Asia was booming in the 1980s, India's national income grew at an annual average rate of about 3.5 percent: derided by Indian economists as the "Hindu rate of growth" – the rate at which the economy "keeps growing no matter how badly [the government's] economic policy is formulated."[11] That formulation, "Nehruvian socialism," had by the end of the 80s produced the most regulated and protected, closed, subsidy-ridden, inefficient and corrupt major industrial economy outside of eastern Europe.

From the 1980s, and against the background of the "Asian miracle" in which India was a non-participant, its industrial development policies came under increasing criticism. They kept India far behind South Korea as an industrialized nation, for example, although the countries were on a par of underdevelopment in the 1950s. By 1991, the Indian economy was virtually bankrupt. The "conditionalities" of the International Monetary Fund's rescue package and the Indian government's ready acceptance of it added up to the end of "Nehruvian socialism." Import restrictions were lifted, the public sector was opened to competition from private sector enterprises, their regulation by government was eased and foreign investment encouraged. For a few years during the mid-90s, the Indian economy grew at the extraordinary – for India – annual rate of 7.5 percent. It has since been brought down to the accelerated "Hindu rate" of 5 percent in response to downturns in the international economy and in the Indian government's enthusiasm for reform: dampened, in no small measure, by the persistence in India of what Pranab Bardhan calls "equity politics" – something for every one of the growing number of groups that have the political muscle to sustain a demand for it.[12] "The opportunity created by the crisis [of 1991] ... dissipated. With no crisis in sight, the old political games involving various vested interests came back into play and the pace of reforms dropped dramatically."[13]

Equity politics and vested interests have their home in the public sector. It is the legatee of Britain's bureaucratic empire and yesterday's economic nationalism. In a wide variety of fields, from the manufacturing of drugs to gold mining, the public sector accounts for about one-quarter of the production of Indian factories. Many of these are "sick units," neither productive nor profitable. But they serve the interests of those whom they employ, their suppliers and labor unions; the bureaucrats who manage the factories and the politicians who use them to bestow grace and favor. Predictably, the shedding of such enterprises by a democratically elected government, through "disinvestment" – the public sale of a portion of their equities – and privatization, is likely to be sluggish. And sluggish it is.

Alongside the public sector, in the "mixed" Indian economy, private enterprise manufactures a full range of capital, intermediate and consumer goods, operates banks and manages hotel chains, wholesales and retails. Globalization notwithstanding and its consequent penetration of the Indian market by foreign multinational corporations, India's industrial economy remains overwhelmingly owned and operated by Indians. The great family conglomerates of the old economy, makers of everything from soap to steel, and lesser *crorepatis* (multi-millionaires) who profited under yesterday's industrial policy continue to profit under today's. Indian companies of the new high-tech economy – Wipro and Infosys, for example – and the new service industries prosper.

So, too, do smaller fish. Aided by a government policy of reserving certain product lines for their manufacture, thousands of small-business families and entrepreneurs all over India have made small-scale industry into a dynamic sector of their country's economy. These industries of the urban petite and moyenne bourgeoisie have increased their output more than twenty times over since 1970, and they produce about 35 percent of India's exports. In addition to small-business families, whose number has more than quad-rupled over the past decade or so, two other groups have added their number to India's urban middle classes. First are the 24 million university graduates who provide India with one of the world's largest national pools of technically and scientifically trained personnel. In India, as elsewhere, universities have been the factories for the production of candidates for embourgeoisement, and for adding numbers and social variety to the urban middle classes. Second are millions of skilled and semi-skilled workers whose bread-and-butter trade unionism has produced pay packets large enough to nurture middle-class aspirations for their children.

No more than Indian industry, has Indian culture been colonized from abroad. It is as powerful and persistent as any culture on earth. It has, of course, borrowed from the European West over the past two centuries, as it borrowed from the Muslim West in earlier centuries. But in almost all things, Indian culture is distinctively Indian. Indian Christianity and Islam are distinctively Indian. The recurring call of Hindu zealots for the "Indianization" of their Christian and Muslim countrymen is as preposterous as would be a call for the "Americanization" of American Jews.[14] For all their borrowings, Indian music and art – including film music and modern and pop art – remain distinctively Indian. So too, Indian cuisines. Most of the books read by Indians are written by Indians and published in India. English-language publishing flourishes in India, but so too does publishing in Indian languages. No worse nor better than the ordinary run of Hollywood films, the ordinary run of Bollywood films provides the foundation for an extra-ordinarily powerful and pervasive popular culture that is distinctly Indian. It will be clear, I hope, from subsequent chapters that India's political culture has mixed its Indian *masala* into Western parliamentary democracy and taken it for its own, as earlier, India did with other exotic imports such as chili, tea, the violin, nineteenth-century British bureaucracy and railways.

India can govern itself. The political center of Indian society has been occupied for more than a half-century by the Republic of India. In form, it is a quasi-federal, democratic republic whose political authority is consti-tutionally apportioned between a central parliamentary government in New Delhi, the Centre, and parliamentary governments in all twenty-eight of the Union's constituent states and some of its seven territories. Fifty years ago, political democracy was an exotic transplant in India. Against all odds, parliamentary democracy has become successfully domesticated, although less as an ideology, perhaps, than as a way of doing political business. Unless disqualified for some particular reason, all adult Indian citizens are enfranchised to vote for the national parliament, their state legislative assembly, local government or municipal council. The Indian electorate is the largest in the world. The proportion of it that usually votes, between 55 and 60 percent, is larger than it is in the United States and, I believe, no less well-informed or more gullible. By any comparative measurement, parliamentary democracy in India is genuine, stable, and adapted to its social environment.

For two decades in the states and three decades at the Centre, the Congress Party of Mahatma Gandhi, Jawaharlal Nehru and Indira Gandhi monopolized power. These were the years of one-party dominance. They were followed by some more years of unstable coalitions alternating in government with a fading Congress Party. Nowadays, coalition government has become the rule in the states, and a multi-party National Democratic Alliance led by the "Hindu nationalist" BJP (Bharatiya Janata Party – Indian people's party) rules in New Delhi. Thirteen elections for the lower house of the national parliament, the Lok Sabha, have been held since 1952. In six of them, and any number of times in state elections, the party or parties in power have been voted out. And they have gone out. This is my acid test for parliamentary democracy: when, in a reasonably free and fair election, a government is voted out of power, does it surrender its control of the army and the treasury, the home ministry and the national broadcaster, pack up and move to the opposition benches?

In India, as elsewhere, but perhaps more so in India, it is the interests of the middle classes that are best served by parliamentary democracy. As elsewhere, there have been lapses in India's democracy. Ballot boxes have been stuffed and "lost," politicians' hirelings have "captured" polling booths, criminals have exerted political influence and become politicians, political workers have been beaten, politicians have been murdered, voters have been bribed and intimidated, campaign funds have been extorted and collected from black money hoards. From 1975 until she was voted out of power in 1977, *and went* – perhaps, her finest hour – Prime Minister Indira Gandhi, in effect, suspended the workings of India's parliamentary democracy with her tyrannical and self-serving "emergency." Although their power is respected and feared, politicians, in general, enjoy no great reputation in India. There has been hardly a ministry, in the states and at the Centre, unsullied by the evidence of corruption. But by comparative third world standards, the improbity of Indian politicians, though certainly condemnable, is not much more than ordinary. What is extraordinary, by any standards, is that India has become one of the world's stable parliamentary democracies: that Indian politicians and bureaucrats have managed with more than workaday success to govern democratically and to integrate into one quasi-federal union a population that is generally poor, illiterate, dispersed, parochial, anti-democratic in its cultural biases and larger and more socially diverse than the population of Europe.

Parliamentary democracy, particularly at the state and local levels, has been India's general solvent for threats to domestic order. But when stubborn threats resist dissolution in parliamentary politics, Indian governments have not hesitated to meet violence with violence. The power of the gun is often abused, in India as elsewhere: by police brutality and corruption, indiscipline and partiality, bashings and killings of prisoners, stagings of "encounters" in which "militants" are murdered, insensitivity to the plight of the poor and socially despised. But by and large, state violence has been used successfully in India. Explosive tensions between castes and religious communities have usually been contained. In general, though not without violence, balances have been struck between the rights of Indian citizens to mount civil dis-obedience campaigns and the concerns of governments to dismount them. There have been a number of armed insurrections in independent India: in districts of West Bengal and Andhra Pradesh, in Punjab, perennially in Assam and tribal areas of the northeast, and with no apparent end in sight, in Kashmir. None have threatened the stability or the integrity of the Indian Union. At no small cost in life and to human rights, all have been suppressed or contained. Some have been reconciled.

In little more than half a century, India has fought three wars and a major battle with Pakistan and its proxy *mujahidin* and one disastrous war with China. Nowadays, New Delhi's relations with a nuclear-armed Pakistan are poisonous, and with a nuclear-armed China, uncertain. India's very expensive efforts to maintain a modern military establishment are driven by the usual forces, international and domestic, but among them is an intelligent appreciation of the need to defend itself against real and potential enemies. And India can defend itself. It can make nuclear weapons and send them off by ballistic missiles of its own making. Its military services are well-armed, well-disciplined, well-trained, well-led and subordinate to their political masters. This was most recently demonstrated in the "Kargil War" of 1999.[15]

The Indian Army is one of the world's largest and probably one of its best. In recent years, India has put into service a formidable, state-of-the-art "blue water" navy, complete with missile-armed corvettes, an aircraft carrier and modern submarines. The Soviet Union, once India's major arms supplier, has returned to the job as Russia. India's military forces can not only defend it against any present or prospective threat, they can as well show the tricolor. India is clearly the great power not only in South Asia but on the Indian Ocean's littoral, and it expects to be acknowledged as such. In the 1980s, that was the message of New Delhi's interventions into the internal affairs of Sri Lanka, the Maldives and Nepal. India is increasingly dismissive of any claims by Pakistan to parity with it, and increasingly insistent on being recognized with China as one of the great powers of Asia.

Looking forward from the first decades of the nineteenth century, Tocqueville saw in the United States and Russia what we, looking forward from the beginning of the twenty-first century, may already see in China and reasonably anticipate in India:

> There are at the present time two great nations in the world, which started from different points; [their courses are not the same] but seem to tend toward the same end. ... Both of them have grown up unnoticed; and while the attention of mankind was directed elsewhere, they have suddenly placed themselves in the front rank among the nations, and the world learned [of] their existence and their greatness at almost the same time.[16]

The societies of India and Indian society

When humankind's attention is directed to India, it will find a society that has, like Europe's, the diversities of a continent and the unities of a civilization. Moreover, these diversities and unities extend to the boundaries of the subcontinent which India shares with Pakistan, Bangladesh, Sri Lanka, Nepal and Bhutan. Within these boundaries, as within Europe's, political borders have changed over time and correspond only partially to ethnic boundaries and sometimes cut across them.

To take only the recent past: Early in the sixteenth century, Mughal invaders, out from Afghanistan and led by Babur, the founder of his line, began to build their Indian empire from existing Hindu and Muslim principalities and their fragments. That empire began to disintegrate from the middle of the eighteenth century. At its most extensive, under Aurangzeb, the last of the Great Mughals, his family's patrimony reached from Kabul to the Bay of Bengal, and from the Himalayas to the borders of what is now Tamil Nadu (see map 2). As the Mughal empire disintegrated, the British began to build their empire from its remains. By the middle of the twentieth century, when the British finally surrendered it, their Indian dominion had become the modern world's largest, most valuable and best-administered bureaucratic empire. It was partitioned into the republics of India and Pakistan in 1947. In 1970, Pakistan's eastern province rebelled and seceded with the aid of Indian arms to become Bangladesh. The Republic of Sri Lanka – until 1948 the British colony of Ceylon and not administered as part of the Indian Empire – is certainly a political and social division of the subcontinent. India was ceded the French territory of Pondicherry in 1956; it seized Portuguese Goa in 1961; and it annexed its protectorate, the Hindu

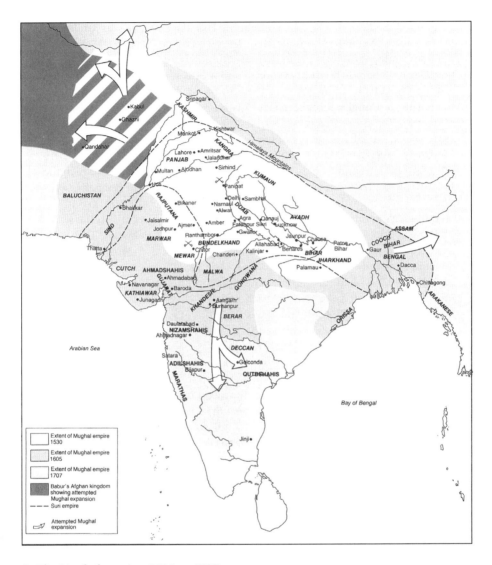

Map legend:

- Extent of Mughal empire 1530
- Extent of Mughal empire 1605
- Extent of Mughal empire 1707
- Babur's Afghan kingdom showing attempted Mughal expansion
- Suri empire
- Attempted Mughal expansion

Labels on map:

Kabul, Gnazni, Qandahar, Srinagar, Kishtwar, Mankot, KASHMIR, KANGRA, Himalaya Mountains, Lahore, Amritsar, Jalandhar, PANJAB, Multan, Ajodhan, Sirhind, KUMAUN, BALUCHISTAN, Uch, Panipat, RAJPUTANA, Bikaner, Delhi, Sambhal, Narnaul, Alwal, DOAB, AVADH, Bhakkar, Jaisalmir, Amber, Qanauj, Lucknow, SIND, Jodhpur, Ajmer, Fatehpur Sikri, Gwalior, ASSAM, Javnpur, Chausa, Ranthambor, BUNDELKHAND, Allahabad, Ratoa, COOCH, MARWAR, Chitor, Kalinjar, Benares, Bihar, BIHAR, Gaur, Thatta, Chanderi, MEWAR, JHARKHAND, BENGAL, CUTCH, AHMADSHAHIS, MALWA, GONDWANA, Palamau, Dacca, Ahmadabad, Navanagar, GUJARAT, Baroda, Chittagong, KATHIAWAR, Junagadh, KHANDESH, ARAKANESE, Asirgarh, Burhanpur, ORISSA, BERAR, Arabian Sea, Daulatabad, NIZAMSHAHIS, Ahmadnagar, DECCAN, Satara, Golconda, ADILSHAHIS, Bijapur, QUTBSHAHIS, MARATHAS, Bay of Bengal, Jinji

2 The Mughal empire, 1526 to 1707

kingdom of Sikkim, in 1975. The remaining Himalayan kingdoms are Indian protectorates: Nepal less so than Bhutan.

All the subcontinent's present international borders cut across ethnic boundaries. There is a Hindu majority and a Muslim minority of almost 85 million Bengalis in India, most of them in the state of West Bengal. Across the border in Bangladesh, there is a Muslim majority and a Hindu minority of about 130 million Bengalis. Until its discovery by cannabis and trekking enthusiasts, Nepal was best known in the West as the homeland of those doughty mercenary soldiers, the Gurkhas. Over Nepal's eastern border, there are 2.5 million Indian Nepali-speakers who want a "Gorkhaland" state in the Indian Union. Travelling eastward to Punjab: Punjabis, like Bengalis, were divided by the partition of the British Indian Empire. There are about 40 million Punjabis in India, almost all Sikh and Hindu, mostly in the states of Punjab and Haryana. In the Punjab province of Pakistan, there are approximately 100 million Punjabis, almost all of them Muslim. Among all Punjabis, Indian and Pakistani, the "dominant" caste is Jat. Sindh is in Pakistan, but there are about 3 million Sindhi-speakers in India. Now moving southward: more than 60 million Tamils live in India, most of them in the state of Tamil Nadu on the subcontinent's southeastern tip. Less than 100 kilometers away, across the Palk Strait, in Sri Lanka there are another 3.5 million Tamils. In their rebellion against the Sinhalese majority-dominated government of Sri Lanka, its Tamils have been the recipients of covert and not-so-covert moral and logistical support from Indian Tamils. In 1987, the Indian government became embroiled in two years of bloody, futile "peace keeping" in north and northeastern Sri Lanka. India's prime minister, Rajiv Gandhi was assassinated by a Tamil suicide bomber in 1991. The Sinhalese are ethnolinguistically related to the people of the subcontinent's north. Two thousand years ago, the Sinhalese were among the first people to receive the Lord Buddha's message from India.

Religion and religious communities spill across the subcontinent's political borders. India's Muslims, its largest minority, number about 120 million. There are approximately as many Muslims in Hindu-majority India as there are in either Muslim-majority Pakistan or Bangladesh. Together they account for the world's largest geographical concentration of Muslims, more than one-third of their world population. Across political borders, subcontinental Islam is as distinctively subcontinental, as European Christianity is distinctively European. Pakistan's Hindu population is minute, but Bangladesh, following Nepal, has the third largest Hindu population in the world: about 13 million.

Languages, too, cross the subcontinent's political borders. Bengali is the official language of West Bengal and Bangladesh. In both, there is a passionate attachment to their same language. Hindi is the official language of the Indian Union. Urdu is the official language of Pakistan. At the level of ordinary, day-to-day communications, Hindi and Urdu are basically the same language: except that they are written in different scripts and Urdu has a larger vocabulary of Persian and Arabic loan words and phrases. Because it is the language of Muslim high culture on the subcontinent, Urdu was chosen to be the official language of Pakistan. But Urdu is the mother-tongue of only a minority of Pakistanis, most of them migrants from India. The homeland of Urdu is around and about Delhi. Although they would now identify their language as Hindi, there are probably more Urdu-speaking Hindus in India than there are Urdu-speaking Muslims in Pakistan.

English is the distinctive and distinguishing language of the sub-continental haute bourgeoisie. It is their tool and their symbol. For the lesser bourgeoisie, English is the language of aspiration and opportunity, now more than ever, as India is joined to the global economy. A mastery of written and spoken English is the sine qua non for entrance into the elite bureaucratic services, the officers' mess, the executive suite, the upper reaches of the professions, the circles of artists and intellectuals who are invited to international conferences, the editorial rooms of influential newspapers and journals, the professorates of leading universities, the student bodies and old boys' associations of "great public schools" and fashionable colleges, the company of the distinguished, the beau monde of the best people, the celebrations of the rich, the right clubs and, now crucially for India, the world of the Internet and of India's burgeoning information technology industries.

This reality is little affected by surges from time to time, place to place, and political party to political party of the assertive populism of Indian politicians who decry the use of English and declare that Indian languages alone are truly and self-respectfully Indian. English-language adepts are, to be sure, a minority on the subcontinent, but they are its elites. They are the directors of modernizing change. Their ostensible, public style is modern and they are the exemplars of modernity. In India, their society has become attainable by the upwardly mobile, the beneficiaries of bourgeois revolution. For better or worse, and with varying success, it is English-speaking elites who are leading the subcontinent into the modern world and the modern world into the subcontinent.

Within India itself, diversities abound: of ethnicity, religion and in regard to both the modes and means of production. Along with Sanskrit, which is of great cultural, religious and sentimental significance, but spoken by hardly anyone, the Indian constitution "schedules" 17 widely spoken languages – really language groups. Hindi, across most of north India, has by far the largest number of designated speakers, about 400 million. The half-dozen languages after Hindi, and the approximate number of speakers attributed to them are: Bengali in the northeast (85 million), Telegu in the southeast (80 million), Marathi in the west (76 million), Tamil in the south (64 million), Urdu primarily in the Hindi-speaking north (52 million), Gujarati in the west (50 million). Speakers in these and all other scheduled language groups are geographically concentrated, as are speakers of European languages in Europe. Other than Sindhi (2.5 million, the language in India of migrants from Sindh, now a province in Pakistan), Urdu and Nepali, every scheduled language group provides the official language of one or more states of the Indian Union – Hindi in the states of northern India, Bengali in West Bengal and Tripura, Telegu in Andhra Pradesh, Marathi in Maharashtra, Tamil in Tamil Nadu, Gujarati in Gujarat, Kannada in Karnataka, Malayalam in Kerala, and so forth. In each state, the majority of its population or a substantial plurality are reckoned to be speakers of its official language.

Of India's ethnic diversity, however, its constitution's scheduled language groups and the official languages of its states are only the surface. Language-speaking in India, as elsewhere, is only a central trait in an ethnic complex of traits. The Marathi-speakers of Maharashtra, for example, are an ethno-linguistic group. They belong to a society that is distinctly Marathi, not only in its language, but in its history, social structure, religious practices, literature and art, customs and manners, diet and dress. The ethnic distinctiveness of Marathis is no less than that of Swedes or Spaniards, for example, nor more than that of Bengalis or Tamils. Moreover, the first language of most people is unlikely to be the scheduled language attributed to them, but rather one of hundreds of "mother-tongues" – dialects – that politicians and their linguists have grouped together to form a scheduled language group.

Some mother-tongues are themselves central traits in an ethnolinguistic complex and some are more or less assimilable than others in the inclusive ethnolinguistic group indicated by its scheduled language. Some mother-tongues that have been grouped together in a scheduled language are mutually intelligible and some are not. In every state there are minorities, whose mother-tongues are included in other states' scheduled language groups or in none of these. About 38 million people speak mother-tongues that are not included in the constitution's scheduled language groups. Most of these people belong to tribal groups, of which there are hundreds in India. In the northeast, some tribal groups – Nagas, Mizos, Bodos, for example – have fought protracted guerrilla wars against the government and/or their non-tribal neighbors to preserve or reclaim their tribal identities. In response, New Delhi has since the 1960s complemented its violent repression of tribal uprisings with attempts to mollify tribal demands by creating six states in each of which particular tribes are a majority or a substantial minority. In 2000, the Indian government carved from three existing states in the

Hindi-speaking north, three new states: all of which have substantial tribal minorities and established tribal political movements.

Groups differentiate themselves from one another by caste within virtually all non-tribal ethnic groups throughout India. Ideologically, caste is an institution of Hinduism. But there are castes and quasi castes among Muslims, Christians, Sikhs, Buddhists, Jains and Jews. Legitimately, one becomes a Hindu caste member only by being born of parents, both of whom were born into that caste. Caste membership can be renounced or revoked, but one can never, or hardly ever, except through subterfuge, join or be joined into a caste other than that of one's parents. Caste is the group into which one must marry to remain a member in good standing and to endow one's children with caste membership. According to the traditional or prescribed occupations of their members, by sumptuary taboos and commensal restrictions, castes are customarily differentiated as being of relatively high or low ritual-cum-social status. Though this is less the case now than it was in the past. Caste systems too are changing. Virtually all castes are areally centered and exclusive to the people of a large ethnolinguistic division. Telegus have their castes, Malayalam-speakers have theirs, and so forth. Castes are, in Tonnies' famous term, *gemeinschaft*, "communities of fate": "us" as differentiated from "them." There are thousands of castes, and quasi castes, their fragments and aggregates in India. Second only to families, of which they are demonstrable or ideological extensions, castes provide the Indian countryside with its basic social and political organizations.

To their operations as Hindu societies' basic social units, castes have readily added the function of representing their members' interests in the rough and tumble of Indian politics: as interest groups, vote banks, party blocs and even parties. Caste is an ordinary consideration in pre-selections of party candidates and post-elections divisions of the spoils. Representatives of their castes contest for membership of virtually every institution that has access to public resources: state ministries, university councils, municipal corporations and village *panchayats*. Castes have become so integral a part of the Indian political scene that it is hard to picture it without them: these organizations of Hindu inegalitarianism that vitalize and are vitalized by Indian parliamentary democracy

Cutting across large ethnolinguistic and even caste differences in India are diversities of religion. Sikhs belong to the same castes and often the same families as their Punjabi Hindu neighbors. Within the same non-Hindu tribal groups and some of the same castes of south India, some segments are Christian and some are not. The most important lines of religious diversity, however, are between Hindus and Muslims. Muslims are everywhere in India. Forty percent of them live in the Hindi/Urdu-speaking north, where they are 11 percent of the population. Jammu and Kashmir, famously, is the only state of the Indian Union to have a Muslim majority: of about 65 percent.

In Kerala, West Bengal and Assam, Muslims are between 20 and 25 percent of the population. Everywhere in India, Muslims are part of their local society. They live in the same villages and towns as non-Muslims, they speak the same mother-tongues and read in the same languages. Hindu castes and Muslim quasi castes, though generally separate from one another, are usually parts of the same local societies. Though less now than in the recent past, Hindus and Muslims of the same local societies sometimes professed more or less the same religious beliefs and performed some of the same or similar religious rituals.

From the latter half of the nineteenth century, Hindu and Muslim politicians, aided and abetted by the British government of India, began to imagine and invent the agglomerations of their coreligionists as two separate religious "communities" that menaced each other with secular competition and sacred contagion.[17] British "constitutional reforms" and other imperial legislation of the early twentieth century – the 1905 partition of Bengal province and the Punjab Alienation of Land Act of 1900, for example – politicized communalism. Strife between religious communities followed. Its usual form was and is the communal "riot": an occasional short-lived volley of arson and assault between Hindu and Muslim neighbors in pursuit of a local quarrel. From the middle of the 1920s, communal riots became ordinary, recurring events on the Indian political scene. Muslim divines accelerated their efforts to purify their humble coreligionists' faith from the taints of Hinduism, and thus to distinguish them from Hindus. Hindu revivalists fulminated against trespasses of Muslim conquerors and proselytizers on *Bharat Mata* (Mother India).

While census-takers and scholars began increasingly to appreciate the similarities between Indian Hindus and Muslims, they began increasingly to think of each other as different. The partition of the subcontinent between India and Pakistan in 1947 was accompanied by a communal bloodbath in Punjab and Bengal. In the towns and cities of independent India, communal riots are, again, ordinary and recurrent. Encouraged by increasingly militant, well-financed and ideologically oriented communal organizations, tensions between Hindus and Muslims and the incidence and destructiveness of communal riots have steadily increased. From December 1992 and into the new year, there occurred the first communal rioting on a subcontinental scale since Partition. In the north Indian temple town of Ayodhya, Hindu zealots, cheered on by their politicians, wrecked a mosque, the Babri Masjid. In the folklore of Hindu revivalism, the mosque was built on the ruins of a Hindu temple – Ram Janmabhumi Mandir – that marked nothing less than the birthplace of the Lord Ram and was desecrated and destroyed on the order of a Mughal emperor. Initially, the incident sparked murderous riots in several towns across northern India, in Mumbai, and in cities in Pakistan and Bangladesh. What followed was the opening of a festering wound in communal relations, now simply called "Ayodhya." It is no closer to healing in 2002 than it was a decade ago. Hindu zealots are determined to rebuild their Ram temple on the Babri Masjid's ruins. Muslim defenders of the faith are determined to stop them. A confrontation between them in February 2002 resulted in an explosion of murder, arson, pillage – the most bloodstained communal rioting since 1992. The BJP-led government that Ayodhya brought to power and that now stands between the communities is widely mistrusted, on the one hand by Muslims and, on the other, for its apparent betrayal of the Lord Ram, by the forces of *Hindutva*, "Hindu nationalism."

India is as economically diverse as it is ethnically and religiously hetero-geneous. It is like a vast museum of technology. Agricultural techniques vary from the slash-and-burn of some tribal people to laborious cultivation by tens of millions of hardscrabble farm families; to Green Revolution, capital-intensive, market-oriented farming by cultivating entrepreneurs. Through Indian towns and cities, streets spill over to their footpaths with carts, bicycles and rickshaws pushed and pulled and pedaled by men and boys; donkeys loaded with sacks of goods; vehicles drawn by horses and bullocks and camels; motor scooters, three-wheeled goods and passenger carriers; over-aged and overloaded trucks and buses trailed by their stinking black exhaust; sleek new Japanese-model hatchbacks, Tata 4x4s, and light com-mercial vehicles. Modern buildings are built with the labor of women hod-carriers who scale bamboo building frames with pots of bricks and mortar balanced on their heads. Modern technology is used to build modern engineering and electronic equipment. The small business sector includes *karkhanas* (workshops) that bang and clang with a family's labor on the ground floor of its living quarters and the sleek offices of computer software suppliers and advertising agencies. In Bangalore, there is a twenty-first century, state-of-the-art, internationally competitive information technology industry. In Mumbai, an intricate fit of nineteenth-century technologies – trains, bicycles, hand-written codes and manpower – delivers daily and with great efficiency home-cooked, hot lunches to thousands of the city's office workers.

The lines that separate Indians into ethnic groups, castes and religious communities are hatched and cross-hatched with the lines of class. Among the 180 million or so Indians who live in cities with populations of over 100,000, proper cities, and particularly among those in modern industrial and professional employment, class consciousness and conflict are facts of urban life, no less than they are in comparable cities elsewhere. In villages and small towns, class consciousness is not so clearly articulated and class conflict tends to be absorbed or incorporated into patron–client relationships and factional and caste conflicts. But even here, in the countryside, wealth and power are intruding more heavily than they have in the past and even displacing the traditional caste criteria of social status.

Finally, different Indians live in different moral universes. The difference is most pronounced between that modern universe inhabited by the educated, urban, upper-middle class, and the universe inhabited by villagers. The difference manifests itself as a matter of course in the non-observance by villagers of laws made in New Delhi: for example, injunctions against the practice of untouchability, child marriage, female infanticide. On the issue of *sati*, the difference is profound and emblematic. Two recent incidents of widows immolating themselves on their husbands' funeral pyres, in 1987 and 1999, attracted national media attention. It seems clear that both Roop Kanwar, an educated young women from an upper caste family, and Charan Shah, an elderly Dalit, chose to die as *satis*: women who embody the Truth. Embarrassed Indian governments reacted by (unsuccessfully) trying to make a homicide of the first case, and ruling the second a suicide. In the modern universe, the official attitude is that widows who immolate themselves on their husbands' pyres do so prima facie as a result of coercion or despair, or both, and that the practice – thankfully, a rarity nowadays – is barbaric, obscurantist, misogynous, corrupt, "a pagan sacrifice," a dark secret of India's past, a national disgrace, a matter for police or psychiatrists. In the village universe, throngs of villagers worship at the shrines and temples dedicated to *satis* of the past. There the deaths chosen by Roop Kanwar and Charan Shah are thought to manifest courage and dutifulness that transcend death, and they are honored as additions to the role of those women who bless and are blessed.[18]

How do the unities of a civilization give coherence to a society so diverse as contemporary India's? What, in other words, makes an Indian society? It begs rather than answers the question, I know, to say its Indian-ness. But that is perhaps a way to begin. What constitutes Indian-ness? Certainly, it is no less a quality than European-ness; and like it, Indian-ness is something resembling a complex of characteristics which those who share identify with themselves and each other, and by which they distinguish themselves from others and are distinguished by others. I would include among these more or less shared characteristics: myths and mythologies, memories of the past, the sense of a common fate – now and in the future, religious, philosophical and intellectual traditions, political ideologies and modi operandi, emotional and affective conventions, self-perceptions and notions about others and the world in general, prejudices and stereotypes, ideas about morality and propriety, affinities of social structure, language, physiognomy – actual and perceived – music, art and architecture, diet, dress and adornment. Indian-ness partakes of the sacred and the mundane; and arbitrarily and only for the sake of expository order, we might untangle, divide and consider these characteristics under the following headings.

First, second and permeating almost all of the sacred, both giving life to the characteristics of Indian civilization and living in them, are Hinduism and Islam. Hinduism and Islam are not only different religions more or less separating their faithful – benignly, usually, although sometimes not – but as well components in an Indian civilization more or less shared by Hindus and Muslims. Hinduism is first, both in its antiquity, its numbers, and its Indian-ness. A religious cosmography, Hinduism's concern is with the whole order of the universe and everything in it. Its location, however, is in India and among Indians. All the world's major religions save Hinduism settled and resettled in places that already had long histories. The histories of Hinduism and India began together and have remained, almost exclusively, together. Like other religions, Hinduism was the font of a great culture whose monuments decorate its world: in words and music, brick and mortar, metal, stone and paint. But, really, Hinduism lives in Hindus.

It lives in their daily lives all over India: in the families, castes and villages where most Hindus live. In no small measure, these are Hindu institutions. To be born into a Hindu family is to be born into a caste. To be born into a caste is to be born a Hindu, there is virtually no other way. To be born a Hindu is to have a caste place, however notional, in Hindu society. Hindu society is for most Hindus their village. Its rules are for the most part Hindu rules. Proper relationships within a family between young and old, male and female, husbands and wives; legitimate marriages, births, adop-tions, inheritances; appropriate behavior within a caste, among its members and between castes, among their members; right deportment, occupation and exchanges of goods and services within a village – all are prescribed, thought to be prescribed, represented as being prescribed by Hinduism.

The great gods and goddesses of the Hindu pantheon are everywhere in India. The rituals in their worship vary from place to place, they are known by various names and recognized in varying iconographies, they share their devotees' ardor with local gods and saints, they may be worshiped as idols or as emanations of the One that is the essence of All. But everywhere are Ram and Krishna, Siva and Ganesh, Laksmi and Saraswati, Parvati and Durga. Their images are present and revered in homes and temples, shops and factories, government offices and schools, buses and rickshaws, bodily decor-ations and amulets, shrines by the wayside and in the middle of city streets. Their stories are celebrated in great festivals, commemorated by pilgrims, carved and painted, read, recited, acted, danced, sung and, now, broadcast, screened, televised and preserved forever on videotape and DVD.

No less than great and folk culture, is popular culture in India infused with Hinduism. Though not hung in art galleries and museums, the most popular genre of painting in India today is graphic art: par excellence, the illustrations that decorate the tops of calendars. Mass-produced prints are available, with or without calendars, framed or unframed, in bazaars all over India. The illustrations are usually portraits and they usually portray Hindu gods and goddesses. They are in extensive use not merely as decorations but as icons. Sculptors, who have for generations carved marble idols of gods and goddesses for Hindu temples, nowadays use calendar art portraits as their models. Calendar art merges its Hinduism into the films: the visual art supreme of popular Indian culture. India is the largest feature-film-producing country in the world. Every day a number of Indians roughly equivalent to the population of Australia go to the movies. India's best known and most parodied films are the Hindi-language features of Mumbai's Bollywood, but there are other film industries all over India that make movies in virtually all of its most widely spoken languages. Nearly every Indian film industry produces its repertoire of dramas that celebrate the Hindu pantheon and Hindu virtues. The goddess Santoshi Ma, who first manifested herself to urban housewives, was brought into the Hindu pantheon by her calendar art portraits and a Hindi film of the 1970s, now preserved for the faithful on videotape. In the 1980s, Indian television presented it viewers with what has undoubtedly been the most widely attended recitations of the Hindu epics *Ramayana* and *Mahabharata* in their millennial histories. These days, every god and goddess has "his [and her] day on the tube" in apparently endless series of television "mythologicals."[19]

Indian politics is suffused by Hinduism. From the Republic's inception, some of its most contentious political questions have been provoked by Hinduism. Thus, although Indian society is overwhelmingly Hindu, the Republic of India is a constitutionally secular state. To what extent should the government of such a state try to support moral principles derived from the religion of most Indians, for example, by banning the slaughter of cows? To what extent should it try to reform social practices of the Hindu majority, for example, by prohibiting the giving and taking of dowries and the marriages of children? To what extent should it try to enforce its constitutional mandates to interfere in the social practices of the majority, for example, by prohibiting the practice of untouchability? To what extent should the government of a Hindu-majority nation and a secular state insist on legislating one secular civil code for all Indian citizens when the apparent preference of India's Muslim minority is to retain *shari'ah* law as its civil code?

The communal conflict over the Ram Janmabhumi Mandir–Babri Masjid first surfaced in the late 1980s. From then until the present, there has been no more bitterly fought and argued question in Indian politics than that of *Hindutva*: its compatibility with the Indian state's constitutional commitment to secularism and its impact on India's religious minorities – particularly Muslims. *Hindutva*, made manifest in Ayodhya, is certainly the most massive and turbulent force below the surface of Indian politics. Millions and millions of Hindus – young and old, left and right, rich and poor, high caste and low – would like their government to be not simply Indian but Hindu. This has been reflected over the past decade or so in the coincident increase in the occurrences and savagery of Hindu–Muslim, inter-communal violence and the spectacular rise to power of the BJP. From a party of the Hindu petty bourgeoisie of north Indian towns, the BJP has risen to become the leading party in a nationwide National Democratic Alliance (NDA) that rules at India's Centre. Even within the NDA, however, *Hindutva* is a vexed question. Virtually all the alliance's parties other than the BJP reject *Hindutva* as an ideology or a program. The BJP's allies are in the NDA not to affirm an ideology, but to win elections and share power. So, for the time being at least, secular opportunism – the guiding "ism" in Indian politics, as it was in the beginning and is now – has mooted the question and shelved the ideology. But, for the first time in the Republic's history, India has at its Centre a governing party that Muslims, in general, mistrust and apprehend, and it is attached to a "family" of Hindu revivalist organizations which they despise and fear.

Second only to Hinduism is Islam, an integral part of India's Indian-ness. Over most of north India, Muslim *durbars* (princely courts) had come and gone over six centuries until the nineteenth. Things Islamic and Muslim and large populations of Muslims have been in north India for eight centuries. The social and religious practices of these Muslims have been profoundly, characteristically affected from their having grown over the centuries among converts from Hinduism and in a Hindu heartland. No less profound and characteristic have been the contributions from Islam and Muslims to the Indian-ness of contemporary Hindu society. Incorporated into the devotions of many ordinary Hindus all over India, for example, are the *dargahs* (tombs) of Muslim Sufi saints. Any number of these, in terms of their patronage and to all appearances, have been transformed into Hindu shrines managed by Muslims.

Certainly and not surprisingly, in the items of India's composite Indian-ness, the defining ingredients are more often than not provided by Hinduism. But Islam's contributions to the *masala* have been great and undeniable. From the patronage of Indian Muslim potentates and magnates, composites emerged in art and architecture, music and dance. In high and popular culture in all their manifestations, Islam has left its mark on Indian-ness. Sufis, no less than Hindu devotionalists and mystics, *bhaktis*, and people who drew their inspiration from Sufism and *bhakti*, gifted India from the eighth to the sixteenth century with an unrivalled capacity for religious benignity and tolerance – a capacity which it may yet rediscover. Of the Sufi–*bhakti* enterprise, Kabir, the revered poet of the late fifteenth century, leaves us with this snapshot:

> O servant, where dost thou seek me?
> Lo! I am beside thee.
> I am neither in temple nor in mosque:
> I am neither in Kaaba nor in Kailash
> Neither am I in rites and ceremonies,
>   nor in Yoga and renunciation.
> If thou art a true seeker, thou shalt at once see me:
>   thou shalt meet me in a moment of time.
> Kabir says, "O Sadhu, God is the breath of all breath."[20]

Bhakti, which had its beginnings in what is now Tamil Nadu, spread northward in the centuries that followed the eighth until it engulfed the subcontinent. Sufism came into India from the north. It shared with Hinduism a belief in God's immanence. Like Hindus, and particularly *bhaktis*, Sufis expressed their devotion in music and dance. Like their Hindu counterparts, there were miracle-working Sufi saints. They gathered *murids* (disciples), as did *bhaktis* gather their *shishayas*. Some Sufis belonged to religious orders, and some of these claimed and/or were acknowledged to be orthodox in their Islam. But there were orders outside the *shari'ah*. There were Sufis who belonged to no order: preachers of sermons, singers of songs, God-intoxicated mystics who said, with Kabir, that they were neither Muslims nor Hindus. They were God's lovers, visionaries, ecstatics, comforters, prophets, miracle-workers. Not entirely but enough, *bhakti* and Sufism melded into one another, particularly in north India. Sikhism is an amalgam.[21] But the largest product of the devotionalist ferment that pervaded medieval India is the subcontinent's Muslim population of half a billion and a distinctively subcontinental Islam that reaches from village roots to high culture.

In south India, in general, there are fewer Muslims and less of Islam, but there, too, they are part of the Indian fabric. Because Arabs were in the spice trade from the eighth century and India's Malabar Coast was one of its locations, Muslims are 20 percent of Kerala's population. Andhra Pradesh, whose Muslim population is about 8 percent, has its capital in Hyderabad. Until 1947 it was the capital of India's leading Muslim prince, the Nizam, its most famous Muslim court and a major center of Muslim high culture on the subcontinent. What is now the state of Karnataka, with a Muslim population of about 11 percent, had been within the orbit of Muslim imperial politics and religious proselytization from the early fourteenth century, and during the eighteenth was ruled by a short-lived but vigorous Muslim dynasty. Tamil Nadu, virtually the only part of the subcontinent that was beyond the furthest extent of even the Mughal empire, has a Muslim population of about

5 percent. No less than their coreligionists in the north, Muslims in south India are integral parts of those local and regional societies that patch and blend into the fabric of Indian society.

The creation of Pakistan ripped away only the edges. But, often with tragic consequences, the Indian fabric has not been for Muslims everywhere, and at all times, protective and secure. For too long, conservative Muslim politicians looked to Congress's one-party dominance to protect their power and influence in the Muslim community and to provide it with a vote bank's security. It was the security of political stultification. Now, the present and future are uncertain. For many Muslims, the BJP remains the party of Ayodhya: of Hindu politicians who slandered Islam and defamed Indian Muslims, and cheered while Hindu thugs wrecked the Babri Masjid and afterward led a campaign of murder and arson against the Muslims of northern India and Mumbai. The cumulative effect of violence and uncertainty has been to undermine Muslim confidence in the fabric. Yet they have no other. They are part of it, and it of them. Hinduism and Islam in India are analogous to Christianity in Europe in this sense: they are at once major sources of cultural cohesion and social conflict.

Indian-ness partakes of the mundane no less than of the sacred. Vital parts of India's composite civilization have been derived from its experiences of British imperialism. Indeed, virtually every major public institution in India derives from those experiences: the use of English, homeopathic medicine, the post office, the railways, the army, the bureaucracy, the legal system, the Westminster model of government. All have been domesticated, integrated into the composite: become Indian institutions. As any traveler on Indian railways can attest, they are distinctively Indian. The Anglo-Indian legal system has become the Indian system. English has become Indian English. It was, I think, the eminent psychiatrist and public intellectual Ashis Nandi who quipped that cricket was an Indian game invented in Britain. Much the same might be said about parliamentary democracy. Other than the tiers of rural self-government (*panchatyati raj*), every major public institution that bears directly or indirectly on India's parliamentary democracy – suffrage, an elected parliament of two houses, cabinet government, a bureaucracy and a military subordinate to political masters, a free press, modern universities, public education – were all, for India, "invented" in Britain. But they play as an Indian game. The Lok Sabha is a very Indian parliament. Parliamentary elections in India are very Indian. As bourgeois revolution proceeds, the Indian polity becomes more and more prominent as a cohering force in Indian society.

Second only to religious celebrations, election campaigns and political demonstrations of one sort or another have come to provide India with its great public festivals. They are festivals in affirmation of Indian nationality, replete with their appropriate Indian luminaries, *mantras*, rituals, iconography, hagiography and demonology. These are well-known and immediately recognized, though taken with a pinch of salt. Politics are an ordinary topic of conversation among ordinary Indians. Politicians and their *tamashas* (celebrations) may be held in general and increasing disrepute, but that politics translate into influence, wealth and power, loans and jobs, electricity, schools and paved roads is widely appreciated. Widely appreciated, too, is that the prizes of politics go to those who can compete for them and that the competition takes place within the arenas of an Indian polity. To men and women who were, or whose parents were, just a short time ago imperial or princely state subjects, citizenship in democratic India promises, at least, the rights and dignity of participants in the determination of their fate and their children's. To Indian bourgeois, in whose lifetime their country was scorned and ridiculed for its backwardness, the Indian Union promises citizenship in a great power.

The economic dimensions of Indian civilization have been greatly enlarged by capitalist development. It has created Indian markets for goods and services. A perquisite of Indian citizenship is privileged access to these markets. And it is largely a privilege of the middle classes. The doctor from Tamil Nadu who practices in Delhi. The manufacturer in Kolkata who sells his goods in Karnataka. The farmers in Punjab whose wheat is consumed all over India. A decade of economic liberalization notwithstanding, government still looms large in the Indian economy. The public sector, owned and managed by the central and state governments, accounts for about one-fifth of the output of India's factories. India's major banks are in the public sector. Directly and indirectly, government decides who pays taxes and receives subsidies; the supply of money and the availability of credit; how black money is to be turned green, foreign direct investment treated, and capital markets regulated; what resources are allocated for infrastructural development; which "sick units" in the public sector are to be "disinvested" or privatized and how the interests of their managers and employees are to be protected. In a word, the government has made involvement in the Indian economy, at least for the middle classes, a crucial characteristic of their Indian-ness.

Over the centuries, there have developed among Indians, as among Europeans, ordinary continental similarities and familiarities. So for all their diversities, Indians are likely to recognize as Indian rather than something else the food that other Indians eat, how they look and act, their styles of life and ways of going about things, their histories and languages. In recent decades, all of this has been made increasingly recognizable by rapidly expanding communications media and educational facilities. Feature films and television dramas shot on location all over India identify to their audiences unfamiliar people as Indians and unfamiliar landscapes as parts of India, and make these familiar according to the Indian cinema's tried and true formulae. India Radio's network has grown from six stations in 1947 to almost 200 now, and they reach just about 100 percent of the Indian population. Since 1959, India has built one of the largest television networks in the world. Until the mid-90s, television broadcasting was largely a government monopoly and its programming was heavy on government propaganda, news, social up-lift and education, but light on fun. Nowadays, Doordarshan (the government channels) competes with a host of Indian and foreign cable providers – Star TV, Zee TV, CNN, for example – for audience share and advertisers' rupees. The channels resound with sitcoms, movie re-runs, game shows, as well as programs that are meant to inform and enlighten and in many cases do so – for Indians about India and the world. Either in their own homes, 75 million of them, or in those of their neighbors, most Indians nowadays are at least occasional television viewers. Over 20,000 periodicals circulate in India, of which about 1,600 are daily newspapers: published in English, every scheduled language, and other Indian languages and mother-tongues.

Governments in India have largely failed to provide adequate systems of free, public primary and secondary education for citizens. Nonetheless, literacy has increased substantially over the years, as have enrolments in secondary and primary schools, and in all cases the gender and probably the caste gap has narrowed. The languages used in most mass media communications and in education at all levels are provincial, but most of the ostensible messages are Indian: in popular culture, current affairs, geography, history, the social sciences, sport, fun. The underlying message is: This is India and you are its citizens.

Part I

The changing countryside

My discussion in part I is of the Indian countryside's basic social institutions, from the smallest to the most inclusive, and how they are all changing. Families, with particular regard to their female members, and villages are the topics of chapter 1. Chapter 2 focuses on that unique Indian institution, caste. Class, in its several manifestations, is the topic of chapter 3. In chapter 4, I discuss ethnolinguistic homelands-cum-states of the Indian Union. Religion, and particularly Hinduism, as it affects these institutions and is affected by them, is part of the discussion in general.

Although the institutions of part I vary considerably in their structure from one place to another, I have tried with whatever success to describe them generally for a non-specialist audience. My own experiences have given a north Indian bias to my descriptions. I describe the institutions in part I as changing and emphasize their participation in bourgeois revolution. In doing this, I have necessarily, though not exclusively, focused my discussion on rural middle classes.

Chapter 1

Families and villages

Families are the oldest, most prevalent and enduring social institutions everywhere in the world. In Indian villages, families prevail and endure as the basic social institution. Villagers think of their villages as the homes of families. The homes of individuals are in their families. Villages are the basic arenas of cooperation and conflict among families. Families are the constituent units of the larger, inclusive institutions that are described in the chapters that follow.

Families

If in *Anna Karenina*'s first paragraph, Tolstoy had extended his observations from happy and unhappy to ideal families, he might have said of these that they exist in reality nowhere and intrude upon reality everywhere. So it is in India. The basic family unit is, as elsewhere, the household. In the Indian ideal, however, the household is the home not of a nuclear but of an extended family. A family that is both described and idealized as the Hindu or, more accurately, Indian joint or extended family.

Of the ideal Indian joint family, grandfather is the patriarch. Grandmother is his deputy: in charge, particularly, of day-to-day household management, women's and children's affairs, the calming of troubled waters and the smoothing of ruffled feathers. Living under the same roof and taking their food from the same hearth are the couple's married sons and their wives, unmarried sons and daughters, married grandsons and their wives and unmarried grandsons and granddaughters. Children are usually married early.

When sons and grandsons are married, their wives are brought with them to live as in-laws in grandfather's house and their children become the household's children. When daughters and granddaughters are married, they are sent to become in-laws in their husband's households and their children become the children of those households. Marriages are celebrated as the crucial events in a family's life cycle. They are regarded as family affairs of the utmost importance. They are almost certain to have consequences for the family's harmony, reputation, prosperity, integrity and, ultimately, its very survival. The primary function of marriage is to produce sons. Marriages result from the careful arrangements of worldly and responsible adult members of the household and not from the serendipity of brides and bridegrooms, innocent and fanciful children. The ties that bind the household are consanguinal, not conjugal.

With its center in the household, the family is expected to serve its members as a moral community, a productive enterprise, a purchaser and consumer of goods, and a support group. A man is expected to behave in his village as a member of his family. He has no higher moral duty as a householder than to act on his household's behalf. A villager's neighbors are likely to judge his actions as wise and good if they benefit his family. The costs of a villager's actions that are foolish and bad are likely to be assigned to his family. Within the family, ordinary conflicts are anticipated and tolerated, but best closed to the outside. The family that is all for one and one for all behaves properly and appropriately.

The productive enterprise of most middle-class village families is in cultivable land. They are farm families. Of the family's enterprise, grandfather is normally treated as the actual or titular director. But his sons are his coparceners. Other than children too young to work, all members of the family contribute their labors directly or indirectly to the family's enterprise and all draw their sustenance from it. The work of villagers who are neither landholders nor cultivators nor middle class is also generally done as a family enterprise.

Not only dependent children, but the aged, the ill, the maimed, the handicapped, the widowed and orphaned, the unemployed and underemployed, the downcast, the despondent and the down-and-out are meant to be cared for by their families. The social services provided by a variety of institutions in the West are in the provenance of families in India's villages. In times of need, villagers turn to their families, and they are expected to do the needful. Universally, and at the very least: "Home is the place where, when you have to go there,/ They have to take you in."[1]

When grandfather dies or retires or becomes incapacitated, his position as family head descends, ideally, on his eldest son, and the household carries on as before. More likely, however, and still compatible with the joint family ideal, when grandfather dies, his sons partition the family's real and other property equally among themselves and establish their own, separate households. These give the appearance of being nuclear families when their children are young, but ideally they are joint families-in-becoming and will become so when sons marry and bring their wives home to live.

As a customary general rule, only grandfather's sons or grandsons inherit any of the family's real property at his death; although his widow may hold part of the family estate as a lifetime annuity. Her sons are bound in family duty to care for her and any other widows of the household and to assume responsibility for arranging their sisters' weddings and providing their dowries. If grandfather had had no sons or grandsons, the family's real property would properly pass at his death to his brothers or more distant kinsmen in his father's line. Women's inheritances do not come primarily from their husbands' but from their fathers' families: they come when they marry and in the form of money, jewelry, clothing, household and other movable goods. Their dowries. In Hindi, they are called *stridan*: the gift to a woman.

Like all family ideals, this one affects reality more than it reflects it. While the joint family household certainly persists in reality, its ideal structure is exceptional and real families do only imperfectly what they are meant to do ideally. Fortuitous circumstances and ordinary human imperfections account for some of the gap between the ideal and the real, but some of it – of particular concern here – is accountable to family adaptations to the exigencies and opportunities of life in contemporary India. In any case, the gap is not so wide as to separate the ideal from having its effects on the real. Far from it. For most Indians, family ties take clear precedence over all others; they bind closely and as a matter of course a more extended group than the nuclear family of parents and their unmarried children. Extended or extra-nuclear family organization is based almost invariably and exclusively – with some exceptions – on descent through the male line and male kinship. Groups of exceptions, now decreasing in number, are among some tribal people and a few matrilineal groups in Kerala. Another group of exceptions, fairly recent and probably increasing, are the elderly or widowed parents of urban middle-class families who retire to their daughters' households.

Sometimes the gap between the ideal and the real is the apparent result of family demography. There are families without sons, and sons without fathers. There are families whose sons are unmarried children. Sometimes the gap is a matter of choice. There are fathers who choose not to have their sons live with them, and sons who choose not to live with their fathers. The ideal does not prevent such choices, although it might prompt and shape relevant explanations and rationalisations, inferences and gossip.

Where joint family households have been more or less established, they may be more or less disestablished at any time before the patriarch's demise. In the Indian folklore of family disharmony, the proverbial saboteurs of the family's consanguinal jointness, the agents of subversive conjugality, are the household's daughters-in-law. They live within the interstices of the binding ties of blood, only caught in them but not a part of them. In the presence of the family's hierarchy, daughters-in-law are expected to show no particular concern for their own children other than as children of the household, nor are they expected to show any signs of affection for their husbands or to court any. Joint family etiquette suits joint families. And privacy is hard to come by. The proper relationship of daughters-in-law to the patriarch is one of respectful distance; to the matriarch, one of obedience and deference to her status as their husband's mother. It is the duty of daughters-in-law to behave compatibly with their husband's parents, rather than their duty to behave compatibly with their sons' wives. If brothers- and sisters-in-law are compatible, then well and good; if not, there are no sibling bonds to take the edge off even ordinary incompatibility. In a word, daughters-in-law are the most likely members of the family to be disaffected. Or to be blamed for the disaffection of their husbands.

The shoe may, of course, fit; or it may be purposely misfitted to disguise tenuous and attenuated ties among the household's men. Daughters-in-law live in the moral communities of their husbands' families and are expected to behave accordingly, but they are not really of them. The moral community's substance is the family's substance: the ties of blood among men. When these seem not to hold, a daughter-in-law's disaffection is a family affliction that merits sympathy and indicates a specific flaw rather than a general weakness. Scapegoats vary in kind but are universal in their use. Oblations to ideals! It will come as no revelation to observers of the Family of Man that fathers and sons and brothers are quite capable of mistrusting and despising one another without the connivance of their wives.

Disaffection can wreck a joint family household. Disaffection can also be one of any number of reasons for a household to vary from the joint family model. Convenience, preference and necessity are reasons. Household dynamics provide reasons, as do social and economic dynamics outside the family and beyond its control. The capacity of Indian families to contrive variations on and from the joint family model provides our first example of the Indian genius for preserving the valued substances of social institutions by allowing and even facilitating circumstantial changes in their form.

So, for whatever reasons, a husband and wife may live separately from his paternal household, with their children, under their own roof, taking food from their own hearth. But they may choose not to separate the husband's portion of the family's holdings, and continue to cultivate it as if they were unseparated members of his father's household. Or, they may choose to separate the husband's portion and cultivate it separately, but continue, for example, to accept his father's authority in making marriage arrangements for the couple's children and the husband's responsibility for contributing to his sisters' dowries. Or, they may not accept his father's authority or the husband's responsibilities to his sisters, but for the sake of appearances, domestic peace, whatever, act as if they do – or, act as if they don't. In general, there is a sort of continuum in Indian village family organization. At one pole, there is the archetypal, model joint family: patriarchal, patrilineal and patrilocal. At the other pole, there is the model nuclear family of parents and dependent children. Between the poles, and tending toward one of them, are myriad variations, of which the sketchy illustrations here are only a sample.

In lieu of contributing his labor to the work of cultivation, the adult son of a farm family household may remit some of his income from an urban occupation. Such remittances are common. For many farm families, they have become an important source of income. Usually, they secure for the remitter his coparcenary rights in the household's land holdings and, otherwise, his good standing as a family member. He may continue to live in his father's household and commute to work, depending upon its location and circumstances and his proclivities and those of his family. Or his wife and children may continue to live in his father's household and he may return to it regularly, irregularly, often, once in a while. Or his nucleated family, living apart from his father's household and seeing little of him, may be managed by his wife as its de facto *karta* (eldest male). Or his wife and children may live with him in an urban nucleated family: really a conjugal module, more or less, of his father's household. Or they may live with him in an apparently proper, sociologically standard urban nuclear family; although they may (or may not) preserve some ties his father's household.

In contemporary India there has been an enormous growth in the number and variety of urban occupations and their accessibility to villagers. This is the consequence of developments that we have yet to discuss: industrialization and urbanization, the development of transport facilities and services, the growth of education and the use of regional languages in occupations where English was once the medium. For village families, urban occupations are perhaps most notable as producers of remittance income. For poorer households, remittances may mitigate underemployment. Often, in modest household enterprises, in land or otherwise, more people are doing the work that could be done as well or better by fewer people and, consequently, more people are being sustained by a family income that could better sustain fewer people. Sending sons off to work in town and harvesting their pay packets or postal money orders provides some relief. For better-off and well-to-do village households, remittance income may be one among other substantial benefits they receive from sons who work in towns and cities across India and around the world – benefits of their participation in bourgeois revolution.

There is no evidence in the various studies of Indian village families to indicate that there are nowadays fewer households which approximate the joint family model than there have been in the past. Based upon what evidence there is, the observations of the sociologist A. M. Shah suggest changes in the social location of joint family households. And these are consistent with different patterns of bourgeois revolution. Thus, while in the past there was a disproportion of joint family households among well-to-do, upper caste families, nowadays, among one section of these families – the socially and spatially mobile professionals – the joint household is giving way to the nuclear. The "business class," however: "... from the richest industrialists down to petty shopkeepers, is steeped in joint family culture. So, also, is the [urban] lower middle class ... ."[2] And so is the political middle class. In the succession to political office, in the ministry in virtually every Indian state, in the hierarchy of virtually every political party, politics is as often as not a family affair.

Middle-class families hold to joint family ideals and to variations from it as a result of increases in life expectancy and the "formation and accumulation of household assets due to economic development ... and [the] use of joint household organization for upward economic and social mobility."[3] Increasingly, for middle-class farm families, upward economic and social mobility leads in one generation to membership in the urban professional middle class. Thus, a farm family that aspires to invest in a career in medicine, for example, for one of its sons, must be able to afford the considerable opportunity and out-of-pocket costs of his education through university. As a means of insuring its investment, among other things, the family may choose to arrange a suitable marriage for its doctor-to-be while he is still a dependent student, thereby precluding his own arrangement of an unsuitable marriage when he becomes a self-supporting practitioner. Then, there will also be the costs to his family of maintaining his wife (off-set, to be sure, against her dowry) and, perhaps, their children. If the investment produces a successful urban medical practice, the household can look to it as a source of substantial remittance income.

Some of this can be reinvested in land, in urban careers for other sons of the household and in substantial, good-husband-catching dowries for its daughters. Having a successful doctor in the family should also enable it to ask for substantial dowries and brides from well-to-do and well-connected families, otherwise facilitate its access to the well-to-do and well-connected, provide a reliable hedge against life's contingencies and a cosy retirement for grandfather and grandmother. But, however tied economically and otherwise to the village household of his father, our hypothetical doctor is almost certain to live apart from it. Any lucrative medical practice will certainly be in a town or city. There, our doctor will live in a modern, urban, more-or-less nuclear family of his own. At least until his sons marry. Or until one or both of his or his wife's aged parents come to live with him – another variation on the joint family model. Or, his family may in time become as unambiguously nuclear, in reality if not in ideology, as its Western counterpart.

Families, of course, need wives and mothers. Now, modern wives and mothers suit modern, urban, more or less nuclear families. Modern wives are educated women: women who can share their husbands' interests, be their companions, entertain their friends and colleagues, raise their children to succeed in the modern world, manage their households and cope with city life. As India produces more and more modern men – it has, we know, become a supplier of doctors to the world's cities – the demand for modern Indian wives increases. To meet this demand and benefit from it, relatively well-to-do village families began doing some years ago what would have been unthinkable to them in past generations. They started investing in university educations for their daughters. By and large, the initial motivation for doing this was to meet the demands of modern men for modern wives. For a village family that can hope to make an advantageous marriage for its daughter and sees the advantages of having a successful modern man for a son-in-law, its daughter's education, along with her personal and familial attributes and her dowry, of course, form part of her family's negotiating package. Many of India's modern men are New Men, first-generation-up-from-the-village, and so increasingly are many of their modern wives. Whatever currently motivates their families' interests in educating them, many of these modern women will sooner or later do the work for which their education has pre-pared them: school teaching, medicine, law, government service, university lecturing, business management, engineering and so forth. Whether or not an educated wife aspires to a working career, inflation and the increas-ing availability and attractiveness of modern consumer goods to modern families may simply be more than her bread-winning husband can manage on his own.

In pages to follow, we return often to a discussion of village families in the context of bourgeois revolution. A first, summary statement is perhaps appropriate here. Among the many other ways that better-off and well-to-do village families accelerate bourgeois revolution and reap its rewards are through their investment of family resources: first, to educate and accom-modate the trained personnel necessary to that revolution; and second, to do this as a family enterprise, more or less assuring the family, thereby, of some return on its investment.

Thus far, I have only alluded to women as members of their families. I want now to put them and their condition at the center of my discussion.

Variations from the joint family ideal structure do not ordinarily include organizational ties between a man and the families of his mother, wife or sisters. Within the joint family household and its extensions, however varied, organizational ties are lineal. And a man has no lineal ties to the families of his mother, wife or sisters. Women are family members only individually and in their own right. Hindu women take their *gotra* (or clan) membership from their fathers, but it is little more than the inheritance of a prohibition against marrying a man of the same *gotra*. Otherwise these women are lineal members de facto of neither the families into which they were born or married. To reiterate, with the exception of a handful of matrilineal groups, extended family organization throughout India, within families of whatever caste or religion, accords only with the line of male descent.

It seems likely to me that this remarkable consistency has contributed in no small measure to the equally remarkable preservation of the family as the basic social institution in Indian villages and in the society at large. Simply, the organizational unity of the family based on male descent, its integrity, is under no threat of being eroded by some competing family tie. Sons-in-law who are particularly enterprising or disaffected at home can anticipate no spear-blunting invitations to change their organizational ties and move to the distaff.[4] Where people's interests are in an organization, their allegiances are likely to be there too. Again, the Indian village household is an organization through which work is done and income shared, goods and services consumed, property passed on, marriages and careers arranged, children reared, life's contingencies provided for. And it is an organization of the spear *alone*.

On the distaff side there may be close *personal* ties. The families of a man's mother, wife and sisters are, after all, kinsfolk. To contain the ambitions of men of their lineages, Rajput princes and noblemen customarily sought alliances amongst their mothers' and wives' male relatives.[5] The affectionate relationship between a brother and sister separated by marriage and his solicitude for her children is proverbial in India. Proverbial enough to be celebrated by a holiday in the Hindu calendar, *Rakshabandan*, and to invest the Hindi word for wife's brother – *sala* – with the additional meaning of a term of abuse.

Depending upon their families and their families' circumstances and, of course, their own attributes, wives may be regarded as drudges in their in-laws' households or as important and powerful members of them. Daughters may be regarded as burdens or blessings. Grandmothers as no more than their husbands' shadows, or no less than their *maires du palais*. Typically, women of ordinary cultivating and artisan families do not only the universal women's work of housekeeping and childrearing, but contribute their toil to the household's work of cultivation and artisanship.

Well-born and well-to-do families typically regard it as unseemly for their women to work in village fields and lanes, or even to leave their courtyards more often than they have to. Village families, Hindu as well as Muslim, give witness to their respectability and affluence by more or less secluding their women. Behind the household purdah (curtain) in village India are kept those universal tokens of family honor and stability: women who are meant to be chaste, obedient and economically dependent (and are unnerving when they are not). Purdah may be no less than an emotionally, intellectually and physically harmful confinement. Or it may be no more than excusing the family's women from tedious work outside their households. Inside, women of middle-class village households are likely to be busily engaged in a wide range of crucial family undertakings that vary from sifting and winnowing harvests and gossip, to the usual chores of homemaking and childrearing, to those managerial activities – like marriage arrangements – that enhance a worthy family's worthiness and maintain its cohesion.

Ironically, the costs of family cohesion are borne disproportionately by its women. Indeed, unequal treatment of women, including their lineal exclusion, contributes to, if it does not sustain, that cohesion. With some appreciation, no doubt, of this connection, but motivated by Gandhian and Western liberal solicitude for women's welfare, the government of India began in the 1950s to legislate in favor of greater gender equality. Known generally as the Hindu Code, this legislation has been supplemented and complemented over the years by other laws, and together they form a comprehensive code of personal and family law for India's religious majority. Primarily, this code provides laws for marriage, separation and divorce, adoption of heirs and inheritance of family property.

In principle, though not in practice, this Hindu Code and its extensions are radical reforms. They bring under the law matters, like inheritance in grandfather's household, which village families have customarily regulated themselves. Their regulations were generally based on time-honored caste usage and sanctioned, however knowledgeably, by Hindu injunctive scripture. When disputes arose, these were customarily adjudicated by such amorphous, ad hoc and extra-legal bodies as caste and village councils. Disputes over family matters were sometimes brought to British Indian courts. Here, too, judges handed down decisions based on their understanding of Hindu (or Muslim) injunctive scripture and relevant and applicable customs and usage. Nowadays, an Indian court would apply the appropriate provision of the Hindu Succession Act of 1956 and its amendments.

This and other acts of the Hindu Code and its extensions were meant not only to incorporate into one set of laws the myriad family customs of thousands of Hindu castes, but to reform them. And to do so largely for the benefit of women. With *shastric* (Hindu injunctive) sanction, customary usage regarding the inheritance of family property, for example, is much the same in most Hindu castes as it is in grandfather's: women have no right, or only a limited right, to inherit real property. The Hindu Succession Act, and its amendments granted grandfather's widow and daughters some inheritance rights in the household's real property, but fewer than those retained by his sons, and no coparcenary rights. Other major legal reforms of customary Hindu family rules provide for civil marriage and divorce, a family's right to adopt girls, prohibitions on the giving and taking of dowries, a minimum marriage age for boys and girls, and the right of a girl married during her childhood to repudiate that marriage before attaining her majority.

These reforms are, by and large, only of the statute books. The Indian government and, even more, the governments of Indian states are apparently unwilling or unable to enforce their legislation for the equal treatment of Hindu women within their families. For Muslim women there is not even a legislated code. Their family law is that of the *shari'ah*: the legal code of Islam. Under Islamic law, the women of a family have lesser rights in the inheritance of property, for example, than its men. Nowadays still, in litigation over matters within a Muslim family, the courts of the Indian Union apply their understanding of the *shari'ah*. The government of India has the constitutional obligation to bring Hindus and Muslims under a "uniform civil code." Why, after more than a half-century, is there still no such code? Why, in 1986, did a "secular" Congress government in New Delhi give legislative sanction to the *shari'ah*'s rules on divorce? And why, when it was in opposition, did the "Hindu" BJP demand in the name of "secularism" the legislation of one uniform civil code, but now in government denies any intention to legislate it? In chapter 6, we take up these and related questions regarding Hindu–Muslim relations in contemporary India.

An extension, in effect, of the Hindu Code's reformism was the Dowry Prohibition Act of 1961. But it has been ground to dust in the post-Independence march to Hindu respectability and embourgeoisement by families in their tens of millions. The traditionally and generally accepted association of dowry marriages with high social status has not been effaced by Gandhian or liberal reformism. Almost certainly there has been an increase over the past decades in the practice of dowry marriages, largely through its adoption by upwardly mobile castes. Among the middle classes, particularly, there has probably been an increase also in the monetary value of dowries. The fiction that they are daughters' inheritances rather than the purchase price for sons-in-law has become increasingly palpable. Indian women's groups have brought to light a number of hideous instances in which brides with discrepant dowries were brutalized and even murdered or driven to suicide by their married families. The extent of this horror is unknown but, like domestic violence elsewhere and in other forms, much of it is probably hidden.

Hidden also is the contribution of dowry marriages to one of modern India's darkest secrets: female infanticide. The usual weapons on the domestic killing fields are outright murder and the murderous neglect of female children. Though forbidden by law, amniocentesis and ultrasound have been put to use in recent years as contrivances for female foeticide. Over the century, the number of females in the Indian population per 1,000 males has steadily declined: from 972 in 1901 to 929 in 1991. The 2001 Census of India recorded an increase to 933, but that may be attributable to other causes: the increase of female life expectancy, for example. In any case, the increase is slight and it should be set against a child (1–4 years of age) mortality rate for girls that was more than 40 percent higher than it was for boys in 1992–93, and a sharp decline since then in the ratio of girls to boys in the age group from birth to six years old.

That the benefits of development, through bourgeois revolution and otherwise, are going more to men than to women and that the costs of development are being borne more by women than by men are to the women's movements of India and their friends matters of grave concern. These were first and most fully articulated in a landmark report of 1974, entitled *Toward Equality*, prepared and presented by a government-sponsored Committee on the Status of Women in India. In its conclusion, the drafters of the committee were "forced to observe" that the:

> ... revolution in the social and political status of women for which constitutional equality was to be only the instrument, still remains a very distant objective. While there is no doubt that the position of some groups of women have changed for the better by opening to them positions of power and dignity, the large masses of women continue to lack spokesmen who understand their special problems and [are] commited to their removal in the representative bodies of the State.[6]

Over the three decades since *Toward Equality* was published, have Indian women progressed any further toward equality? There has certainly been some progress with regard to literacy and education. Their importance to the long-term improvement of the condition of Indian women is, as far as I know, questioned by no one. Nor is there any question about the contribution of female literacy to general welfare. That literate mothers are more likely than illiterate mothers, for example, to tend effectively to their children's health and education, has been fairly well established. The female literacy rate which was 22 percent in 1971 had more than doubled to 54 percent in 2001. The female literacy rate was less than half the male rate of 46 percent in 1971. By 2001, the gap between the female literacy rate and the male literacy rate (76 percent), had narrowed by about 20 percent. Even narrower now is the gap between the literacy rates for girls and boys in the current school age population (10–19 years old). That gap has virtually disappeared in urban India, as it has between city girls and boys in the rates of their attendance in educational institutions at all levels.

But, while India's urban population continues to grow by leaps and bounds, from 20 percent in 1971 to 28 percent in 2001, most Indians still live in their villages. And there, the condition of women compares unfavorably with that of their urban sisters. Among women in the Indian countryside, illiterates are 70 percent: twice the rate of illiteracy for both rural males and urban females. Among matriculates in rural India, there are half again as many males as females and twice as many graduates. Less than 6 percent of rural females are matriculates and less than 1 percent are graduates. The percentage of urban women who have matriculated (23 percent) is roughly four times greater than the percentage of women matriculates in the countryside (6 percent). Among women who live in towns and cities, the percentage of graduates (9 percent) is ten times greater than the percentage of women graduates who live in villages.

It may be that bourgeois revolution in the Indian countryside has increased the value of sons as family resources and the cost of daughters as family liabilities. I have already suggested this. Nonetheless, it may also be that some of the general prosperity that has accompanied bourgeois revolution is going to women. I can, perhaps, suggest this by making some comparisons between the states of Bihar and Punjab. I pursue these comparisons in other contexts, and it seems apropos to introduce them here.

Thus, of the major agricultural states in India, Bihar is the least well-developed and Punjab – the home, par excellence of both Green and bourgeois revolutions – is the most well-developed. At prices current in 1996–97, per capita income in Bihar was estimated to be the lowest of any Indian state: Rs3,835, up 44 percent from 1990–91. The per capita income in Punjab at prices current in 1996–97 was estimated to be Rs18,213: up more than 150 percent from 1990–91. This great difference in their wealth notwithstanding, Bihari and Punabi parents demonstrate no appreciable difference in their preferences for male children. This is reflected in the states' sex ratio: in both, lower than the Indian average, and lower in Punjab than in Bihar. It is also reflected in the disparity in mortality rates between male and female children, high in Punjab, but twice as high in Bihar.[7]

For women who survive childhood, however, their life chances are quite different in impoverished Bihar than they are in well-to-do Punjab. Here are some straws in the wind! In Bihar, the female literacy rate in 2001 was less than 35 percent, up approximately 30 percent from 1971, and little more than half the male literacy rate in 2001. In Punjab, the female literacy rate in 2001 was more than 65 percent, up approximately 40 percent from 1971, and about 85 percent of the male literacy rate in 2001. In 1999–2000, the enrolments of girls in Bihar's primary schools (grades1–5) was approximately one-third lower than it was in Punjab. In its upper primary grades (6–8), the enrolments of girls in Bihar was approximately one-third that of the enrolments in Punjab. The drop-out rates for girls from primary and upper primary grades is more than twice as high in Bihar as it is in Punjab. With a female population of more than three times that of Punjab, Bihar enrolls in its high schools' final grades about 10 percent of the girls enrolled in grades 11 and 12 in Punjab's high schools.[8] The positive relationship between urbanization and general prosperity in India is well established; and I have suggested the benefits to women of urbanization. In Bihar, the urban pop-ulation, 6 percent in 1971, was estimated to be 15 percent in 2001. By contrast, Punjab's urban population, which was 3 percent in 1971, had grown to about 32 percent in 2001.

Along with general prosperity, there is at least one other phenomenon related to urbanization that stands to benefit women. It is in what I have elsewhere described as "the aristocratic nature of Indian society and its interface with modernity"[9] and it applies to those "some groups of women" referred to in *Toward Equality*. More specifically, it is the growth of exem-plary *inequality* between high status urban women and the general run of urban men.

To begin, we must attempt to explain why in every country of South Asia, all of whose societies are male-dominated – whatever the religious majority of their population – there has been at least one woman prime minister, and in Bangladesh and Sri Lanka, two. In these places, where the aristocratic principle of political inheritance has been subsumed rather than replaced by the political principle of democratic election, the claim to power of all these women was that they were the conjugal or consanguinal legatees to the *gaddi* of some "great man." In recent years, however, in India, these heiresses have been followed into political power or prominence by other women whose connection to some "great man" is either irregular – a "protégée," for example – or non-existent, and who can be fairly described as self-made. We must try to explain this too.

My preferred explanation (there are several) is that all these women – and a growing number of others in virtually all areas of modern, urban Indian life – are the beneficiaries, initially, of the general, gender-unrelated inegali-tarianism of South Asian societies. Simply, Jack is neither as good as his master *nor his mistress* in a hierarchical society, in an aristocratic social order, in a social order of castes and status groups. In these societies, the exercise of power by high-status women over low-status men is of long standing and commonplace: by upper-caste ladies-of-the-house over their families' sweepers and laundrymen, by middle-class matrons in first-class railway compartments over the "coolies" who carry their baggage, by female shopkeepers over their male employees, by educated women in professional employment over the office *peons* (menials) who fetch and carry their files.

To such ordinary examples of superordinate women can now be added countless other examples which are extraordinary in comparison to the position in various public arenas enjoyed by women 30 years ago. In a word, women in considerable number have moved into superordinate positions in virtually all urban occupations. For whatever these statistics are worth (and they are probably at least indicative), in the 1991 Census of India's category "professional, technical and related workers," the percentages of males and females are equal. In the category "administrative, executive and managerial workers," the percentage of women is very small. The men's percentage is six times greater than the women's, but this is probably not much different than it was in the recent past – and in some places still is – in the West. So, while there has been a marked decline in the percentage of women workers in India's factories and mines, there has been an increase – far less substantial in numbers, but more substantial, perhaps, in social and multiplier effect – in the prestigious, urban, role-model, superordinate occupations enjoyed by women.

Few of these women are "aristocrats." A disproportionate number of them, certainly, are from middle-class, upper-caste homes in which education is valued. They are an extension and an expansion of 1974's "some groups of women." But as it is with India's New Men, an increasing proportion of upwardly mobile women are from very ordinary caste backgrounds. Whatever their castes, what distinguishes all these women from their male subordinates is not birth but class. Only their model is aristocratic. Bourgeois revolution is their vehicle. Bourgeois revolution is at the interface between the aristocratic nature of Indian society and modernity: translating status based on birth into status based on class. In its celebration in 1992 of India's New Woman, the news magazine *India Today* had this to say:

> It is the middle class, educated urban woman who is carving a niche for herself ... . The phenomenal growth of a large middle class ... during [1980s] is responsible for this new woman.[10]

A field in which the New Woman is notably under-represented is politics: ironically, but explicably, in the land of Indira Gandhi. Certainly, at the leadership level, there are women: her daughter-in-law wears Indira Gandhi's crown as the Congress Party's supremo, and virtually every other party has its leading women. Uma Bharati of the BJP, Jayalalita of the AIADMK in Tamil Nadu, Mayawati of the Dalit BSP in Uttar Pradesh, Mamata Banerjee of the Trinimool Congress in West Bengal: these are only a few, and there are any number of lesser female lights in less prominent leadership positions in politics. *But*, fewer than 10 percent of the candidates elected to the Lok Sabha in 1999 were women, and it has never been much higher than that. In state legislative assemblies it is much the same.

Considering that the great majority of parliamentary and legislative assembly seats are in the countryside, and that the countryside is the particular habitat of the patriarchal family, and that at election times in the countryside – as everywhere – political parties are more interested in votes than in social reform, and that politics in the countryside (to quote Mr Dooley) "ain't beanbag," this is not terribly surprising. For some time now, a proposal has been before Parliament to reserve one-third of Lok Sabha and state legislative assembly seats for women, in much the same way as seats are reserved for "scheduled tribes and castes." But the proposal has been stalled by OBC-dominated parties. They argue, quite rightly, that reservations for women, as such, would increase the legislative representation of upper castes at the Centre and in the states. They want proportional reservations for OBC, tribal and Dalit women within the one-third reservation for women. In the Lok Sabha elected in 1999, as in past elections, the vast majority of women members belong to what Mayawati calls the A and B teams of *Manuvad* (Brahminical Hinduism): the BJP and Congress.

At every tier of India's national system of rural, local self-government – *panchayati raj* – one-third of the general seats must be reserved for women; and of the seats reserved for OBCs, tribal people and Dalits, one-third must be apportioned to women from these groups. That is the law according to the 73rd Constitution Amendment Act of 1992. Apparently, it is the boldest step yet taken by the Indian government to position village women to serve the interests of village women through local politics, to provide village women with representatives from amongst themselves, "who understand their special problems and [are] committed to their removal ..." That village women have special problems separate from those of their menfolk – in the whole unfulfilled agenda of the Hindu Code, for example – is self-evident. Is the Amendment Act likely to serve those interests? It is too early to say with any certainty. But, for the foreseeable future, at least, I have my doubts.

First, *panchayti raj* institutions have been in the countryside since the late 1950s. State politicians have tended to view them, and particularly their *sarpanchas* and *pradhans* (elected heads), as competitors and spoilers with some capacity to intimidate and threaten by virtue of their positions as state-subsidized patrons of lesser patrons and wider-than-village client networks. With much the same view of these *dehati* (village) politicians, civilian and police bureaucrats who work in the countryside have been no great friends of *panchayati raj*. So, most states have allowed these institutions to languish and/or they have brought them under the control of politicians and bureaucrats. It was ostensibly for this reason that Parliament passed the 1992 Act. But under it, the powers assigned to *panchayats* have not been expanded.

They remain entirely dependent for their funding on state governments, and they retain sufficient power under their enabling legislation to hobble their *panchayats*. The 73rd Amendment Act provides state politicians and bureaucrats with no reason to be any friendlier to *panchayati raj* institutions now than they were before 1992.

Second, though usually less than one-third, there have always been women in *panchayati raj* institutions. Many states reserved positions for them before 1992. And generally, like their male counterparts, they represented the interests of their families, clans, castes, and factions. Whether with greater representation and the guarantee of elevated positions in the *panchayati raj* hierarchy, women members will become champions of women's issues remains to be seen. But the embeddedness of village women in their families, the family centeredness of villagers, the expectation among villagers that respectable women will be guided by their menfolk and their families' interests, persistent low levels of literacy and education among village women give little cause for optimism. Seven years after the enactment of the 73rd Amendment, this was one knowledgable observation of the position of women in *panchayati raj* institutions:

> ... Women have class and caste identities, not just ... gender
> identit[ies]. In fact, gender as a phenomenon hardly ever appears
> in a pure form. It is almost always alloyed with caste, class and
> religious factors. In matters where there is a clash between gender
> and caste or class, we cannot expect women to align themseleves
> with other women, going against their caste or class loyalties.[11]

To another observer, the women elected to be *sarpanchas* in Maharashtra, "... replicate rural power structures and deeply embedded patterns of dominance and inequality."[12]

Nirmala Buch is more optimistic about the effects of the 73rd Amendment. She notes the entrance into the *panchayati raj* system of "a large percentage [of women] from families of lower socio-economic strata." But she presents no evidence to suggest that most or many of these women are active participants in *panchayat* affairs, or that they speak for women's interests, or that they are, in fact, representatives in their own right rather than proxies for their menfolk – the good *sarpanchpatis* (*sarpanch* husbands) behind, not every, but many, good woman *sarpanchas*.[13]

My guess is that the impetus for gender equality in the Indian countryside is coming less from women *panchas* and *sarpanchas* than from the exemplary superordination of urban India's New Woman. Equality is a new idea in India – whether between genders, castes, classes, or people, in general – and it sits uneasily in a society whose norm is *homo hierarchicus*.[14] I think that in the first instance, the gender issue in India is less equality for women than exemplary access for women to superordinate positions in urban public life. Their example is part of the ethos drift of modernity – including the values of gender equality – which proceeds from the cities: carried by an intelligent and energetic women's movement, the underlying egalitarian ideology of parliamentary democratic politics, the gutsy New Woman heroines of television and movie dramas. Greater gender equality may follow into the countryside. But the pace will inevitably be slow. As caste inequality is built into the social ideology and structure of village life, so are some crucial aspects of gender inequality. Not wife-beating certainly, but the non-inheritance of land by females, for example, is probably basic to the maintenance of the patrilineal family. And there are changes in Indian society that run counter to the drift toward gender equality: the growth in the spread of dowry marriages, for example. In sum, on the road to gender equality in Indian villages it would be well to expect slow going.

Villages

The great and powerful in India, as elsewhere, have their protégés and minions. Ordinary villagers depend upon their families. Family ties are virtually the warp and woof of the Indian countryside's social fabric. Again, of every ten Indians, more than seven are villagers: more than 700 million people, living in 600,000 villages all over India. Another 100 million-or-so live in towns with a population of less than 20,000: for the most part country towns, as much a part of the countryside as the villages they service.

All along the 4,000 kilometers of India's coastlines, there are villages of fisherfolk. Tribal villages dot the subcontinent, more heavily in some areas than in others. But all over India the great majority of villages are places of sedentary cultivation by families of small-holders. They might be called "peasant villages," except that the cultivating middle classes that run them are no longer peasants. No longer subject cultivators. Nowadays, Indian village families, particularly of the cultivating middle classes, are part of a wider society: as caste-fellows, coreligionists, language users; as producers and consumers of goods, services and revenues; as citizens and voters.

Over most of India, villages are clusters of residences surrounded by fields that their resident families cultivate. Within the residential cluster, the village proper, in northern India an apparent warren of baked mud and brick buildings, neighborhoods are most frequently marked off by the lines of caste and religious community. A quarter, at some distance from other village neighborhoods, is often marked off for families of Dalit castes. Interspersed within the neighborhoods there are more or less public facilities. These are, typically, places for worship, wells or reservoirs which supply water for household use, small shops and, increasingly, a building or buildings that are used as primary school, medical dispensary, council chamber, accommodation for official visitors.

Country towns are likely to have a large population of cultivating families who live and work in much the same way as do villagers. Otherwise, country towns are the sites of a variety of facilities, run by local people and outsiders, which provide villagers with their closest substantial link to the wider Indian society. Places where they show movies are in country towns. Shops which sell goods made in factories all over India are there, as are merchants who buy villagers' produce for resale in distant markets. The police, offices of the civil bureaucracy, courts and lawyers, post and telegraph services, bus and train stations, branches of national and state banks and local *sarafs* (moneylenders), high schools and hospitals, proper temples and mosques are in country towns.

Apart from transients brought by their work to country towns and migratory farm laborers, India's rural population is, in general, stationary. Families emigrate from villages to towns and cities, but not usually from towns and cities to villages, nor from one village to another. In north India, marriages between children of the same village are usually taboo, so brides emigrate from their natal to their in-laws' village. The men of a village are likely to have been born there, as were their fathers and grandfathers. Whether or not they are born in their husbands' village, most Indian women are likely to spend most of their lives there and are less likely to venture from them than village men.

Autonomy and autarky are matters of more or less. Most Indian villages today are less to much-less autonomous and autarkic than they were in even the recent past, not to say in the golden ages of foreign and native romanticizers of Indian rusticity. Still, the ongoing, day-to-day and closest relationships of all sorts that most villagers have are within their villages. Often these relationships have been inherited and will be passed on. They are relationships of generations. The closest paternal kinsmen of a household's men are likely to live in their village: brothers, uncles, cousins, nephews. Other demonstrable kin are there as well, although the kinship tie may be distant or attenuated. The geographical spread of castes is invariably wider than any one village, but it is primarily within their villages that families and family members of the same caste relate to one another as castefellows. It is within their villages that people have daily experience of their caste and, indeed, the customs and usages that shape that experience may vary from village to village. It is primarily within their villages that families and family members of one caste or community relate to people of other castes and communities. The parameters of these relationships, their etiquette and taboos, and the hierarchical positions of some castes relative to others frequently vary from village to village.

Relationships of production among villagers are still largely within their villages. In times past, all over India, these relationships were more or less regulated and given sacred sanction by what anthropologists call *jajmani* systems. These were relationships of exchange within villages whereby landholding families received from families of occupational specialists and others – potters and laborers, for example – certain specified services and remunerated these with certain specified quantities of grain or portions of land. From each according to the station to which they were born! Thus, was the *dharma*, the sacred order of things, maintained. On both sides of the exchange, *jajmani* relationships were heritable. They were relationships of generations. *Jajmani* systems and the secularized patron–client and employer–employee relationships that succeeded them are subjects of my discussion in chapter 3. But we may anticipate its conclusions here.

Modernity in the forms, for example, of the increasing availability to villagers of cash, opportunities and compulsions to work outside their villages, factory-made goods, outside markets for their agricultural products, Green Revolution technology, have largely dismantled *jajmani* relationships. Between them, however, and the secular connections of superiority/subordination that succeed them – patrons to clients, employers to employees, creditors to debtors, masters to servants – there are some striking similarities. They are both village-centered. Connections are likely to be between villagers of the same village. The superior parties to the connection are likely to be landholders. The patron–client relationship of generalized superiority/subordination that characterized *jajmani* systems tends to persist in contemporary economic relationships. State legislated land reform in the 1950s, which virtually disestablished non-cultivating, absentee and urban landlords throughout India, may well have increased the village-centeredness of productive relationships. It has probably been decreased in more recent decades, however, by the growing commercialization of Indian agriculture.

In the past, before Indian independence, the most regular involvement of baronial, princely and imperial regimes in the governance of the subcontinent's villages was to collect their taxes and, less dependably, to keep the peace. Village government as such was usually supplied by ad hoc village councils: in northern India, *panchayats*. These customary *panchayats* ought not to be confused with the statutory institutions of *panchayati raj*. In form, if not in substance, the two share little more than a name. Customary *panchayats* and their modi operandi were either tenuously or not at all connected in any official or legal sense to the state. Their rules were provided by injunctive scripture and caste and communal conventions. *Panchayat* governance was largely a matter of the ad hoc arbitration of disputes among villagers by upper-caste and landed village elders. If it seemed appropriate or prudent, they would arbitrate in consultation with leaders of relevant families, castes or communities. Women, needless to say, played no apparent part in the business of customary *panchayats*.

The government of customary *panchayats* was of the village, by and for its well-to-do and well-born families. They maintained the order of things by holding to the ways things had always been and accommodating their village to the ways in which things were changing. The tax collectors' *raj*, the state – its land tenure legislation, its law courts, its police and civil bureaucracies, its railways – changed things. But from day to day, landed *panchas* and *sarpanchas* – *panchayat* members and heads – patrons to their clients, ruled their villages.

To some extent, they still do: in statutory law, now, as the hierarchs in *panchayati raj* institutions. The intentions of its founders notwithstanding, the system has been less successful in filtering democratic development downward from state capitals than in percolating upwards to state capitals the village interests of well-to-do farm families. Nowadays, many of these are less well-to-do than were their predecessors. The countryside's New Men are small-holders from OBC family households. For them, as for the upper-caste and larger small-holders with whom they share power in the countryside, however uneasily, their villages enjoy a political importance gifted to them by India's parliamentary democracy. Upward from *panchayati raj* institutions, to state legislative assembles, to the Lok Sabha, villages are at the base of the caste and factional politics that permeate the Indian political system.

Parliamentary democracy has extended the arena of intra- and inter-caste and factional politics to state boundaries. While this extension has affected political relationships within villages, the village centeredness of these relationships remains. So, for example, the considerable political power in their state legislative assemblies of "dominant"[15] and OBC castes certainly affects their castefellows' village relationships, with one another and villagers of other castes. But the political bases of state-level political power for castes and factions are in their villages where their leaders are well-to-do farmers and patrons of less well-to-do clients.

Given the encapsulation of a family's life within its village, and therein its generational continuity and the memories of its generations, it is not surprising that people speak of their family's village as home. When they are away from home, villagers identify themselves and those whom they meet as belonging to their villages. Villages have histories and mythologies. They have reputations, general and specific to groups; and families partake of their villages' good or bad names. Generations, sometimes, after their families had come to the city and moved into the circles of the upwardly and outwardly mobile, Delhiwallas and Bombayites will tell you that their (paternal) families belonged to such-and-such a village. Villages have not only corporate identities, they are primordial locations.

Clearly villages are something other than societies in which families exchange goods and services and no more. But what other are they? Are they communities? If we keep to our definition of community as a group of people who think of themselves as "we" and act accordingly – often in juxtaposition or opposition to "them" – then villages are probably less communities than arenas in which communities meet. As families are the basic units of Indian society, so villages are its basic arenas. In the Hindu ideal, the metaphor is otherwise: villages are society's basic organisms, all maintained by the natural functioning of each of their parts in natural synergism with one another. Those who were born to treat with the gods, do so; those who were born to rule, rule; those who were born to produce wealth, produce it; and those who were born to toil, toil. The villages they sustain are microcosms of the divine order of things.

In village reality, I have already intimated, conflict and competition among groups are no less usual than cooperation. What is unusual in villages is villagers behaving as villagers rather than as members of their families, castes, religious communities and factions. Although less so now than in the past, groups of villagers separate themselves from each other in the rounds of their daily lives by what they eat and whom they eat it with, how they dress, where they live and obtain their domestic water supply, what work they do and won't do, whose patron or client they are, who they defer to and who defers to them, what they worship, where and how. Even on village occasions, like weddings and *melas* (festivals), villagers are likely to participate as members of their group and in such ways as to demonstrate its separateness from other groups and, less now than in the past, its place in some putative village hierarchy. Government community development schemes failed to serve the poor in the 1950s and *panchayati raj* has best served the middle classes from the 1960s, in some measure because both were predicated on the incorrect assumption that villages are communities rather than arenas. A belated correction to this is to some extent contained in the 73rd Amendment Act's elaborate provisions for reserved positions in all *panchayati raj* institutions: compulsory for women and "scheduled tribes and castes," and permissible by the states for OBCs.

Chapter 2

Caste

What is caste? Of all Indian social institutions, caste is the most exotic to Westerners, the furthest removed from our experience. We may look through the forms of Indian family and village life to recognize the substance of Western lives. We may have no difficulty in recognizing from Western experiences the substance of patron–client and class relationships in Indian villages. But we have no castes. We speak of "castes" when we refer to apparently impenetrable social barriers: in apartheid South Africa, for example, or in outback Australia, or in the segregationist American South. But as a composite social form, caste in India is uniquely Indian. As a composition of parts – a tapestry, to choose a convenient metaphor – caste in India is unrecognizable to Westerners. Our discomfort with its strangeness tempts us either to disparage caste's uniqueness by pulling and tugging it to fit our experiences of class and status, or to devalue Western experiences because they seem irrelevant to an understanding of caste.

Negatively put, the central commitment of this chapter is to avoid these temptations. Caste is of the warp and woof of Indian civilization, and Indian civilization is of the warp and woof of caste. We avoid the temptation to social-science hubris by understanding that the tapestry of caste is the work over millennia of a great civilization. We may avoid the temptation to abandon as useless our own Western experiences by examining the tapestry's composition, by scrutinizing it for recognizable strands. Of these there are many: social hierarchy and snobbery, ascription and status, race and ethnicity, class and power, sumptuary regulations and taboos, notions of causality and contagion, beliefs about ritual purity and pollution, things divinely ordained and myths about our "imagined communities"[1] and who "we" and "they" are.

By connecting our experiences to its parts, we may come to a recognition of the composite. Put positively, our commitment is to understand caste as something that is both peculiarly Indian and essentially human.

The first step to understanding is to make clear what we are trying to understand: simply, to name it properly. We need to say what we mean by "caste." It comes to us from the Portuguese. They were the first Europeans in modern times to build their settlements in India and to become familiar with Indian society. But what the Portuguese meant by "caste" is not what we mean. In one word, cognate with "chaste," the Portuguese named a complex social system for what seemed to those Europeans most exotic about it: the segregation of people into groups and their hierarchical arrangement on the apparent criterion of heritable and unalterable degrees of religious purity. But, more than likely, there has never been unanimity among castes as to what constitutes religious purity. Other criteria – occupation, for example – were used by castes to segregate themselves. And yet other criteria – for example, political power – determined their ranking: and, nowadays, more than ever.

But more detrimental, perhaps, to our understanding, "caste" embodies a misconception. In one word, the Portuguese conflated two characteristics of any society that are best understood as distinct though related: referent social ideologies and the social groups that refer to them.[2] Westerners, for example, distinguish between and relate Christianity and Christian denominations, Judaism and congregations of Jews, Marxism and communist parties. We are able to make (and refine) similar distinctions and relationships with regard to "caste." Not by relying on that European term, however, at least initially. But by working our way to it through Indian terms.

Varna dharma is a referent ideology. According to it, mankind is divided into four categories, *varnas*, which are ranked according to their religious purity. There is an order, *dharma*, among them. Like any ideology, *varna dharma* favors the group that propounds it. In this case, Brahmins. *Varna dharma* is a Brahminical ideology. Brahmins come in at the top. Other ranks do not necessarily concur, and some either ignore the ideology or vehemently reject it. But having said that, we must begin somewhere. As a point of departure, *varna dharma* has the advantages of being a well-known, well-articulated and well-constructed ideology. We can dismantle it as we go along. Moreover, while other ranks deny the validity of the *varna dharma* hierarchy and their placements in it, there is a general acceptance among them of social mechanisms related to the ideology – segregation based on notions of purity/pollution, for example – and of the rightness of a social order based on hierarchy.

The social groups that refer themselves to this ideology or are referred to it by their neighbors are numbered in thousands. They are localized in regions of the subcontinent where they comprise local society. They are ranked by others or by themselves, often indeterminately and contentiously, according to a variety of locally interpreted, determined and defined criteria. The generic names for these groups are different in the different regional languages of India and in their local dialects. In the language of anthropology and Indian studies, in general, they are usually called *jatis*: their name in Hindi pluralized in English. In everyday English, they are called castes. In the pages that follow, I stray somewhat from my usual preference for everyday English to use *"jati"* where it seems meaningful: usually as a small, face-to-face, kinship-based group in the context of village life. But what, then, is "caste"?

"Caste" suggests extensions of *jati*: larger, more inclusive and less face-to-face and demonstrably based on kinship. In its least ambiguous meaning, caste is the furthest extension of *jati* endogamy. *Jati*-sanctioned marriages are between brides and grooms of the same caste, and caste-legitimate children are born of such unions only. Otherwise, it is a matter of more or less. There are distinctions without clear differences, as there are in social systems based on class. An example may help. Imagine a spectrum with *"jati"* at one end and "caste" at the other, and place on it the Jats – one of northern India's largest and most successful castes of cultivators. At the *"jati"* end we have Jat farmers who have lived in their same villages for generations, who are related to one another, know all about one another, have regular pleasant and unpleasant dealings with one another, dine with one another and generally marry into known Jat families in neighboring villages. At the "caste" end of the spectrum, we have millions of Jats. They share a caste identity, but are mostly unknown to one another and spread across thousands of square kilometers of northern India. That Jat population – Hindu and Sikh – is probably larger than the total number of Swedes, Danes, Norwegians and Finns in Scandinavia.

Shading from *"jati"* into "caste," and with no clear dividing lines between them, are *jati* extensions into caste. Smaller than the whole caste and more face-to-face, but larger and less face-to-face than their *jatis*, are caste fragments of Jats which identify themselves by lineage or clan or region and vary in their general social standing from, say, very ordinary farmers in parts of Rajasthan to powerful landholders in western Uttar Pradesh and Punjab. Even within these regional variations, Jat *jatis* differ from village to village in their social standing, how they relate to *jatis* of other castes and they to them. There are face-to-face, personal, family and professional relationships between urban Jat families that share none of the usual *jati* ties between villagers. Outside of their *jatis*, there are formal and informal associations of Jats – welfare societies, factions in *panchayati raj* institutions and university faculties, cliques in political parties and state ministries, patronage networks among Jats in public service, vote banks in the hustings, and so forth. Thus, my use of both *"jati"* and "caste" makes no clear distinction between the entities to which they refer. Sometimes, it may seem to readers, and quite correctly, that I use *"jati"* when I might just as well have used "caste," or the other way around, or that I use the two terms synonymously, or almost so. I plead guilty to the sacrifice of some terminological consistency.

Varna

Varna dharma is a religious ideology and ideal of Brahminical Hinduism. Its ostensible claim to acceptance among Hindu believers is that it is ordained by God. It is sacred. Its historicity is uncertain and of no particular concern here. Some scholars think, but are by no means certain, that *varna dharma* originated in the meeting in northern India more than 3,000 years ago of darker complected indigenes with fairer complected Aryan migrants or invaders from Central Asia. There are mythological descriptions of this in the earliest Sanskrit hymnals, and one meaning of *varna* – among others – is color. We have no idea whether *varna dharma* ever really existed as a hierarchy of social groups, based on skin color or color-coding or anything else. It does not now and even if it did at some time in the distant past, that would be quite irrelevant to its importance in India today. Unlike Christianity and Islam, Hinduism is disinclined – or has been until recently – to search the historical past for validation, and the validity of *varna dharma* is not as a memory of the past but as a living, albeit contentious, ideology. Understanding *varna dharma* is our first step to understanding *jati* and caste. But where, in an introductory essay do we begin? Where do we end? The body of relevant literature – religious and scholarly, esoteric and contentious – is vast.

But these are the questions and the obstacles that confront anyone who aspires to a terminable examination of doctrine in any religion. A preacher's style of doing the job is to choose a text, elaborate on it but not wander far from it. It is a style that aspires less to profundity and the exhaustive and definitive discussion of theologians than to making a point with economy, clarity and intelligibility to laypeople. Without a preacher's purpose, of course, it is a style appropriate to our discussion of *varna dharma*. Our first text is a frequently quoted creation myth of Hinduism. It appears in the *Rig Veda*, the oldest of the Sanskrit hymnals and one traditionally revered by some Hindus as the revealed and recorded word of God. According to the myth, the world and the *varna dharma* were created in the same primeval sacrifice. The Cosmic Spirit, called Purusha, whom we may think of in this context as the One, offered himself to the gods as an oblation, and:

> When they divided [him], in how many different portions did they
> arrange him? What became of his mouth, what of his two arms?
> What were his two thighs and his two feet called? His mouth
> became the Brahmin; his two arms were made into the Rajana
> [i.e. Kshatriya]; his two thighs [loins], the Vaishiya; from his two
> feet the Shudra was born.[3]

Not all, certainly, but many of the parameters of any religion are set out in its
creation myth. "As it was in the beginning, is now and ever shall be …" In the
beginning, God tells His human creatures, or at least suggests to them subject
to subsequent elaboration: I am who I am; you are who I made you; and this
is the deal. We know from the first chapters of Genesis, for example, that God
of the Abrahamic religions – Judaism, Christianity and Islam – is omnipotent
and transcendent, and that the progeny of His creature, Adam, are imperfect,
free to make their own decisions and responsible for them, redeemable
through God's mercy, and in His judgment essentially equal.

In much the same way, Hinduism's conception of humankind and its
relationship to God is suggested in the story of Purusha's sacrifice. Purusha is
the one source of humankind's ancestry, but these ancestors are not one but
four. Their progeny are the *varnas* whose ordained functions are unequally
important to the maintenance of the organic whole: the cosmos created from
Purusha. The Brahmin (priest), through the organ of speech, invocation,
prayer and instruction, maintains the divinely ordained order of things
in which Purusha is immanent. The arms of the Kshatriya (warrior-ruler)
enforce among human creatures their acceptance of the divine order of
things, including the *varna dharma*. The Vaishiya generates the wealth
which priests and rulers must have to perform their ordained functions. The
Shudra serves the whole by providing his toil in the service of the other,
superior *varnas*.

These superior *varnas*, in subsequent elaborations of the ideology, came to
be known as "twice-born." Brahmins, Kshatriyas and Vaishiyas were thus
grouped into another sacred category that increased the hierarchical distance
between them collectively and non-twice-born Shudras. The Shudra category
was in turn subjected to ideological bifurcation. There were those Shudras
who toiled at respectable, clean occupations and lived respectable, clean
lives. But there was a lower order of Shudras whose toil, though necessary to
the maintenance of social order, was so unclean, as were their living habits,
as to put them beyond the pale of ordinary social intercourse. They and
their progeny were *panchama*, a fifth category of people who were *achhut*:
untouchable.

What is self-evident is that in the ideology of *varna dharma* all men are created unequal. They are endowed by their Creator with unequal capacities in order to perform functions of unequal importance to Him. Their positions in His hierarchy accord with their functions. Their functions and their positions are not only divinely ordained, however, but having been ordained by nature's God, God of the cosmic organism, they are also natural. The organism as a whole functions best when its parts perform those specialized functions that nature has equipped them to perform. The mouth can form the sacred, world-sustaining syllables, the arms cannot. The arms can wield the sword in defense of the *varna dharma*, the mouth cannot. *Varnas* are the parts specialized by nature to maintain the cosmic organism.

This anatomical metaphor for the naturalness of inequality and hierarchy is succeeded in Hindu literature, and certainly in popular Hinduism, by a zoological metaphor. Its medium is the beast fable. You cannot train a tiger to nibble grass. You cannot train a goat to hunt. Capabilities and potentialities are in nature not in nurture. To act on the contrary belief is to invite disappointment, or embarrassment, or disaster. Like other animals or species of animals, men have their breeds and, of course, these have different and unequally important capabilities and potentialities. The generation of wealth is a more important social function than the performance of societies' menial tasks. Vaishiyas are the best generators of wealth because they are naturally acquisitive. Shudras are the best servants because they are naturally servile. In the Hindu ideal, the *varna dharma*, Man, as Louis Dumont argues, is properly *homo hierarchicus*.

Inextricably connected to *varna dharma* and serving to reinforce it are two other Hindu ideals: *dharma* and purity/pollution. Our use again of the word *dharma* is noteworthy. In *varna dharma*, *dharma* applies to society and its best meaning is "order." The best meaning of *dharma* as applied to individuals is "duty." The two meanings are crucially related. When a society is properly ordered, people do their duty. When people do their duty, society is properly ordered. Social order lies in *varna dharma*. But wherein does individual duty lie? That question takes us to the core beliefs of Hinduism, and back again to *varna dharma*.

Dharma-karma. *Dharma* is inextricably connected to the law of *karma*. It is an "inexorable" law, according to Mahatma Gandhi, "impossible of evasion." "Whatever a man sows, that shall he reap."[4] God does not determine our fate. Our gift from Him is the capacity to determine our own fate: to make choices, to sow according to our will. The reaping takes place after we have experienced the incident of death and in the incident of subsequent birth or in a final release from these incidents. Depending upon how we sow in this lifetime, we reap in the next. The Brahmin who has sown badly will be reborn as less than a Brahmin. The Shudra who has sown well will be reborn as more than a Shudra. Whoever has sown perfectly will escape rebirth, will attain *moksha*: oneness with God, liberation from the cycle of re-birth and re-death.

Wherein are the instructions for proper sowing? In the rule of *dharma*. Our text here is the *Bhagavad Gita*. Originally in Sanskrit, it is an epic poem of Hindu faith and one of the world's great works of religious literature. The *Gita's* scene is a battlefield. The battle is about to begin. The opposing armies are in position. They are armies of opposing kinsmen. One of their chiefs, Arjuna, grieves. Whichever army wins, many brave warriors of both will be slaughtered, and it will be a slaughter of kinsmen by kinsmen. Whichever army wins, there will be mourning women, orphaned children and social dislocation, *adharma*. Arjuna confides his grief to his charioteer. His charioteer is Lord Krishna, God incarnate. He comforts Arjuna, but instructs him, in effect, to get on with it, to prepare himself to fight the battle. That is his duty. Arjuna is a Kshatriya and his *dharma* is to fight. The divine and even the social consequences of his doing what he must do, fight, are neither within his capacity to determine nor to judge. The man who is concerned with consequences, attached in some way to the results of what he does, is necessarily inhibited in the performance of his duty. The man who best serves God, society and himself performs his *dharma* and is detached from its consequences. Our duty is set out in nature: by gender, age and – as in Arjuna's case – by *varna*. The general rule is this: "Better is one's own *dharma* though imperfect, than the *dharma* of another well performed." [5]

The rule of *dharma* supports the *varna dharma* ideal largely by prescribing proper and rewarding behavior. By contrast, the rules of purity/pollution support the *varna dharma* ideal largely by proscribing improper and penalizing behavior. The sum of the rules is this: avoid pollution. Concern with religious purity or cleanliness is not, of course, peculiar to Hindus. Leviticus (and its exegeses), for example, provide Jews with an elaborate set of dietary and sexual rules for doing that which is clean and not doing that which is unclean in the eyes of God. Although Hindu rules of purity/pollution are in substance of this religious genre, their systematic elaboration is in form so strikingly similar to our modern conceptions of health/sickness as to invite their use as an analogy.

Thus, purity/pollution is like health/sickness; as applied not to the substantial body, however, but to its insubstantial essence: soul, for lack of a better word. Some people's souls are relatively pure, others are relatively polluted. In Hindu ideology, the state of purity/pollution of the individual's soul is understood not as some metaphor but as an actual state of being, much as we regard an individual's health/sickness. The ordinary and individual purity/pollution of people, like their ordinary and individual health/sickness, is from time to time adversely affected by circumstances. Women during their menstrual periods and families in mourning, for example, are in extraordinary states of pollution that pass in time and in response to the appropriate purificatory treatments. Much as infections are treatable by antibiotics.

But there are also ordinary states of purity/pollution that are congenital and untreatable. These attach to people not as individuals, but as members of their *varna*. The higher God has placed a *varna*, the purer He has made those who belong to it. The purity/pollution enjoyed by individuals by virtue of their *varna* is, at once, indicative of sacred status and requisite for the proper performance of the duties prescribed by that status. At the top in Brahminical Hinduism's *varna dharma*, the Brahmin, whose prescribed functions require the greatest purity, is the most pure and least polluted. At the bottom, the Shudra, whose functions require the least purity and are the most polluting, is the least pure and most polluted. Individuals cannot enjoy a purity greater than that inherent in their *varna*. But they can suffer a greater pollution. Like the flu, pollution is contagious. It threatens its victim's chances in this lifetime and the next. It limits his abilities to perform his prescribed and organism-sustaining duties. The ways to keep from greater pollution are in the performance of one's own *dharma* and in the avoidance of pollution's contagion. It is primarily the conception of pollution as contagious that provides the reinforcing connections between the ideologies of purity/pollution and *varna dharma*.

The most widely recognized carriers of pollution's contagion are water and prepared food. There are Hindu dietary rules which, in form similar to those of Leviticus, proscribe certain food and drink. In Hinduism it is considered sinful to kill cows, and the consumption of beef is universally proscribed. But nature prescribes different diets for different *varnas*. A diet that is vegetarian and teetotal is generally considered to be appropriate for Brahmins and Vaishiyas. Flesh and alcohol, on the other hand, are appropriate for a Kshatriya's diet. While the dietary rules of Jews separate them from Gentiles, the dietary rules of Hindus separate the *varnas*. Hindu commensal rules (rules about whom to eat and drink with and from whom to accept food and water) do the same. These are rules for the maintenance of purity and the quarantine of pollution. In sum, *varna* members maintain their endogenous levels of purity/pollution and quarantine pollution when they drink and dine only with one another, take water and prepared food only from one another or from members of purer *varnas*, and give water and prepared food only to one another or to members of more polluted *varnas*. Here is the nexus between the ideologies of purity/pollution and *varna dharma*: rules about eating and drinking affirm the separateness of the *varnas* and the hierarchy among them.

Jati and caste

Some of the most obvious differences between *varna dharma* ideology and *jati* and caste societies we have already noted in passing. There are four *varnas*, but a myriad of *jatis* and thousands of their inclusive castes. The divisions of *varna dharma* go to the borders of Hinduism. *Jatis* are local and castes are rarely found beyond the borders of ethnolinguistic regions and some do not even extend to these. While the notion of a social hierarchy is generally accepted, many *jatis* and castes reject the legitimacy of the *varna dharma* hierarchy and/or the places assigned to them in it by their neighbors. In what were Brahminical strongholds in south India, the fourfold division of the *varna dharma* hardly exists. Where it exists in the rest of India, it does so in local variations. In many of these, not all *jatis* which call themselves Brahmins accept the Brahminical credentials of all other *jatis* that call themselves Brahmins. The village roost is not necessary ruled by some Brahmin *jati*, and when it is it may be as a result of the *jati*'s wealth and power rather than its reputation for ritual purity. Some Brahmin *jatis* enjoy no such reputation.

Jatis and castes do not function as synergic parts of one imagined organic whole, one Great Society. Rather, they work variously in cooperation or competition or conflict with one another in separate but overlapping social arenas: villages, development blocs, districts and states. The *varna dharma* is a Hindu ideology, but *jatis* and castes are Indian. Among that 18 percent of India's population that professes Islam, Christianity, Sikhism, Buddhism, Jainism, Judaism, there are what might be called, for lack of better words, quasi *jatis* and castes. These are groups which follow some characteristically caste-like customs and usages, but sanction them with no reference to Hindu sacred ideology. In the ideology of *varna dharma* converts from Hinduism can change their faith, but they cannot change their breeds. In fact, some do – scribal caste (Kayastha) converts to Islam, for example. Others cling to them – for example, Brahmin converts to Christianity. The best translation of *jati* is "breed."

In villages, commensal rules provide not only a prop for *jati* and caste and notions of some hierarchical arrangement among them, but guidelines for daily behavior. With whom should men share their water pipes? Who should women allow in their kitchens? With whom is it comfortable to dine? Some scholars argue, it might be noted in passing, that caste endogamy is merely an historical or logical corollary of caste commensality. In a word, a man is in greater danger of becoming polluted from eating impure food or drinking impure water than from having sexual contact with a woman whose *jati* is less pure than his own. Sexual contact outside of marriage between men and women of different *jatis* is generally considered to be improper. But it is nonetheless commonplace. Villagers often wink at it, particularly when the contact is between a man who is relatively powerful and of a higher *jati* and a woman who is relatively powerless – frequently, the man's servant or dependant – and of a lower *jati*. This sort of exploitive sexual relationship does not, of course, imply an invitation to dine. *Godan or The Gift of a Cow*, is an epic novel of Indian village life, written in 1936 by the foremost Hindi novelist of his times, Premchand. In it, the mother of a Dalit girl chides her Brahmin lover:

> You think you are very pious. You'll sleep with [my daughter] but you won't touch food cooked by her.[6]

Corollary or not, while caste rules of endogamy have become virtually absolute, *jati* rules of commensality have become increasingly situational. Nowadays, villagers live not only in their little societies but in the Indian world outside their villages. Their villages, too, are parts of the world outside. More and more are the situations in which more and more villagers, particularly men and their grown children, find it difficult or inconvenient or unpleasant to abide by their *jatis'* commensal rules. More and more, Indians travel. At a tea stall near a railway station or a bus terminal, in a market town hotel or on an Indian Airlines flight, how can one know who prepares and serves the food? For the millions of villagers who work or attend schools and colleges in the city, who prepares and serves their meals and in what company are they eaten?

Hindus have adjusted their commensal rules to the compulsions and temptations of the world outside their little societies in much the same way that many observant Jews have adjusted their dietary rules: observance at home, but observance less well or not at all away from home. If the logic of the rules is to be internally consistent, then, of course, both compromises are irrational. Food that is prepared by someone who is polluted is polluting wherever it is eaten. Meat from an unclean animal is unclean wherever it is eaten. But if the logic of the rules is to facilitate the survival of the group, then both compromises are rational and functional. Within their little societies, where circumstances are more or less controllable by them, *jatis'* observances of commensal rules contribute to maintaining their separate identities, their members' sense of being secure among their own kind, and probably some order within villages. Outside of their families' homes and beyond village borders, *jatis* cannot control the observance of their commensal taboos. So, rather than discredit their authority by exercising it futilely, they forgive non-observance and profit from the non-observant. The dining habits of villagers who work in the city may be suspect, but their remittances are welcome and contribute to their families' wealth and their *jatis'* prestige.

In practice, there are no commensal rules of universal and uniform applicability. Not infrequently, the same *jatis* of different villages apply their rules differently. Here members of *jati* A take water and food from members of *jati* B, there they do not. Here and there, *jatis* that have been ranked as low by their esteemed neighbors, will reject their right to do so by refusing to take water and food from them. In general, customary commensal taboos are giving way, at least in part. Members of touchable Hindu *jatis* may be as loath as ever to take food or water from members of Dalit *jatis*, but among touchable villagers, at least in public places, there is probably more eating, drinking and smoking together across *jati* lines today than there has been even in the recent past.

It may be that villagers' non-observance of commensal taboos in town and en route is weaning them away from observance inside their villages. The new political modus operandi of parliamentary democracy has taken on some ideological overtones that may be shading the landscape of purity/pollution. High-caste politicians who would win the votes of their lowest caste constituents must woo them over tea. Dalit ministers, and there are many of them, expect invitations not only to dine but to be honored. The most recent past President of India is a Dalit. The Chief Minister of Uttar Pradesh, India's largest state, is a Dalit. It may follow that as village hierarchies respond to the modern world by becoming increasingly secular and less sacred – class intruding on caste – commensal taboos become increasingly irrelevant to the structure of village hierarchies and, thus, to the concerns of villagers. When the certainty of old ways gives way to new ways, much of the fabled conservatism of Indian villagers, their preference for what was yesterday's tried and true, gives way as well.

In the *varna dharma*, ideal groups are separated from one another by their members' inherent capacities. These are made manifest in the hereditary occupations of their groups. Castes, in general, have and are usually known by their hereditary occupations: priest, warrior, merchant, farmer, mason, smith, potter, carpenter, tanner, sweeper and so forth. Nowadays, however, many and in some cases most *jati* members do not follow their caste's hereditary occupations or follow them only in part. In village India, social honor and degrees of purity/pollution are still assigned to *jatis* on the basis of their hereditary occupations – whether or not *jati*-fellows still follow them. But, with some exceptions, people are not expected or compelled to do what they were born to do. Members of artisan castes may be farmers or moneylenders, and no one expects them to work as potters or carpenters or masons. Brahmins who can choose to become white-collar professionals, rarely choose to become *pujaris* (temple priests). Their touchable neighbors may coerce members of a Dalit *jati* into doing some polluting task associated with their hereditary occupation – disposing of dead animals, for example

– although nowadays they do the non-polluting work of farm laborers rather than the polluting work of tanners and cobblers.

Although farming and trading are the hereditary occupations of some castes, villagers, in general, regard these as occupations open to members of any *jati*. The social status accorded to families whose holdings are the same, however, may vary on the basis of their *jati*. Some villagers, from choice or necessity, combine their hereditary occupation with other work. A well-to-do farmer will also lend money. An impoverished mason will work as an agricultural laborer. Villagers may more or less reserve some hereditary occupations for members of the appropriate caste. Often, but not always, the job of temple priest is reserved for Brahmins. Some non-Brahmin castes, however, produce their own priests. Villagers will patronize a family of potters, if they are still at their wheels. But families and family firms that are not of potter caste may also make and sell clay pots. There is in India today a full range of occupations that no one regards as the hereditary work of any caste. These are the occupations of towns and cities, of modernity: from rickshaw pulling to neurosurgery.

There is usually some connection between a person's hereditary caste occupation and her or his modern job. It is frequently indirect and often something like this: to some degree and for better or worse, the hereditary caste occupation of a person's family affects his or her chances in modern, urban society. Village families of higher status and more valued skills enjoy greater potential access to wealth than do families with lower status and less valued skills. Well-to-do village families enjoy greater potential access to high status and valued skills than do poor families. The status, skills and wealth enjoyed by a village family affect its capacity to prepare its children for modern jobs. But, in all this there is also a disconnection. The valuations of purity/pollution that are attached to hereditary caste occupations in India's villages are frequently detached from modern occupations in its towns and cities.

So, for example, because the men in a hypothetical Brahmin family were trained for generations as temple priests, literacy is one of the family's skills and intellectual training is one of its experiences. Let us add to the family's income, the *maf* (beneficence) it enjoys from the gift of a landholding to support its temple. The sum of all this, for our purposes, is that the family is well situated to choose and pay for a medical career for one of its sons. Our hypothetical doctor! That doctors may be in regular contact with death and human excreta takes nothing away from this doctor's Brahminhood nor the high status of medicine as a modern occupation. In the doctor's village, *jatis* whose hereditary caste occupations, practiced or not, involve regular contact with death or human excreta – like leather workers and sweepers – are Dalit.

Much the same observation that we made earlier about *jatis'* non-application of their village commensal rules beyond walls of their villages, can be made about the non-application of their usual assessments of purity/pollution to modern occupations. They are applicable to those situations and spheres of activity in which *jatis* exercise no control or in which their attempts to exercise control would likely be unsuccessful, unprofitable and undermining of their authority.

Not entirely, but determinately by their rules of endogamy, *jatis* and castes mark and monitor the borders that separate them one from the other. But where and how and by whom are social hierarchies among them marked and monitored? As it is with us, so it is with them: social hierarchies are determined and monitored in the play of legitimacy and power. We revisit the *varna dharma*. Certainly, it is a Brahminical ideology. But its currency is general. And even those who deny its validity must wrestle with it. It is Hinduism's quintessential legitimation of power: an ideology that postulates a God-given, universally valid hierarchy.

On the ground, however, caste hierarchies are like the castes that comprise them: not universal, but regional and local. In these hierarchies, whether or not particular Brahmin *jatis* or castes are able to sustain their claims to *varna dharma* primacy depends in no small measure on their power. It may be reputational power. Chitpavans of Maharashtra, Nambudris of Kerala, Iyengars of Karnataka, Kulin Brahmins of Bengal, for example, belong to groups that are generally regarded as *pukka* Brahmin. Village families belonging to these castes may receive the deference of their neighbors, although they understand that power and wealth reside elsewhere – in a *jati* of non-Brahmin landholders, for example.

The *varna dharma* does not provide for that. It is not a secular hierarchy. But on the ground, it is receptive to secular inputs. In no particular order, the sacred and secular combine. A Brahmin *jati* may combine its reputational power with the power of landownership and *panchayati raj* position to secure its place in the local hierarchy. In the Indian countryside, priestly power can be potent. In order to protect their place in the local hierarchy, Brahmins may use their priestly power to legitimate the authority of landholders. That was more or less the hierarchical arrangement of Brahmins and Rajputs in parts of Rajasthan. In other parts, Rajput noblemen of indisputable Kshatriya *varna* demanded hierarchical precedence over Brahmins. Dalits may deny the legitimacy of any such hierarchy, but be forced by their powerlessness to abide by its rules. A *jati* of cultivators may be quite indifferent as to who occupies the notional hierarchical top, but feud endlessly with another *jati* of cultivators over which of them enjoys the higher middle rank. In the middle, occupied by many and often most *jatis*, rank order is less than determinate, often varies from village to village, and has little or nothing to do with the *varna dharma* and almost everything to do with who has more land, more clout in the upper tiers of *panchayati raj* and in the state government.

There are always castes or caste fragments, generally larger than their village *jatis*, that claim more exalted hierarchical positions than are accorded to them by their esteemed and powerful neighbors. These claims have sometimes been manifested in a process of social mobility that was named "sanskritization" by one of India's leading anthropologists, the late M. N. Srinivas.[7] As Srinivas presented them in the 1960s, many of the facts of sanskritization are no longer current. But, for us, the scheme itself retains its usefulness. It enables us, at once, to appreciate the age-old importance of sacred considerations and sacred hierarchy in village India and to observe their accelerating erosion in changing India by the modern forces of politics and economics.

A movie script about a sanskritization campaign of 40 years ago would read something like this: Prompted by some change in fortune, a *jati* or caste fragment or caste – let us name it "Charhaiya" climber – begins to claim a more exalted place in the *varna dharma* than that accorded to it by its neighbors. They, more than likely, refer to the Charhaiyas as Shudras, or imply such a reference in the regard and treatment that they accord to its *jati*-fellows in their villages. But they are mistaken, say leading Charhaiyas. Really, the Charhaiya suffers Shudra status because of some cruel twist of fate or the machination of some malign force in the immemorial past, or because of the enmity of neighbors or their jealousy or their self-interested persistence in error. In God's truth, appropriately documented, the Charhaiyas have always belonged to the Kshatriya *varna*. Having made this claim, Charhaiya leaders then encourage *jati* families to model or remodel their behavior – dietary and commensal, familial and occupational, sartorial and so forth – on the behavior of another local caste whose *jati*-fellows are generally regarded in their villages as enjoying the Kshatriya status to which our Charhaiyas aspire.

A fight ensues. Where status – whether Kshatriyahood or knighthood – is valued as a resource or as a means of access to resources, those who enjoy it and even those who do not are likely to guard it against the claims of arrivistes. These confront not only those who say "they are not as good as we are," but those who say "they are no better than we are." In Indian villages the menu of such confrontations includes social ostracism, economic boycott, harassing litigation, political vendettas and physical violence. In order to vindicate their claims – even partially, here and there but not everywhere – after many confrontations over many years, the Charhaiyas will have to give as good as they get. They will need secular resources: political, psychological, and economic. The *varna dharma*, let us say, is the hierarchy which the Charhaiyas recognize as legitimate and in which they want to sanskritize themselves upward. Their success or failure is less likely to be decided by arguments about purity/pollution or *dharma-karma* than in clashes of secular interests. Paradoxically, however, the Charhaiyas' sanskritization campaign tends to affirm the *varna dharma* hierarchy by processing in sacred form the secularly motivated and advanced ambitions of an upwardly mobile group.

Though strewn with obstacles, winding, full of pitfalls and traversable only by the most determined and resourceful travelers, the path of sanskritization goes socially upward. Even, perhaps, to the village top. But not to the India top. That top is urban. From the village's social boundary, where sanskritization breaks off, the road to the India top is "westernization." Srinivas identifies it as such, and most of its regular travelers as reasonably well-to-do urban families of twice-born castes. Their road leads to membership in the modern elite of India's great cities. The roads of sanskritization and westernization differ not only in who travels them but how they travel. So, for example, as its village women give witness to the Charhaiyas' upward mobility by sanskritizing themselves or being sanskritized into purdah, the city women of twice-born westernizing families move out of home into practicing medicine, publishing magazines, managing boutiques, climbing the bureaucratic ladder.

Our concern here is not with westernizing urban families. We return to them later. Here, we want to update to 2002 our picture of caste mobility in the countryside; and, in the process, look again at caste, in general. Not entirely but considerably, our sanskritization script of 40 years ago is dated. Thus, in 1960, and particularly before Independence, the changes in fortune that prompted castes to embark on sanskritizing campaigns were likely to be serendipitous, not of their making: some change in government policy or an economic downturn or upswing, for example, that incidentally affected them. Mostly, they were castes of peasants, and it is in the condition of peasants to have their fate determined by others.

The world in which *jatis* of peasant castes worked, lived and in which their sanskritizing campaigns were mounted were their villages. These were not entirely, but mostly, closed arenas in the Srinivas's model. No more. Nowadays, there is an unprecedented resource flow directed toward the countryside from government agencies and the great world: Green Revolution products and technology, benefits of compensatory discrimination and anti-poverty programs, development grants and loans from *panchayati raj* institutions and state governments, schools and enhanced educational opportunities, possibilities for urban employment and remittance income. Access to these resources and to the agencies that dispense them has been opened to villagers by the institutions of parliamentary democracy, the nexuses between political parties and castes, by increased literacy and education, opportunities for travel, government business in Indian languages. Village arenas nowadays are encapsulated by *panchayati raj* institutions, political parties, state legislative assemblies, the Lok Sabha. The status and power enjoyed by castes in these encapsulating arenas translates into status and power for their *jatis* in their villages.

The battle for resources is increasingly secularized. The *varna dharma* hierarchy is devalued. Jealously guarded in the past by those who benefited from them, many sacred symbols have either slipped out of use or into common use: the "sacred thread" of the twice-born, the Kshatriya name-title "Singh," who wears what, defers to whom, is properly addressed by what title, rides on horseback in his wedding procession. The usual secular rewards of high sacred status – influence, deference, *mafs* and so forth – have either disappeared or pale in comparison with the rewards of wealth and power. The sacred survives in the ancestor myths which serve to affirm the separation of castes, one from the other. In the hierarchy sanctified by the *varna dharma* creation myth, the sacred survives less well.[8] Where it counts, where the resources are and where they come from, status and power are determined not by relative degrees of purity/pollution but by wealth and political muscle.

OBC caste-fellows, India's New Men and Women, though customarily accorded no more than the sacred status of touchable peasants, seem to feel no great compulsion to sanskritize nowadays. Parliamentary and *panchayati raj* politics and capitalist economic development are their vehicles for upward mobility. Distinctions of economic class among *jatis*, which have always been a feature, however thinly veiled, of local hierarchies, have become an outstanding characteristic and one that accords less well, more ambiguously than it has in the past, with distinctions of sacred status. The demands for appropriate status by those who succeed in the pursuit of wealth and power makes the sacredness of *jati* hierarchies increasingly notional and the process of sanskritization increasingly irrelevant to social mobility. Next to the well-to-do Yadava agricultural entrepreneur, son in medical college and in-law in the Bihar ministry, who after all is his family's *pujari* (priest) but a Brahmin servant? Finally, the roads to sanskritization and westernization sometimes merge nowadays. So, as the matrons of upwardly mobile village families move into relative seclusion, their daughters are being sent to universities to learn to be modern wives and to cope in the world's cities. Upwardly mobile village families are traveling on the paths of sanskritization *and* westernization.

Now, what do *jatis* and castes do? What functions have they performed, do they perform, and what are the social implications of these performances? *Jatis* and castes are the basic particularizing institutions in the Indian countryside. Socially, India is an identity of particles. The metaphor changes from "tapestry" to "mosaic." People belong to particular families, *jatis* and castes, villages, ethnolinguistic and religious communities. It is as such that people generally think of themselves and behave, and are thought of by others and treated. *Jati* and caste particularize families, their places in their villages, Gujaratis and Tamils, Hindus and Muslims. Indian society is vast. But it does not, in the countryside, certainly, have masses. It is not a mass society. Its amenability to bourgeois revolution may have its roots in this. It may be that a society of particles is less amenable to mobilization for proletarian or ethnic revolution than to adaptation, however coincidental, to the opportunities of parliamentary democracy and capitalism.

Nowadays in India, the relatively new secular ideologies of parliamentary democracy and capitalism and the social realities that refer to them – legislative assemblies and elections, factories and class conflict, for example – impinge increasingly on the lives of Indian villagers. But, as I have suggested, the new has not so much replaced the old as been accommodated by it. Not only has the accommodation been successful thus far, but systems of accommodation have evolved – with regard to commensality and work, for example – whose capacities have no apparent limit. The little societies of Hinduism have centuries of experience in accommodating themselves to the new and secular, or non-Hindu: to Muslim and British rule. Too, it might well be that people who believe that *homo hierarchicus* is the essential and natural order of things are better able than others of us to sustain their faith while accommodating it to changes which alter inequalities but seem always to retain them.

Jatis and castes do more than particularize villagers and provide them with pecking orders. Over the centuries, *jatis* and castes have functioned as sodalities and regimes in their villages and integrators of a great subcontinental civilization. In a family-centered society, *jatis* and castes are demonstrable and conventional extensions of the family. The family has been the bastion, and the *jati* and caste its walls. Without relinquishing their usual defensive function, castes nowadays have also moved to the offensive, to assault on behalf of their members the citadels of the modern world. They do so from positions of legitimacy and strength. In a society in which faith is still a vital force, referent ideologies that are sacred, however notionally, give social groups that refer to them their credentials. Again, the sacred ancestor myths that affirm the separation of castes have been little effaced in changing India. However riven by clan feuds, family vendettas and personal hatreds, a caste enjoys the status of that mystical bond of blood which is so difficult to deny to those who claim it, and even to our dismay and discomfort identifies those of our own. In Rajasthan, another name for *jati* is *khun*: blood.

Until Indian independence, virtually all activities within villages, of defense and offense, from hearths to fields, were monitored and regulated by *jati* families and the *panchayats* of villages and *jatis*. The tax collector's *raj* intruded into village life, and sometimes crucially – in matters of land revenue, for example – but was usually no more than tangential to it. Captains of empire knew to leave well enough alone. *Panchayats* and *sarpanchas* wanted to be left alone. Today, villagers have both adjusted themselves to intrusive national and state governments and attempted to colonize them. The adjustments have been variable. Villagers have taken irrigation loans and primary schools with enthusiasm; land reform and family planning measures more selectively. They have compromised with the laws that bar untouchability and ignored those that ban dowries. In general, their modus operandi has been neither to force change nor to oppose it beyond reason and self-interest, but rather to accommodate it, situate it, profit from it or make the best of it.

More and more, villagers have intruded on, colonized in their own interests, the tax collector's *raj*. In this century, and particularly since India's independence, face-to-face interactions within small groups of *jati*-fellows have been supplemented by caste-wide activity, particularly in state politics: as political parties and blocs in political parties, colonies in the bureaucracy and factions within ministries, in *panchayati raj* institutions, as welfare societies and interest groups. In general, these are the activities of castes as associations, interest groups: formal and informal. The leaders of caste associations are caste-fellows with the requisite skills and state-wide prestige rather than the requisite age, genealogy, wealth and local reputation that characterizes *jati* leaders. Caste associations are based on shared identity and interests among their members rather than personal identification, and associational concerns are more with irrigation and electrification than ritual purity.

The domestication of parliamentary democracy in India since the 1950s has largely displaced from state legislative assemblies those twice-born reformers of the old school who represented modern and Western values. Their places have been taken by representatives of villagers and castes, their values and their takes on modernity. Nowadays state legislative assemblies sometimes resemble *panchayats*-of-the-whole, in which every caste in the state is represented, albeit unequally. Best represented, almost invariably, and most powerful though often in factions, are large castes whose leading members are well-to-do farmers. The coming to political prominence in the states, first, of "dominant" castes and, more recently, to challenge their dominance, OBC castes, are post-Independence phenomena and crucial events in bourgeois revolution.

In the mosaic of subcontinental Hindu society, its caste particles are the basic units in its integration. The sacred ideologies of Hinduism both legitimate the separation of castes and integrate them into a society characterized by its Indian-ness. There are notable regional variations between *jati* and caste societies, particularly between north and south India. But certainly more striking than these regional differences are the subcontinental similarities of castes one to another in all the basic characteristics that we have attributed to them: endogamy, commensal rules, notions of *dharma-karma* and purity/pollution, ancestor myths that affirm or deny the *varna dharma's* validity, a persistent belief in *homo hierarchicus* as the natural order of things. It is no less striking that these similarities are more than anything else the consequences from time immemorial of countless references and cross-references of separate *jati* and caste societies to common ideals. Until recently *jati* societies in the villages of different regions in India were barely aware of each other's existence, much less were they in direct contact with one another. There was some contact at pilgrimage sites, but most of these are local and regional. Hinduism has never had a subcontinental church ruled from its center, nor has there ever been a subcontinental state which sustained the Hindu *dharma* from its center. What has been subcontinental are sacred ideologies and their flawed *jati* and caste references, and nothing has contributed to the cultural identity of India more than these.

Muslim quasi *jatis* and quasi castes

We know that as Christianity developed in Europe it was profoundly influenced in its high culture by the Greco-Roman civilization that preceded it and in its popular culture by the folkways of the pagan villagers and townsmen who became Christians. It should not surprise us, then, that Islam as it developed on the subcontinent was similarly influenced by Hinduism and Hindus and that their influence was profound. Indeed, possibly more profound than the influence of pre-Christian Europe and Europeans on Christianity. After all, Islam did not develop on the subcontinent as successor to a moribund Hinduism, but as another faith in a vibrant and forever-changing civilization of Hindus. Moreover, in contrast to the Abrahamic religions, Hinduism is neither exclusivist nor creedal. Thus, it erected no substantial barriers – until the late nineteenth century – to those who chose, at once, to become Muslim and remain Hindu.

Islam on the subcontinent is the faith of Muslims who are in their overwhelming majority the progeny of converted Hindus. Their conversion was effected largely by a variety of regular and irregular Sufis or influenced by Sufism. At its most orthodox, Sufism has important theological and ritual similarities to Hinduism. At its most heterodox, Sufism was virtually indistinguishable from the Hindu *bhakti* movements of medieval India. Typically, Hindu converts came to Islam not as individuals but in groups: in *jatis* and caste fragments, usually, of middling to lowest Hindu rank. Like Hindu castes, these groups of Muslim converts have over the ages fragmented or fused with other groups to become new groups. But groups they remain, hundreds of them, in an Indian society tessellated into groups. In social terms, at least, there is no Muslim community in India. Only Muslim communities.

For the most part, these Muslim communities live among Hindu communities. Both live as *jatis* in the same villages. In these, Muslims are likely to have their own social structure, but as well to occupy places in village social hierarchies and to participate as families in relationships of production with other village families. In the twentieth century, still, there were Muslim communities which were virtually indistinguishable from their Hindu neighbors, even in their professions of faith and religious rituals. M. Mujeeb in his celebrated *Indian Muslims* gives a number of examples of such communities. Here is one, recorded in 1911, from Purnia district in what is now Bihar.

> In every village could be found a ... shrine dedicated to the worship of the [Hindu] goddess Kali, and attached to almost every Muslim house was a little shrine called ... God's House, where prayers were offered in which the names of both Allah and Kali were used. A part of the Muslim marriage ceremony was performed at the shrine of the [Hindu] goddess Bagvati. Goats, fowls, pigeons and the first fruit of trees and crops were offered [by Muslims] to purely Hindu deities, in particular the village godling ... The most popular deity, among both Hindus and Muslims, was [the Hindu] Devati Maharaj, with his door keeper, Hadi.[9]

The conversion of Hindu groups to Islam was rarely epiphanic or otherwise immediate. But usually through a long slow process, two steps forward and one step back, of acculturation from Hinduism: of "Islamization," a process of generations that for many Muslim communities is still ongoing. For some, particularly poor and newly converted communities, the process may seesaw and zigzag inconclusively. Or it may, over time, from neglect or under the influence of Hindu proselytizing, reverse itself. For some, the process may end in literate, well-articulated Islamic heterodoxy. The Khojas of Gujarat believe that the Prophet's son-in-law, Ali, was the tenth incarnation of the Lord Vishnu. The Ahmadiyyas of Punjab revere God's revelation of a prophesy and to a prophet successive to the Holy Qur'an and the Seal of the Prophets. Some groups of converts to Islam have, and others doubtlessly will, become communities of more or less orthodox Sunni or Shi'ah Muslims. For none is "Islamization" likely to efface the Indian-ness that they share with their Hindu countrymen.

I refer to these Muslim communities as quasi *jatis* or quasi castes. Called by their members *quam* (ethnic group), *beradari* (brotherhood), *zat* (alternative to *jati*) and so forth, these Muslim quasi castes exhibit to some degree some *jati-* and caste-like traits. Such traits among Muslim quasi castes enjoy the sanction of custom and usage. Not, however, the sanction of religion. To the contrary, Islam shares with the other Abrahamic religions a belief in the essential equality of male believers, if not of all of Adam's progeny.

As it is with Hindu castes, the trait most invariably exhibited by Muslim quasi castes is endogamy. Marriages sanctioned by the quasi caste are between its brides and grooms. Exceptions to this rule, as among Hindus, are almost invariably hypergamous: marriages between grooms of higher social status than their brides'. Muslim quasi castes, though less so among the elevated, are socially attached to hereditary occupations. As among Hindus, actual and hereditary occupations may differ, and both are likely to affect the social ranking of quasi castes. Muslim quasi *jatis* rank each other as do Hindu *jatis*, and with much the same indeterminacy and lack of consensus. Muslims acknowledge no prohibitions supported by injunctive scripture against interdining, but relationships of any intimacy are more likely to take place within quasi *jati* or caste ranks than outside them.

It may be, as some argue, that Indian Muslim social structure has been influenced, and not only in its ideology, by the concern of Arab Muslims with purity of descent: their "un-Islamic" legacy from the pre-Islamic Middle East. In which case, that concern meshes neatly with Hindu concern for ritual purity which is, of course, maintained over time by purity of descent – descent from caste endogamous marriages. In any case, the social structure of Muslim Indians resembles much more the social structure of their Hindu neighbors than that of Muslim Arabs.

A widespread scheme of social mobility, particularly among quasi castes in northern India, is, in effect, a Muslim variant of sanskritization. It is sometimes called "ashrafization." In Indian Muslim social ideology, the Ashraf are the functional equivalents of the twice-born in the ideology of *varna dharma*. Defined as pure by descent, the Ashraf constitute the Muslim category of, literally, "nobility." Its subcategories, hierarchically arranged are: Sayids, descendants of the Prophet, from the line of his daughter and son-in-law, Ali; Sheikhs, descendants of the Prophet's tribe or tribes associated with him; Mughals, scions of warriors from Turkestan who gave the world Tamerlane and India its greatest Muslim dynasty; and Pashtuns, the dominant tribesmen-warriors of Afghanistan. It is an illuminating insight into Indian Muslims' self-perceptions of their origins and subsequent careers, I think, that they should conceive of their nobility as entirely foreign. The one Indian exception to this rule tends to prove it. Rajputs are sometimes accepted as a fifth Ashraf category. Muslims who call themselves Rajputs, like the Bhuttos of Pakistan, are claiming Hindu ancestry of warrior stock, from a caste of unimpeachable claim to Kshatriya pedigree, and renowned for its concern with purity of descent.

Like *varna dharma*, then, the classification of Ashraf is best thought of as a referent ideology. It is not a group and its subgroups of people. Rather, it is a social category of subcategories to which groups of Muslims either refer themselves or aspire. Quasi castes that aspire to Ashraf status discover that they are of Sheikh or some other Ashraf ancestry, document and publicize their discovery, model their social behavior after that of some quasi caste of unquestionable Sheikh status, try to arrange marriages with them or, failing that, with some other quasi caste fragment of less unquestionable Sheikh status, and so forth.

Of the quasi-ness of Muslim *jatis* and castes, the essence is their lack of legitimacy in religious ideology: more, their illegitimacy in Islamic ideology. Undetermined and unfixed by anything sacred, the positions of quasi caste fragments and their individual members are more susceptible to change through the influence of money, power and pluck than are the positions of Hindu caste fragments and Hindus. A frequently cited illustration of this is an apocryphal assessment by a Muslim farmer of his social position in western Uttar Pradesh: "Last year, I was a *Julaha* [a weaver by quasi caste], this year a Sheikh and next year, if the harvest is good, I will be a Sayid."[10]

In the general rush to middle-class affluence and respectability, Muslims come from behind. In general, Muslim quasi castes are among the poorest, most illiterate and uneducated groups in India. Internally, they are burdened, on the one hand by apologists who assure them that Islam has all the answers to the problems of the modern world and, on the other hand, by "funda-mentalists" and their *madarasas* (schools) which ignore or reject the modern world. The inward-turning defensiveness of these groups has certainly been encouraged from outside: by their use as a vote bank by Congress, the force of an increasingly aggressive and violent Hindu communalism which denies Islam's Indian-ness and the loyalty of its Muslim minority to India. Still, the participation in bourgeois revolution that nowadays characterizes aspiring Hindu castes, characterizes aspiring Muslim quasi castes as well. And more and more, in the countryside, among Muslims no less than Hindus, models of respectability and its symbols are taken from the modernized Ashraf and other groups, Muslims and Hindus, of modern urban India.

Dalits and untouchability

I have already alluded to untouchability but said little about it directly. It is the condition of more than 165 million Indians. We refer to them collec-tively as "Dalits," the oppressed, the downtrodden. They were renamed as such some years ago by their literary and political vanguard, mostly from Maharashtra. The name change is significant, meaningful and generally used in the media, by politicians and by people like us. "Dalit" implicitly denies the existence of any relationship between untouchability and Hindu sacred ideology. Untouchability is neither in God's order of the universe, nor are untouchables – *pace* Mahatma Gandhi – Harijans, God's people. God has nothing to do with untouchability. Nor does *dharma-karma*. Untouchability is the product of human oppression, and the oppressed can cast it off.

Dalit castes, ubiquitous throughout India, number in the hundreds and in all their characteristics are like other castes. Except that members of Dalit *jatis* are regarded by their touchable village neighbors as carriers of pollution so dreadful as to necessitate extraordinary quarantine. In theory, Dalits are the sources of dreadful pollution because their castes customarily have had particularly unclean living habits – eating carrion, for example – or particular occupations which involve regular physical contact with death or human excreta, or both. Castes whose ancestral occupations are tanning or attending to funeral grounds are usually regarded as untouchable, for example, as are castes of sweepers and launderers. Nais, whose hereditary caste occupation is barbering, are regarded as Dalits in some places and not in others. Many, perhaps most, members of Dalit castes may, in fact, have abandoned their unclean habits or occupations. Nowadays, Dalits are usually agricultural laborers who hold little or no land and work for village landholders. But that is theoretically irrelevant to the sacred status of their *jati* members as village untouchables. That unclean habits and occupations were hereditarily theirs indicates that they are naturally unclean.

Extraordinary measures are necessary to quarantine the contagion of untouchability: more than the usual restrictions on inter-dining and food handling among touchable *jatis*. Typically, Dalit *jatis* are kept residentially segregated in their villages and forbidden ordinary access to village temples, the homes of touchable villagers and the wells and tanks that are the sources of their domestic water supply. The poorest of the village poor are usually Dalits. They live in squalor and misery. Touchable villagers have kept them in their lowly place by holding them in debt bondage or otherwise paying them as little as possible for their labor, sexually exploiting Dalit women, discouraging the education of their children, routinely subjecting Dalits to verbal and physical abuse, and demanding that they acknowledge their lowliness in the ways in which they refer to themselves and defer to their betters. For touchable, and particularly landholding, villagers, Dalits provide the economic services of an exploitable labor pool, and the social and psychological services of *untermenschen*: people to be better than, to look down on, despise, humiliate, ridicule, reduce to servility and groveling.

For the Indian government, however, untouchability has always been a national disgrace. Its constitutional and legal commitment is to rid India of it. That is not only the approved and intended direction of change, but the actual direction. Though the path is not always followed and the pace is slow. I want to discuss untouchability in terms of getting rid of it. To clarify the discussion we can distinguish sacred ways of getting rid of it and mundane ways. Of course, the ways often cross.

Ironically, the same Hinduism which apparently sanctions untouchability, also promises untouchables relief from it. Simply, the sweeper who accepts his *dharma* as a sweeper in this life, will be reborn into the next as a sweeper's better. We can only guess at the extent to which this promise has been a source of consolation and hope to Dalits over the ages. Certainly, it has been a device for keeping them in their place. Not all have been happy to stay there, however. We know that much. There are Dalit caste fragments that have sanskritized their way into touchable Hindu status, although rarely. In general, Dalit castes have lacked the resources, psychological as well as economic and political, to sustain a sanskritizing campaign; and their attempts to do so are often met with particularly bitter resistance from touchable Hindus.

But Hinduism does not provide the only sacred way out of untouchability. It is generally agreed that of those *jatis* and caste fragments that have over the centuries converted to Christianity and Islam, a substantial proportion were Dalit. I assume that many of the converts were motivated by the desire to rid themselves of their untouchability or of its consequences – hunger, for example. To what extent the tens of millions of descendants of these converts are materially better off for their having become Christians and Muslims, is, again, something about which we can only guess. They are, in general, two of the poorest religious groups in India. To boot, Christians and Muslims have their own Dalit quasi castes – so regarded by their coreligionists, as well as by their Hindu neighbors. Still, it is probably true that upward mobility from a Hindu untouchable base is less likely to have occurred through sanskritization than through conversion first, and then social climbing up through Christian ranks or by ashrafization. Doubtlessly, there are perfectly respectable Muslims these days whose ancestors were Hindu untouchables.

From the founding of the Arya Samaj in 1875 to the recent climb to power and prominence of the BJP and the "family" of Hindu groups to which it belongs, the *sangh pariwar* (organization family), the attraction of Christianity and Islam to Dalits has been of great concern to Hindu revivalist organizations. Their response has been to accept that untouchability is an excrescence on Hinduism rather than something sanctioned by it, sponsor programs for Dalit welfare, discourage – sometimes violently – and disparage Christian and Muslim proselytizing and make some efforts to reconvert Christian and Muslim Dalits back to Hinduism. A recent past president of the BJP is a Dalit. It is fair to say, however, that benevolences from the "forces of *Manuvad*" (Brahminical Hinduism) are generally greeted with suspicion and distain by Dalit politicians.

In the decades before India's independence, Mahatma Gandhi and Bhimrao Ramji Ambedkar marked two major crossings of the sacred and mundane ways to rid India of untouchability. Gandhi described himself as a *varna-shramadharma* Hindu: one who believes in the major tenets of the faith. Untouchability was, to him, *the* corruption of the faith. He was a passionate preacher and active campaigner against the "sin" of untouchability. He worked and lived among untouchables. It was Gandhi who renamed them Harijans. In his *ashrams* (headquarters-cum-model communities) Gandhi forbade the practice of untouchability, and he proscribed it for Congressmen. But his way of ridding India of untouchability was much the same as that of the twice-born Hindu reformers who preceded him. It was the way of "uplift" and reconciliation within Hinduism. Harijans were encouraged to give up those things – beef eating and whisky drinking, for example – that supposedly offend caste Hindus. They in turn were encouraged to revalue the work done by Harijans and to accept them as ordinary members of the Hindu fold. In effect, untouchability would disappear by dissolution into Hinduism, by the undoing of the ancient bifurcation of the Shudra *varna*.

Gandhi, of course, was not only a *mahatma* (a Hindu saint; literally, a great soul) but also the Indian National Congress's supremo, and there were good political reasons – which he would not have distinguished from good religious reasons – for keeping within the Hindu fold almost one-fifth of its members, safe from British divide-and-rule tactics to entice them out. Safe for the Congress. But not safe *from* the Congress. That was Ambedkar's argument. In Congress, Dalits would be the powerless wards of a nationalist movement whose reins were held by twice-born and "dominant" Hindu castes. The oppressors! Not safe for lack of the opportunity to develop outside of touchable Hindu domination, as had the Muslims with British patronage, into a separate and powerful constituency in Indian politics.

Ambedkar was a Dalit: from the very large Mahar caste of Maharashtra. He was one of the remarkable men of his age: an economist trained at Columbia University and the London School of Economics, a leading barrister, distinguished academic lawyer and chief draftsman of the Indian constitution. As both an intellectual and an activist, he was the outstanding Dalit politician of the twentieth century. He wanted Dalits out of Hinduism and out of the Congress. Only outside could they free themselves from the sacred contempt and secular oppression of Hindus. Only outside the Congress could they be powerful, and only if they were powerful would their Hindu oppressors heed them. In the years of discussion before the landmark India Act of 1935 was passed by the British parliament, Ambedkar lobbied the British government to establish for untouchables the same sort of separate political identity that they had gifted to Muslims earlier in the century.

The British agreed to Ambedkar's demand. Gandhi went on a "fast unto death" until either the agreement or the demand was withdrawn. Unhappily,

Ambedkar backed down to Gandhi's "Poona Pact" compromise of 1932. It more or less indicated what has become the grand strategy for abolishing untouchability in independent India. Dalit castes were to be regarded as an integral part of Hindu and Indian society. But in order to realize that integration, they would be made the beneficiaries of compensatory and protective discrimination.

In the years immediately after Independence, Ambedkar organized and led untouchable political action in Maharashtra. But no more than any other party, could his Republican Party compete with Congress. In the last years of his life he led a mass conversion of Mahars to Buddhism. He must have understood that people lacking in self-esteem are unlikely to mobilize themselves successfully for political action. In order to hold Dalits in thrall, Hinduism had forbidden them self-esteem. They could only gain it by choosing not to be Hindus. Ambedkar said that while he was born a Hindu, he would not die one. He need not endure oppression. By an act of will, he could cast it off. Thus, he prefigured the change of "untouchables," "ex-untouchables," "scheduled castes," "backward classes," "Harijans" to "Dalits." There are now about 8 million Buddhists in India. Most of them are Mahars. Buddhism has become a major faith of Ambedkar's caste-fellows and of some north Indian Chamar/Jatavs (leather-workers, by caste). But whatever they may have gained in self-esteem from their conversion, in their villages the social positions and material conditions of these Buddhists generally remain those of Dalits.

In independent India, the mundane ways for getting rid of untouchability have been marked out over the past half-century. Three ways are, more or less, government directed; a fourth, of increasing importance, is autonomously political.

First, through the law. The Indian constitution expressly abolishes untouchability. It prohibits any government agency or private establishment that maintains public facilities – wells and temples, for example – from discriminating or acting in any way *against* any Indian citizen on the grounds that he or she belongs to a scheduled caste. The constitution and laws pursuant to it make any such discrimination or action a criminal offense. In addition, there are laws which are meant, explicitly or implicitly, to benefit Dalits. Manual scavenging – cleaning latrines and disposing of dead animals by hand – which is almost entirely the work of Dalits, and bonded labor, which is the condition of a disproportionate number of Dalits, have both been outlawed by the government. A disproportionate number of Dalits are landless, and they were meant to be the disproportionate beneficiaries of land redistribution schemes and mandated minimum wages for agricultural labor under land reform legislation. None of these laws have been adequately implemented.

Second, through compensatory and protective discrimination. The Indian government pioneered in this area, now widely known among English-speakers by its American euphemism, "affirmative action." Its rationale, though not its modus operandi, has been much the same in India and the United States: only by allowing a period of unequal advantage to those sections of society that have been most socially disadvantaged can they ever be brought to a level of equality with the generality of their fellow citizens. Discrimination *in favor of* disadvantaged groups is explicitly permitted by the Indian constitution.

Its framers were in no doubt but that the most generally disadvantaged, oppressed and brutalized of their fellow citizens were those whom the constitution, following British imperial nomenclature, lists as "scheduled castes and tribes." Here my discussion of compensatory discrimination is confined to scheduled castes: Dalits. Scheduled caste representation in the Union parliament and state legislative assemblies is guaranteed. This is done by reserving for Dalit candidates *alone* the right to contest about 15 percent of parliamentary and legislative assembly constituencies. All adult residents in these constituencies are enfranchised, but the candidates – of all parties and none – must belong to scheduled castes. Seats are also reserved for Dalit candidates in proportion to the relevant "scheduled caste" population at all levels and in all leadership positions in all *panchayati raj* institutions. Places in educational institutions, including universities, are reserved for Dalits, in proportion to their numbers; and relaxed terms of admission and scholarship schemes are available to them. Places in all grades of employment, from executive to menial class, in Union and state public services and in all government-owned corporations are reserved for scheduled castes. To facilitate their employment, particularly in the higher grades, ordinarily applicable qualifications – age limits, educational requirements, experience and so forth – are relaxed for Dalit applicants.

Third, through anti-poverty programs. Although there are state-sponsored programs – free meals for school children, for example – anti-poverty programs are generally the responsibility of the Government of India. These are not specifically targeted at Dalits, but they are disproportionately represented among those below the poverty line: about one-and-a-half times more than the official figure (27 percent) for the population in general. Thus, at least in theory, Dalits would be the disproportionate beneficiaries of anti-poverty programs. These are, basically, of three sorts: food subsidy, rural works and self-employment.

The food subsidy program accounts for about 55 percent of the spending on anti-poverty programs. For many years, the non-poor surreptitiously and with official connivance availed themselves of the program's benefits.

These were more closely targeted to the poor in 1997, and apparently with some success. Self-employment programs are basically subsidized lending schemes. They make up about 5 percent of anti-poverty program spending. After not much success, the existing self-employment programs, which lent to individuals, were replaced in 1999 by one program which subsidizes lending to self-help groups. Rural works programs account for about one-third of anti-poverty program spending. They focus on employment generation and, particularly, on the construction of such rural infrastructure development as paved roads.

In general, anti-poverty programs are riddled with bureaucratic sloth and corruption. A recent study of the food subsidy program in Uttar Pradesh found that "... only 40 percent of the grain allotted to the state actually reached the intended beneficiaries: 20 percent was simply not lifted from central storage facilities and the remaining 40 percent was unaccounted for."[11]

Recent reforms in the programs shift some of the responsibility for their implementation to *panchayati raj* institutions. The 73rd Amendment notwithstanding, what is known about the disproportionate influence on these institutions of the non-poor leaves us with some doubt as to who is most likely to benefit from these reforms. We gain some insight into the Indian government's priorities and compulsions from figures published by the World Bank and India's National Council of Applied Economic Research. Poverty alleviation programs account for some 6–7 percent of the central government's spending, "or 1 percent of GDP."[12] Subsidies to rural middle classes – explicitly for fertilizer and implicitly in the non-collection of charges for electricity, irrigation and credit – are estimated at 2.5 percent of GDP.[13]

Fourth, through Dalit political action. This, of course, is not directed by government, but rather facilitated by government-sponsored compensatory discrimination and as a consequence of parliamentary democracy. The icon and inspiration for Dalit political action is Babasaheb (revered father) Ambedkar. Dalits have not forgotten his "Poona Pact" defeat, and they have not forgiven Gandhi for his victory. They do not want to be Gandhi's Harijans: people of a God who sanctions their untouchability, who stigmatizes them from birth as the lowliest breed of humanity, who colludes in their oppression.

Appropriately, Dalits, by that name, first appeared among Ambedkar's Mahar caste-fellows. In the 1960s, a direct-action group that called itself the Dalit Panthers – in imitation of the direct-action American Black Panthers – appeared and disappeared in Maharashtra. More long-lived and possibly of greater long-term political significance has been a library of Dalit literature, most prominently in Maharashtra. In poetry, plays, novels and short stories, writers who have experienced the awfulness of untouchability describe it for their countrymen. More overtly political are Dalit, or particular Dalit caste vote banks and blocs, in *panchayati raj* institutions, political parties, legislative assembles, bureaucracies and ministries.

In the caste warfare that simmers and regularly comes to a boil in the Bihar countryside, Dalit villagers, armed and trained by Naxalite communists, return push for push and sometimes shove for push against the *senas* (militias) of armed thugs maintained by touchable farmers. Also from Bihar, Ram Vilas Paswan is a Dalit political leader at the Centre. In a left-leaning, OBC-dominated United Front government in New Delhi, between 1996 and 1998, Paswan used his position as Railways Minister to build his very own vote bank in the subcontinent's largest employer. Paswan's party was until recently a constituent in the National Democratic Alliance and he was a minister in the government led by the right-leaning, upper-caste-dominated BJP. He would like to be India's first Dalit prime minister.

Dalit politics have had their greatest success in Uttar Pradesh, the largest state in India. There, a Dalit-based political party, the BSP (Bhujan Samaj Party – common people's association), has become a major player in state politics. Under an arrangement with a BJP searching for Dalit votes, the BSP's firebrand, Mayawati, a Delhi University graduate and a former school teacher, was the state's chief minister for two brief and tumultuous periods in 1995 and 1997. With no ordinary Indian politician's lip-service to parliamentary democracy's norm of an apolitical bureaucracy, Mayawati appointed and transferred officers on the bases of their Dalit caste or their friendliness to Dalit interests, or both. Otherwise, she used scarce state resources to build monuments to Ambedkar and other non-twice-born *bhujan* leaders. For the BSP, any alliance – with OBC parties or with the "A or B team" of Brahminical Hinduism, the BJP or Congress – will do, so long as it yields some share of political power. "We have a one-point program," said Kanshi Ram, the BSP's founder and supremo, "take power."[14] Of all the parties that contested the 2002 state elections in Uttar Pradesh, the BSP won the second largest number of seats. Mayawati has returned to the *gaddi* for the third time: this time with the BJP in tow as her junior partner.

The major obstacles to Dalit politics are two. First, the majority of Dalits are still poor, illiterate, dependent on others for their livelihoods and, therefore, vulnerable to intimidation. Second, "Dalit" is, of course, a collective name for many, frequently competitive and mutually hostile castes. Taken separately or collectively, they are invariably a minority of their states' castes and scattered throughout its electoral constituencies. Thus, because Kanshi Ram and Mayawati are Chamar/Jatavs, the BSP is shunned as a Chamar/Jatav party by some other Dalit castes in Uttar Pradesh. And while the Chamar/Jatavs are one of the state's largest castes, its caste-fellows constitute a majority in no electoral constituency. The BSP's electoral strength is therefore dependent on its ability to enter into alliances, and these have been invariably opportunistic and short-lived. For the third time, Mayawati's tenure on the *gaddi* is dependent on her alliance with *Manuvad's* A team.

To what extent have these four ways in combination contributed, not to the abolition, certainly, but to the abatement of untouchability in India? The best answer, I think, is that they have done so to some predictably disappointing extent and in a fashion consonant with bourgeois revolution. No more than for the general population has change for Dalits been from the bottom up. In spite of constitutional and legal prohibitions against the practice of untouchability, it is still widely practiced, particularly in the countryside, and at times with the connivance or the heedlessness of those who are charged with enforcing the law. There is, however, and not only in Uttar Pradesh, an increasing presence of Dalits in state and *panchayati raj* politics and in civil and police bureaucracies in the countryside. This, coupled with the growing unwillingness of Dalits to grin and bear it, has probably made it more difficult for their unfriendly neighbors to get away with molesting Dalit women or keeping Dalit voters from the polls. It may be that the case load of crimes against Dalits that continues to mount is in some measure a reflection of the increased willingness of Dalits to take their complaints to the police and the increased political pressure on them to register Dalit complaints.[15] It may be that the touchable caste *senas* which terrorize and brutalize Dalit villagers in central Bihar pay a perverse tribute to increased Dalit assertiveness. In the past, Dalits could be intimidated by the mere presence of touchable villagers. Now they need armed thugs to do the job, and Dalits meet their violence with violence.

Reports of violent outrages on Dalit men, women and children by touchable villagers and stories of caste warfare in the countryside are more likely to come from underdeveloped states in which Dalits are particularly poor and degraded – from Bihar, regularly. Such reports are less likely to come from developed states in which Dalits are relatively well-off and relatively well-able to defend themselves. The better off they are, the more able are Dalits to buy or rent or hold onto land. In places where Green Revolution technology is well established, even small-holdings can be viable. The wages of agricultural laborers "increase in real terms wherever growth and the diversification of the local economy are sufficiently strong."[16] After five years of falling agricultural wages in Punjab and rising agricultural wages in Bihar, they were still only 75 percent of Punjab's agricultural wage level in 1999.[17]

We revisit our comparison between Bihar and Punjab. Dalits probably benefit more from general prosperity than from the government's various poverty alleviation programs. Where village dispensaries and schools exist and function, as they do in Punjab, the opportunities increase for Dalits to avail themselves of medical care, to educate their children and to take advantage of their access to discriminatory reservations for opportunities outside their villages. In 1991, the overall literacy rate among Dalits in Bihar (28 percent) was half the comparable figure in Punjab, and Dalit female literacy rate in Bihar (7 percent!) was less than a quarter of the comparable figure in Punjab. Ninety-one percent of Bihar's Dalits were villagers, compared to 79 percent of Punjab's Dalits. Seventy-two percent of Bihar's Dalits were agricultural laborers, compared to 60 percent of Punjab's Dalits.

Even in Punjab, particularly in Punjab, however, there is little hope for the alleviation of Dalit poverty through further land reform. There has been some tenancy reform, in West Bengal, for example, as a result of CPI–M (Communist Party of India–Marxist) state government policy and in Punjab as a consequence of Green Revolution capitalism; but there is little hope anywhere for redistributive land reform. Agricultural reforms, in general, including the Green Revolution, have not favored Dalits. Over the years, the percentage of Dalit farmers – most of them marginal – has fallen, and the percentage of Dalit agricultural laborers has risen. Given the dominance of landholding farmers in virtually all states, any substantial redistribution of land to the landless, Dalits and others, is likely to remain the unfulfilled goal of an earlier generation of Congress Party reformers.

In the bad old days, not so long ago, it was the general practice in Indian villages to deny even a basic education to Dalit children. The sacred rationale for their exclusion from village schools was that their proximity to touchable students and teachers threatened them with pollution's contagion. In more recent years, the great desire on the part of touchable villagers to educate their children and thus prepare them for urban careers as remittance income earners, has made villagers fearful of imperiling their government schools by barring Dalit children from them. Compared to allowing them access to village wells and temples, it has been a minor concession *to* Dalits. But *for* Dalits it has been a major concession. Education is the Dalits' key to the opportunities of employment provided for them by compensatory discrimination. Uneducated, their chances, alternative to agricultural labor, are those of urban drudgery and servility or, worse, virtual helotry in stone quarries and brick kilns. Educated, well-educated, they are employable in the positions reserved for them in the higher grades of public service and government-owned corporations. Nothing is more promising for the Dalit future than education and educated employment.

In 1953, Dalits were less than one percent (133) of the upper two of four categories of central government employees. In 1995, more than 11 percent (20,434) of the upper two categories of central government employees were Dalits. They had not yet reached the quota reserved for them in these employment categories – about 15 percent – but they soon will, if they have not already done so. Moreover, about five times the number of people employed by the Centre work for state and local government and public sector enterprises. On the fair assumption that Dalits serve these employers in their upper echelons in much the same proportion as they do in central employment, there are now upwards of a million Dalit family members who enjoy income and positions of honor that would have been unimaginable to their parents and grandparents. They are the Dalit urban, professional middle class. To date, compensatory discrimination has done more to create a Dalit bourgeoisie than to raise the general social and economic level of Dalits.

But, the story need not end there. As the push for gender equality comes from urban, middle-class women, so the impetus for the abolition of un-touchability is likely to come from urban middle-class Dalits. Aided by the increasing literacy and assertiveness of ordinary Dalit villagers, Dalit officers and politicians serve Dalit interests in the countryside. They know, if they have not always known, that their careers and those of their castes are intertwined. As state governments, of whatever party and caste composition, factor Dalit votes and voters into their political calculations, their civilian and police officers are likely to alter their behavior accordingly. By their example, Dalits who have made it are potential contributors to Dalit self-esteem and discreditors of any lingering belief in the natural inferiority of Dalits.

But in the operation of lifting tens of millions of impoverished and degraded Dalits by tens of thousands of middle-class Dalits, progress is bound to be slow. The belief in untouchability is long-lived and general in the Indian countryside. It is built into the psyches of touchable villagers, into their religious beliefs and the social and economic structures of their villages. Nonetheless, there has been progress and its direction is clear: toward the amelioration of the conditions of Dalits and, perhaps, the abolition of untouchability. In more than half a century of Indian independence and compensatory discrimination, untouchability has not been abolished and Dalits have not gained equality. What they have gained, for the first time in millennia, and it is no small gain when measured against the obstacles to it, is the *possibility* of gaining equality, if not in their lifetimes, then, perhaps in those of their children.

Chapter 3

Class

In the last chapter I indicated that the notionally sacred social systems of Indian villages have, in fact, substantial and growing secular components. These are, primarily, of wealth, power and influence. They are likely to be enjoyed by village households to the extent that they control the productive assets of their villages. In most villages the primary productive asset is land. To the extent of their holdings, then, households which control land are likely to enjoy wealth, power and influence. These are also likely to be enjoyed by households that control capital: money, for example, which can be loaned, bullocks or tractors for hire, access to state or cooperative society development funds or remittance income from urban employment. Some, though not all, village households that control capital also control land. Then, of course, there is the "other half." They control neither land nor capital. They are poor, powerless, without influence and readily exploitable by households that control land and capital. Between a village household that holds ten hectares and one that is landless there exists in all this implies as stark a contrast between wealth and poverty as we are likely to meet in London or Manhattan.

Can we discuss class relationships among villagers? Certainly. They exist, and in my experience and from reports of scholars and journalists, it seems clear that villagers nowadays are acutely conscious of class differences among themselves and between them and non-villagers. Our discussion, however, encounters a major obstacle and one that it must negotiate. It is this: while villagers doubtless have their class relationships, these are mediated largely by affiliations that are derived neither from their class positions nor the class consciousness of their members. What to do? It seems to me that there are two principal ways in which other-than-class-based affiliations, larger and more inclusive than families, mediate class relationships in the Indian country-side. First, they are mediated by castes or religious and tribal communities, or by associations of these groups. Second, class relationships are mediated by the same or different responses or anticipated responses from different classes to class-related stimuli. In addition, patron–client and employer–employee affiliations, factions and *panchayati raj* institutions mediate class relationships. But this mediation is essentially class-based, however rational-ized or disguised.

Some contextual matters before we proceed. First, a general assumption in my discussion is that the states of the Indian Union are the largest and most inclusive arenas in which there are rural class relations. Within these, of course, there are smaller arenas. To be sure, rural interests are well rep-resented in national politics, but there the relations of rural classes are generally with government or urban interests. Second, the definition of class most comfortable to my discussion is one of Max Weber's. I established this earlier, but it bears repeating here. Thus, a class is a group of people whose "typical chance for a supply of goods, external life conditions and personal life experiences" is determined by their similar capacities "to dispose of goods or skills for the sake of income in a given economic order." In other words, and in Indian rural terms, a class is a collection of households which are similarly situated economically. Which share a "market situation." Class groups may or may not be communities or societies. Their members may or may not be conscious of belonging to a class.[1]

Primordial groups as mediators of class relationships

There is perhaps an implication here that caste or communal relationships as such and relationships of classes are somehow distinct, although both may be mediated by castes or communal groups. Indeed, it may be useful in some of our discussion to treat them as distinct, but only for purposes of analysis. For example, to distinguish, on the one hand, social climbing through sans-kritization, and on the other hand, frustrating land reform legislation through the use of political muscle. Our distinction is akin to the physiologist's treatment of circulatory and respiratory systems as analytically distinct. Of course, in neither social nor physiological reality do such distinctions exist. Villagers experience their social systems holistically; as our bodies experience the respiration of air and the circulation of blood.

In real relationships among villagers, those of castes and classes are *not* a duality. They patch in here and there, usually overlapping, in the variegated, variegating fabric of village social life. The patchwork includes, for example, and now more than ever, well-to-do families of quite ordinary caste and well-born families of quite ordinary income. To villagers this is not anomalous but commonplace. To us it is the first clue to an understanding of the role of castes and communal groups in the representation of their members' class interests. For well-to-do villagers and poor ones, well-born villagers and ones who are lowly born, caste and class are not distinct but composite parts of their identities – as are the status groups and classes to which we belong composite parts of our identities.

Castes and communal groups, of course, are not derived from the class consciousness of their member families, nor is consciousness of class likely to be the primary bond among them. Apart from some Dalit castes in which poverty is general, castes and communities generally include families of different classes and exclude families of the same class. Still, however imperfect the fit, near enough has been good enough for castes and communal groups to establish for themselves in democratic and developing India a relatively new, secular and modern raison d'être. They have become representatives of their members' political and economic concerns.

The representation takes place in a variety of ways. There are caste and communal associations which cater for their caste-fellows' interests and are organized in more-or-less associational fashion with elected office bearers, dues-paying memberships, accounts, bylaws, and so forth. There are some well-established caste associations, like those of the Nair and Ezhrava castes of Kerala. In Punjab, the Sikh's central temple trust, the Shiromani Gurudwara Prabandak Committee, is, at once, the apex organization of Sikh religion and the state's political powerhouse. Formidable interest groups such as these provide their members with a wide range of educational, job and welfare services in addition to political influence in state politics. Parliamentary democratic politics and their intimate connection to economic development has prompted the formation, fragmentation and reformation of associations of castes and communal fragments all over India.

There are caste and communal blocs in virtually every state political party organization, legislative assembly and government ministry. In state politics, conflicts between and within these blocs are ceaseless. They may (or may not) be related to such sacred ends as the vindication of a caste's claim to twice-born status, but their means are secular and are made manifest in the clash of secular interests. Moreover, while caste groups, for example, may retain their concern with Hindu social respectability, they increasingly define respectability and mark the routes to it in class terms. Who takes water from whom becomes less and less important, and who has how many irrigated hectares becomes more and more important.

In the struggle for hectares and other assets, castes and communal groups, by themselves or in alliance, have established or captured political parties at the state level. In Punjab, the Akali Dal is the Sikh communal party. It is intimately connected to the Shiromani Gurudwara Prabhandak Committee. But neither the Dal nor the Committee limit their concerns to defending the *panth* (faith). Both are concerned with serving the secular interests of the *khalsa* (Sikh community), and particularly the interests of its farm families.

Since 1967, Tamil Nadu has been ruled by coalitions, one led by the Dravida Munnetra Kazhagam (DMK) and the other by the All-India Anna Dravida Munnetra Kazhagam (AIADMK). Both parties are factions of an older Dravidian movement that was organized to challenge the sacred status of Tamil Brahmins and to oppose their dominance in Tamil Nadu as land-holders and in public administration and the professions. That battle was won some years ago. In 2002, the AIADMK's *amma* (mother) and Tamil Nadu's current chief minister is an imperious Brahmin woman, and the Dravidian movement has fragmented into a struggle over fishes and loaves between splinter parties which represent the interests of their caste con-stituencies.

In the northeast, tribesmen – Nagas, Mizos, Bodos – have fought guerrilla wars against paramilitary forces of the Indian government and challenged it less violently with their own political parties. They want to protect not only their tribal identities but also their economic interests against the incursions of non-tribal farmers, illegal Bangladeshi migrants and Bengalis in general, moneylenders and timber contractors. Central Bihar's simmering class-cum-caste warfare periodically comes to the boil in bloody guerilla warfare. We can identify the antagonists in class terms: the landed versus the landless. But they are organized for battle on caste lines: the caste militias of touchable farmers versus Dalit landless laborers trained and armed by revolutionary communist cadres.

Most NGOs in India are the products of middle-class activists who help to organize groups of poor people to help themselves ameliorate their living and working conditions. The groups are usually identified by their organizers in terms of what their members do or where they live: agricultural labor, work in cottage industries, brick kilns and sweatshops, or earthquake victims in Gujarat, villagers facing displacement by the Narmada River's damming. More than likely, however, the constituencies of these NGOs identify them-selves in terms of what they are: their castes and communal groups.

Uttaranchal, one of three new states created by the Centre in 2000, was carved from Uttar Pradesh. The impetus for its creation was the demand of its large upper-caste population to be freed from the compensatory discrimination extended by Uttar Pradesh to its large OBC population. Everywhere, nowadays, OBCs are at the center of politics and political calculations.

The Second Backward Classes [Mandal] Commission report of 1980 is the OBC charter. It calculated as OBC more than 5,000 castes constituting about 52 percent of the Indian population, and recommended the reservations for them of 27 percent of all positions in the central government's bureaucracies and public sector industries and in all admissions to institutions of higher education. In 1990, these recommendations were accepted by prime minister V. P. Singh. The *"Manuvadi"* BJP quit his National Front coalition, and the government fell. V. P. Singh lost the battle, but the war was won by the OBCs. Reservations for them, not only at the Centre, but in state bureaucracies, state public sector industries and universities have become general throughout India.

Thus, caste membership rather than, for example, family income, was officially made the marker of a household's backwardness, in particular, and more generally, of its class. The Mandal Commission acknowledged and extended the connection of caste consciousness with class aspiration. It legitimated the assertion of class interests in caste terms. Best postioned to assert the class interests of their caste-fellows are castes of OBCs. To the embourgeoisement of OBCs, the "mandalization" of class has given impetus and direction. It has opened to OBC aspirations the opportunities of the city. What upper classes of higher castes have secured by virtue of their wealth and education and what lower classes of Dalit castes have secured by virtue of compensatory discrimination, may now be secured by OBCs thanks to *"mandal."* That has become the shorthand for caste politics. Thanks to *mandal*, OBCs have secured privileged access to money and status in the upper ranks of government employment and university education for careers in well-paying and prestigious professions. Finally, we might note in passing that by following the letter of the Indian constitution's sanctioning of compensatory discrimination to *Other Backward Classes*, as distinguished from compensatory discrimination to *Scheduled Castes and Tribes*, the Mandal Commission and Indian governments have recognized a village marker of crucial importance to OBC castes. Even in the dispensation of political favor, they are other than, different and separate from, Dalits.

In recent years, *mandal* has imparted a certain dynamic to compensatory discrimination. No more or less politically motivated than was V. P. Singh, politicians in at least five states have carved out caste constituencies of MBCs – Most Backward Classes – from their OBC populations. Even that erstwhile champion of Hindu *sanghatan* (union), the BJP, has been unable to resist the force of mandalization. Thus, in 2001, a Social Justice Committee at least as sensitive to the electoral interests of Uttar Pradesh's BJP government as to social justice recommended the following refinements:

[The committee] categorized Dalits into two schedules: Schedule A comprising Chamars, Jatavs and Dhusias; and Schedule B comprising 65 other [Dalit] castes ... Of the 21 percent reservation available for Dalits, the committee ... recommended the reservation of 10 percent for the castes in Schedule A and 11 percent for those in Schedule B ... The Committee has categorized ... OBCs into three schedules ... Schedule A, titled "the backward castes," comprises Yadavs and Ahirs [for whom] the reservation recommended ... is 5 percent. Schedule B comprises eight castes ... [which] have been categorized as "most backward" ... The Committee ... recommended 9 percent reservation for this category. Schedule C comprises 70 "extremely backward castes," including 22 ... castes in the Muslim community. [The committee] ... suggested 14 percent reservation for the castes in Schedule C.[2]

It is enough, I think, to recall and restate some of our earlier discussion about *jatis* and castes to understand why they, in particular, have become primary mediators of their members' class relationships in the Indian countryside. In sum, *jatis* are demonstrable and ideological extensions of families. Castes are demonstrable and ideological extensions of *jatis*. In a society in which family ties are particularly salient, all the legitimate members of people's families, however distant, are their caste-fellows. Intimate social relationships are more likely within *jatis* and castes than outside them. The status that attaches to customary caste occupations is so ideologically fixed that it almost invariably outlives the actual practice of those occupations by *jati*-fellows in their villages. *Jatis* and castes embody consciousness, in depth and breadth, to a degree that is unattained and probably unattainable by most class-conscious associations in industrialized societies. As communities, groups "for themselves" to use Marx's phrase, castes embody group consciousness, monopolize their members' group lives, and inhibit the creation of inter- or intra-caste associations based on class.

In contemporary India, class relations have become increasingly salient to villagers, and particularly in the extra-village political arenas that have become available to them. The mediation of these class relations by castes – under whatever cover, sacred or otherwise – has increased accordingly. But such mediation is no new thing. Sanskritization, as we have seen, was an exercise in which caste and caste fragments demanded sacred status consistent with their class positions. Contemporary mediation of class relationships by castes is most likely to succeed when it is supported by wealth and strength. Success tends, first, to over-represent the interests of "dominant" and OBC castes whose *jati*-fellows own land in their villages; and, second, to over-represent the interests of well-to-do landed households in virtually all castes.

However categorized, as "dominant" or OBC, castes which best represent the class interests of their members combine the virtues that characterize successful groups in most parliamentary democratic systems. Generally, such castes are large, areally concentrated, possessed of relatively well-to-do and respectable "creamy layers," self-confident, attractive as allies, well-connected politically and spokesmen for their own interests. And, above all, they are landed. In village relationships of patronage–clienthood, landed households of whatever castes are the patrons. They are the employers in employer–employee relationships; and in these, too, landed households tend to enjoy the generalized superiority of patrons. Patronage enhances the interest group prowess of the castes of landed households. Clients and employees, for example, are amenable to their patrons' voting instructions.

By contrast, Dalits at the bottom of village hierarchies combine the disabilities of the powerless: poverty, lack of respectability, low self-esteem, illiteracy and lack of education, sickness, dependence on others, a lowliness which serves the economic and status interests of their neighbors. In addition, Dalit families are often clients and vulnerable employees, and that is a disincentive and an obstacle to the organized representation of their interests. Largely through the increasing participation of Dalits as Indian citizens and office-holders, as opposed to village subjects and dogs-bodies, these disabilities have been mitigated to some extent, and in some places more than others, over the past decade. But they are still there.

The mediation of class relations by landed castes tends to favor the interests of their most powerful and prosperous members. They are likely to be the mediators: village patrons and employers, *sarpanchas*, MLAs. In spite of a Supreme Court ruling that compensatory discrimination for OBCs must not go to their "creamy layers," it does: inevitably in a political system attuned to middle-class welfare, and certainly in disproportion to the benefits available below the cream. But that does not appear to have caused any discernable intra-caste conflict between the layers. Caste politics inhibit conflict between intra-group layers, as race politics once inhibited it in the American South. Caste politics also inhibit "creamy layer" alliances across castes. In the next section, however, I will argue that the mediation of class relationships by castes tends not only to over-represent but to aggregate landed interests and, conversely, not only to under-represent but to disaggregate landless interests.

Class interests as mediated by stimuli responses

My observations in this section are meant to be another way of looking at classes in the Indian countryside: not an alternative way, but rather a complementary and supplementary way. First, I want to construct a rough and ready taxonomy of classes comfortable to my definition of class and applicable to a hypothetical Indian village. Then, I want to explain how these classes – without consciousness, neither communities nor societies, entirely the constructs of analysis – are nonetheless capable of acting like classes.

At the base of my taxonomy is table 1, below.[3] Alas, it is no more than a flawed sketch: an approximation. Although the data on which it is based are the most current available to me, they are more than a decade old. Particularly, at the *Large* end of the table, there are *benami* holdings – holdings under false names, usually family members or clients – whose effect is to understate the concentration of holdings among large farmers. Aggregate statistics in this case, and in most cases, obscure regional and other variations. Still, over a time line of 20 years, the table's sketch of an Indian farming sector of small-holding households whose average holdings keep getting smaller is accurate enough. As a model of rural class structure, the table will do.

From the table, I build my hypothetical class structure. First, by reducing its six categories to the usual three, more or less as follows. To make my lower class, I add *Landless* – which accounts for about 30 percent of the rural population, and, of course, none of its holdings – to *Marginal* and *Small*. This

Table 1 Operational Holdings of Farm Family Households

| Size of holding (hectares) | Percentage distribution | | | | | |
| | no. of holdings | | | area of holdings | | |
	1990–91	1980–81	1970–71	1990–91	1980–81	1970–71
Landless	0	0	0	0	0	0
Marginal (below 1)	58	57	51	15	12	9
Small (1–2)	19	18	19	18	14	11
Semi-medium (2–4)	13	14	15	23	21	19
Medium (4–10)	9	9	11	27	30	30
Large (10+)	1	2	4	17	23	31
Total	100	100	100	100	100	100

lower class is actually or effectively landless or tenuously landed. My middle and upper classes are effectively landed. *Semi-medium* and *Medium* constitute my middle class. *Large* is my upper class. Then, I round off my tripartite divison by adding to the incomes of landholding households the money they earn from sources other than their holdings; and to the incomes of *Landless* and other lower-class households, I add their earnings from sources other than the sale of their labor. Village households derive income from urban remittances and investments, interest on loans extended to other village households, rents and other payments collected from lands they hold but do not operate, goods and services supplied by landholding household members to fellow villagers, goods sold to fellow villagers by members of households of landless laborers, and so forth. Finally, if there are in my hypothetical village any households which are entirely non-farming, which derive no income from landholding or agricultural labor, I place them into one of my three categories according to their income.

Analysts of actual rather than hypothetical class relations among rural families might want to use fewer or more, different, or more widely or narrowly based categories. That would depend on who they were looking at and what they were looking for. It is worth reiterating, however, that their categories, like mine, would be the constructs of analysts. They are not the constructs of village households. We categorize in order to better understand villagers' social realities. But our categories are not their social realities. Our categories are the product of our consciousness and not theirs. We cannot, of course, expect conscious action from classes that are not based on their members' consciousness. What we do expect is that our classes will have different "market situations," and in an actual research project, we would test that expectation and categorize or recategorize accordingly. In my hypothetical village, I expect these "market situations" to be roughly as follows, working outward from the middle.

Middle-class village households are generally secure in their sources of income: in their tenure, if they are landholding. Because of ordinary, foreseeable misfortune – a bad season or two – a middle-class village family is likely to be pressed but not ruined. A middle-class village household will hire in and hire out labor, let in and let out land, but primarily by operating the household's holdings (and/or other enterprises) with family labor, it is usually able to produce a better-than-subsistence income. "Better-than-subsistence" is at least in part socially defined and would vary from locality to locality and group to group. But in its general definition, I would certainly include savings: to hedge indebtedness, cover contingencies like the death of a bullock or the repair of a tractor, or the purchase of a water pump, the payment of a dowry, or providing for the investment in a son's higher education. Middle-class village households are at least potentially vulnerable to social, economic and political assertiveness from below and power from above.

Above, upper-class village households hold enough land or capital, or both, to make their livelihoods not merely secure but profitable. Their households are the regular and usual employers of villagers who sell their labor. As well, these households may also be suppliers of capital to other villagers: usually, as moneylenders. As such, they pose a threat to the tenurial security of lower- and middle-class small-holding households. Debt, as they say, goes in like a needle and out like a sword. It is the upper-class households of the village which are likeliest to derive substantial income, influence and prestige from the urban employment of their sons and other relatives and profits from investments in such extra-village enterprises as sugar mills and transport companies. But, even by Indian urban standards, only the most prosperous upper-class village households are truly rich.

Increasing embourgeoisement of upper-class village lifestyles, in and of itself and in relation to the market situation of their households, further differentiates them from the households of their neighbors. Upper-class households own tractors and color television sets. The roles of their men in cultivation are likely to be those of entrepreneur and manager. Some of the men of these households have prestigious and well-paying urban careers. Upper-class village households aspire to both traditional and modern respectability. They take and give large dowries; and send their sons and, increasingly, daughters to university. In their villages, the wives of upper-class households observe the semi-seclusion of respectable matrons, and become increasingly familiar with the modern world in order to perform their traditional roles as household managers. Patron households are likely to be upper-class village households; and nowadays, their webs of patronage and clienthood are likely to extend beyond their village walls.

I have not provided a category for landlords separate from upper-class households. The great estates of non-cultivating landlord households – of either rentier or aristocratic varieties – were, in general, broken up by state government land reforms in the 1950s; and nowadays there are no marked differences in the market situations of landlord and other upper-class village households and decreasing differences in their lifestyles and even their amour propre.

Lower-class village households are insecure in their livelihoods. Those that own any land, farm it with family labor, but they can rarely make ends meet by farming. So, to some substantial extent, family members must supplement household income by working for others – in their fields, factories, brick kilns, and so forth. Through the labor of its men, women and children, a lower-class household earns a subsistence or less-than-subsistence income. It is readily exploitable in its village by upper- and middle-class village households. Roughly half of the landless lower class belongs to Dalit castes, and are therefore socially as well as economically disadvantaged. Many lower-class village households survive only in clientage, which at its worst is debt bondage.

Now, if these classes are the products of our categorization rather than their consciousness and we cannot, therefore, expect conscious action from them, what sort of class action can we expect? For the answer that I propose, I am indebted, again, to a suggestion by Max Weber.[4] We can expect of households which are similarly situated in economic terms similar responses to the same economic or economically related stimuli. So, for example, to the stimulus of some state government's hypothetical decision to enforce its minimum wage scale for agricultural labor, we can expect similar responses from households that I have classed together and different responses from each class: opposition from the upper, a mixed response from the middle and support from the lower.

As I indicated earlier, these responses are likely to be mediated by castes and communal groups and their fragments. They are also mediated through the expectations of politicians. Indeed, we can only hypothesize about class reactions to any state government's decision to enforce the payment of minimum agricultural wages, because state politicians have been almost unanimous in the expectation that any such decision would be an act of political suicide. The same expectation has inhibited state politicians from enforcing other provisions of land reform legislation which disserve the interests of landholding households: ceilings on their landholdings, for example, tenurial security for subtenants, maximum shares for share-croppers, special protection for the small-holdings of Dalit and tribal households. In response to the same expectation, state governments do not tax agricultural incomes, although agricultural production accounts for about 30 percent of India's gross domestic product.

Across India, from village *panchayats* to state legislative assemblies, land-holding interests – my middle and upper classes – are politically predominant over the interests of the effectively landless: my lower-class village households. The salience of land in Indian villages as the marker between haves and have-nots, the worthy and the unworthy, and, perhaps, some mis-application of class analysis has inclined both scholars and journalists – often unconsciously and implicitly – to assume a two-class division in the Indian countryside. There is the upper and the lower, the top and the bottom, those who own land and employ labor, and those who are effectively landless and are employed by the landed. There is, to be sure, an ambiguous middle *something* of small-holders, our middle-class village households, but insofar as they are landed, so the assumption has it, their households constitute the top's bottom. And they would probably respond as such to any proposal, for example, to further extend land reform legislation.

Even before the OBCs' coming of age in the 1990s, however, middle-class households began to assert interests of their own, separate from the interests of upper-class households and sometimes opposed to them. These middle-class assertions are mediated in combination by caste and communal groups and through stimulus-response. At first they peeked through the "farmers' movements" that appeared in various parts of India during the 1980s. Two of the largest and best organized of these were (and still are) the Shetkari Sangathana (farmers' union) of Maharashtra and the Bharatiya Kisan (Indian farmers) Union of western Uttar Pradesh. Both brought out farmers in the tens and even hundreds of thousands to participate in their rallies and agitational campaigns. Both were mixed caste and mixed class movements. Both represented the interests of landholding households.

Of the movements' leaders, the most articulate was (and is) the Shetkari Sangathana's Sharad Joshi. He postulated his movement on a well-visited notion of the 1980s: the "Bharat-India divide" – roughly, the divergent interests of exploited rural and exploitative urban India. In their historical context, thus: *"Bharat* is the notional entity which continues to be exploited by the same policies as those of … colonial rule, even after the British left; … *India* is that notional entity which [inherited] colonial exploitation."[5]

The post-colonial persistence of poverty in the Indian countryside is the work of the "internal colonialism" of urban India; and not, as Delhi's "power circles" would have us believe, the result of the "internal contradiction between the rich farmer and the small peasant." For whatever divides them, they are as one in their demand for " remunerative prices for … agricultural produce." And that is the Sangathana's "single point programme."[6]

Immediately, the program is heedless of the interests of the landless. They purchase most of their agricultural produce, including their food, and depend for their subsistence on low rather than "remunerative" prices. Even among the landed, however, who could agree on remunerative prices, there were internal class issues that had to be finessed if not resolved by the Sangathana. In the late 80s, for example, the Sangathana made three demands on government. First, ostensibly because of drought conditions, the Sangathana wanted farmers relieved from their indebtedness to public and cooperative sector creditors. But, from this relief "loans taken to buy trucks, tractors and drip irrigation equipment [were to] be exempted." From these exemptions, upper-class households would be the sufferers. Second, "a reassertion of the demand for more remunerative prices for agricultural produce." Third, "roughly doubling the minimum wage [for farm laborers] to Rs25 a day," would serve to compensate the landless for higher food prices, and also serve – or at least not disserve – the interests of middle-class families which are themselves suppliers of farm labor. It would certainly disserve the interests of upper-class households which are farm labor's major employers. In a word, the three demands, taken together, distinguish the interests of a rural middle class. And for good reason. It was their numbers that brought the lakhs (hundreds of thousands) to the Sangathana's rallies and the Sangathana to government notice.

Increasingly over the past decade, class conflict in the Indian countryside has moved from farmers' movements more directly into party politics. And it has done so in caste clusters. Those castes which the Mandal Commission joined together in the category OBC, have put themselves asunder in today's politics. Of course, there were always marked class differences within the category: between "backward," "most backward," and "extremely backward," to quote the categorical refinements of Uttar Pradesh's Social Justice Committee. What mandalization did was to give OBC castes something new and valuable to fight over amongst themselves, a new stimulus to respond to competitively: reservations, assured access to urban opportunities for higher education, educated employment, remittance income earning. In the process, Dalit competition for these same scarce resources has been quickened and more firmly emplaced in the arenas of party politics. The Social Justice Committee's recommendations may be understood as a sample guide to the caste lines of class conflict in Indian state politics.

Patron–client and employer–employee relationships, factions and *panchayati raj*

In the Indian countryside, I suggested earlier, the interests of the upper, generally landed, classes tend to be over-represented and aggregated and the interests of the lower, effectively landless, classes tend to be under-represented and disaggregated. Here is the place to pursue that suggestion. And once again, we begin with the exposition of an ideal. It is the *jajmani* system to which we have already referred. Like the joint family ideal, it is best thought of these days as affecting rather than reflecting reality. Though largely defunct as such, *jajmani* systems are still worthy of our notice. They embodied an ideology that persists in the ubiquity, nowadays, of patron–client and asymmetrical employer–employee relations between landed and landless village families.

A village's *jajmani* system was meant to function as its sacred economic order, much as its *jati* hierarchy was meant to function as its sacred social order. They were interrelated parts of the same *dharma*. At the center of a village's *jajmani* system were its households of *jajmans* or patrons. They were usually the village's largest landholders. Although their *jatis* were likely to be relevant to their positions as landholders, they were *jajmans* not because of their *jatis* but because of their holdings. Supplying them with various goods and services were households of *kamins* or clients. Ideally, the goods and services they supplied were according to the *kamin* households' hereditary, divinely ordained caste occupations. So, a household of potter caste, for example, provided its *jajman* household with a fixed supply of baked clay pots.

The *jajman–kamin* relationship was properly heritable, familial, ritualized and performed within the context of a reciprocal relationship between un-equals: of general social superiority of landholding household to general social inferiority of potter households. Members of the two households acknowledged and demonstrated in their social and ritual interactions their relationship of exchange between unequals: in modes of address, patterns of precedence and deference, exchanges of symbolic gifts, participation in each other's ceremonies.

In times of need, potter clients were expected to appeal to their *jajman* households for help: a loan, an introduction, the exercise of some influence. Landholding *jajmans* were expected to call on their potter *kamins* for extra-occupational services: as witnesses in a court case, partisans in a dispute over land, messengers. For their services as potters and otherwise, the *kamin* household had a recognized right to a fixed quantity of the produce from its *jajman* household's fields. Because the patron–client relationship between a particular *jajman* household and a particular *kamin* family household of potters was regarded as an integral part of the village's social order, it was a matter of concern to a group wider than the two households: at least, to their *jatis* and their village elders.

Ideally, this same patron–client, *jajman–kamin* relationship pertained between landholding households and sweeper households, at the bottom of the village hierarchy, and Brahmin households, at the top. Both sweepers and priests were patronized to perform their caste occupations, to do what they were born to do. As it had been with their ancestors, so it was with them and would be with their descendants. Members of the sweeper household were treated with the appropriate disdain, and they were poorly remunerated – usually in kind – for their demeaning (however necessary) services. The Brahmin household was not, certainly in a social sense, *kamin*: a lesser. It might well have been of a higher *jati* than that of its *jajman* household. It was treated with the appropriate respect, even deference, however ceremonious. For their priestly services, Brahmins were well remunerated: sometimes with their *jajman* households' most significant gift, a grant of land, an oblation from their holdings.

Thus *jajman* households separately and their heads together as members of the village's customary *panchayat* enjoyed a surrogate Kshatriya-hood. Their little, village *rajs* worked, ideally, as organic wholes. Their separate parts performed the functions that they were meant to perform and were valued according to their sacred worth. Whoever sat on the Delhi *gaddi* or the viceregal throne in Simla or ruled the *durbar* (regime) in princely states, the economic and political, as well as the social, centers of most villagers' lives were in their villages.

In 2002, *jajmani* systems, as such, barely exist. They have been eroded by virtually all of modernity's encroachments on village life and intrusions into it: the increasing availability and use of cash, factory-made goods (like aluminum pots and plastic buckets), urban occupations and remittances from them, specialist services of all sorts in country towns, *panchayati raj*, compensatory discrimination, the Green Revolution. The erosion has not so much effaced *jajmani* systems as worn them into secular patron–client relationships and asymmetrical relationships between landed employers and landless employees.

So, things change, but remain the same. As it was in *jajmani* systems, landholding households are still at the center of village patron–client and employer–employee relationships. These are still relationships of property, and even more so than before: between households that hold land and those that do not, between farmers and landless laborers. Nowadays, clients and employees may take at least some of their pay in cash, they are likely to be employed as farm laborers rather than in their traditional caste occupations – which many of them no longer follow anyway. Clients may or may not have any inter-generational ties to their patrons' households. Employees may or may not be from the villages in which they work. Clientage and employment are likely to be on the farmer's terms rather than on any *jajmani*-like terms of patron-weighted reciprocity. Farm laborers' unions are virtually non-existent. Clientage and employment are unlikely to be thought of as serving any sacred purpose and therefore worthy of any protection other than that afforded by the sweet will of patrons and employers.

The distinction, in Indian villages, between clientage and employment is only one of more or less generalized subordination. Clientage is a refuge of lower village households, and it can become their prison. Clients need patrons as sources of relatively secure employment in what is usually a buyer's market for agricultural labor. They need or want patrons to help them deal with the often unfamiliar and unfriendly world outside their villages: the world of politicians, bureaucrats and police. Because they have little or no land or capital to serve as collateral, clients need patrons for unsecured loans. Their labor is their collateral, and debt bondage is the most extreme form of clientage. There are millions of Indian village households which live in debt bondage – a disproportionate number of them are Dalit. Patrons may need clients as assured sources of labor during peak periods in the agricultural cycle. They may want clients because it is a good and pleasing thing to be a patron, to have others beholden to you, touching your feet, fearful of your wrath, dependent on your whims. Patrons also need clients to fight their factional battles. Patron–client relationships are the bases of factions.

Village factions are contentious affiliations led by patron households in pursuance of their interests. Their client households are their followers in factional strife: because it is beneficial for them to follow or costly for them to do otherwise. Contentious patron households might be of *jati*-fellows, even of relatives – families of estranged brothers, for example – or they might be of different *jatis*. Where they are of different *jatis*, factional and *jati* conflict may be patched together. Some client households may be of their patron's *jati*, and some not. Some may even belong to the *jati* of their patron's factional opponent. It doesn't matter. If there are no other options, the prudent client is true to his salt. Factional contests may be fought in deadly earnest and they are commonplace in Indian villages. They are pursued through *panchayati raj* politics, litigation, defamation, harassment, boycott and violence. Conventional wisdom, or at least the convention of alliterating wisdom, has it that the usual causes of factional strife in the Indian countryside are: *zamin* (land), *zevar* (movable wealth; literally jewelry) and *zanan* (women).

Since Independence, conflicts between village factions have been incorporated increasingly into the inter- and intra-party conflicts of state politics: into the politics of legislative assemblies and, from the 1960s, *panchayati raj* institutions. From its beginnings in an official report in 1957,[7] *panchayati raj* (literally, conciliar government), had as its intended result to quicken the Indian government's largely unsuccessful, village-based "community development" program. Entrusted to the states as their instuments for local self-government, *panchayati raj* was meant to stimulate development by devolving some political authority for it on to villagers elected by villagers, by encouraging and funding developmental efforts in the countryside and coordinating them with the efforts of bureaucrats and state politicians. *Panchayati raj* was to provide India's villages with local government that was statutory rather than conventional, democratic rather than oligarchical and oriented to change rather than to preserving the *dharma*. But, after more than three decades in operation, *panchayati raj* had fallen far short of achieving these goals. To try again, parliament passed in 1992 the 73rd Amendment Act. It gave constitutional standing to a reformed *panchayati raj* as a more or less nationally uniform system of local self-government.

Although details and names varied from state to state, the original, pre-1992, three-tier system of *panchayati raj* was generally this: by universal adult suffrage, villages in a small cluster of villages elected a *panchayat*. If no women and/or Dalit and/or tribal members were elected, the *panchayat* was often obliged by state law to coopt them. In some states, village *panchayats* elected their *sarpanchas* (presidents). In other states, they were elected separately by popular vote. In general, it was only at this lowest and least effective tier that *panchas* (*panchayat* members) were chosen by direct election. At the upper, effective tiers of *panchayati raj*, the elected chose among themselves. Thus, at the second tier, *sarpanchas* of all village *panchayats* within a development bloc met as a *panchayat samiti* (committee) and elected their chairman from amongst themselves. In most states, bloc development officers sat as members of these *panchayat samitis* and they were the *panchayati raj* tier with most immediate effect on rural development.

With district development officers, the chairman of all *panchayat samitis* in a district met as a *zila parishad* (district council) and elected its chairman from among themselves.

In sum, *sarpanchas* first elected to the village level tier virtually monopolized *panchayati raj* at all its tiers. Given the prevalence of patron–client relationships in the Indian countryside, it will come as no surprise that these *sarpanchas* were overwhelmingly members of village upper-class households: often their youngish, better-educated sons rather than their rustic patriarchs. The factional leader who had at his hearth a statutory *sarpancha* enjoyed a considerable advantage over his rival patron households. His clients constituted his vote bank. And through his *panchayat samiti* and *zila parishad* memberships, he used his access to development funds and political influence to maintain and enlarge his clientele, enrich his household and fight his factional battles.

One effect of pre-1992 *panchayati raj* was to give village factions access to public funds: to fight over them and with them. Another effect was to enlarge the arenas in which village factions contend and to make political influence more readily available to them. The members of *panchayat samitis*, for example, were almost invariably divided into factions which battled over the spoils of development for themselves and their constituents. The chairman of a *panchayat samiti* and his chief rival, the candidate of some opposing faction, were patrons of patrons, in effect: with client-patrons and their clients extending over perhaps 150 villages. Their political influence was considerable, as were its payoffs to them. Ministers, civil administrators and police officers did not underrate their capacities either to be helpful or to do mischief. By all accounts, it was largely because state politicians and bureaucrats were fearful of the power and influence of *panchayati raj* headmen that state governments allowed the system to languish.

Pre-1992, *panchayati raj* became a major contributor to the over-representation and aggregation of landed interests in India's states, particularly of their upper-class village households. Concomitantly, *panchayati raj* contributed to the under-representation and disaggregation of the interests of lower-class village households. However bitter and deadly the contests between rival factions on *panchayat samitis* and *zila parishads*, they were contests among members of the same landed classes, and they proceeded from the aggregation of those classes' interests. It was not a question for them, for example, whether or not there should be some loans to landed farmers, but what the loans should be for and to whom they should go.

By contrast, lower-class village households had no *panchayati raj* institutions in which their interests were represented and aggregated. Rather, *panchayati raj* helped to maintain their clientage. Without it, their patrons would have been neither *sarpanchas* nor *zila parishad* members, so some payoffs of *panchayati raj* were trickled down to maintain the clientage of lower-class rural households. They are poor people, and something is better than nothing. But the cost of that something was the disaggregation of their interests, even as these might be represented by their *jatis* and castes. Hands pressed together, the landless laborer goes for a loan or a political favor to his patron and not to his equally impoverished and powerless *jati*-fellows. In every parliamentary democracy, the interests of the well-to-do tend to be better represented than the interests of the poor. In Indian state politics, this tendency is exaggerated because of the pervasiveness in villages of patron–client relationships between the well-to-do and the poor. Though not, of course, the intention of its draftsmen, pre-1992 *panchayati raj* institutionalized this exaggeration.

The 73rd Amendment Act addressed itself to limiting the effectiveness of *panchayati raj* institutions as instruments for representing and aggregating the interests of the countryside's well-to-do landed households. Specifically, it mandated direct elections for fixed terms to all three tiers of the system, and proportional reservations for the poor – defined as "scheduled castes and tribes" – in every tier and in the offices of *sarpancha* in every tier. By giving *panchayati raj* independent, constitutional standing, the amendment was meant to free the system both from neglect by state governments and absorption into state politics dominated by landed classes.

The possibility of change was certainly a promise of the 73rd Amendment; but to date, a decade after it became law, *plus ça change* …. Over the years, state politicians and bureaucrats, in general, have not grown fonder of *panchayati raj*.[8] Their financial and administrative control over it has been perpetuated and even tightened in many states by their laws to enable the amendment. *Panchayat* elections have been postponed and funds from the Centre withheld. The 73rd Amendment does not empower *panchayati raj* institutions to raise their own funds. So, their purse strings are where they have always been: in state government hands.

Following the amendment, ironically, the continuing control of politicians and bureaucrats over *panchayati raj* has probably been facilitated by the entrance at all its tiers of a large number of *panchas* who are poor, dependent, illiterate and untrained: for the most part, women and Dalits. It is fair to say that the contributions of state politicians and bureaucrats to undermining, in letter and spirit, the 73rd Amendment tend to perpetuate the status quo ante: the absorption of *panchayati raj* institutions into landed-class-dominated state politics. As for the landed classes themselves, the amendment has certainly not disabled them from protecting their own interests. They are still patrons, and they still have clients. As landed households send their wives and daughters to serve their interests from seats reserved for women, so patrons send their clients to serve the interests of landed households from seats reserved for Dalits and tribal people.

It may be that *panchayati raj*'s political and social environment will have to affect *panchayati raj* before it can affect its environment. There are some straws in the wind. Over the past decade, at least, the possibilities of change to the leadership of *panchayati raj* institutions have been clearly demonstrated by OBC castes. Across India, they have loosened, if not broken, the hold of the rural upper classes on *panchayati raj*. With less assistance from the 73rd Amendment than from the push of mandalization and the shove of their own determination and organization, OBC castes have made themselves the dominant forces in *panchayati raj*. And as a consequence, it has become more and more an instrument of the rural middle classes.

Can it be made to work for the lower classes? Perhaps. Green Revolution commercialization of Indian agriculture has inclined rural relationships of superiority–subordination away from patronage–clienthood and toward employment. However slight their liberation from the generalized subordination and protection of patronage–clienthood, employed laborers must now look more immediately to their own resources. They are to some extent both freed and impelled to organize in their own interests. We can only speculate as to the extent that this freedom has been a cause of lower-class organization, but there is no doubt that lower classes are better organized and more assertive of their own interests than they were a decade ago.

Their organization is on caste lines, of course. And not only their numbers and their organization, but the fragmentation of politics into caste blocs and splinters, increases the attractiveness of Dalits as allies. It is as an ally that the Dalit caste-based BSP has come to prominence in Uttar Pradesh. Assistance to lower-class organization is increasingly available from Dalit civil and police officers in the field, from "creamy layer" Dalit politicians and from state politicians of any caste who from time to time must recalculate their numbers. Finally, as it is with women *panchas*, practice may not make perfect for their Dalit colleagues, but it is likely to yield experience and improve performance. Census figures are clear on this: there is a growing number of literate and educated Dalits, who are at least available to seek *panchayati raj* experience and use it in lower-class interests.

Chapter 4

Homelands and states

In India, as elsewhere, the folk have ethnic homelands. The folk belong to those castes and quasi castes, tribal and religious communities that determine and preserve their homelands' characteristic cultures – their languages, customs, arts and crafts, legends, traditions, and superstitions – and pass these on from one generation to the next. Since 1953, the Indian government has used "homeland" as its marker in drawing the boundaries of the quasi-federal states of the Union. For the folk who notionally speak one and the same language, "linguistic" markers indicate their homeland states. Most state borders in the Union are drawn on "linguistic" lines. State borders in the northeast are marked off for their folk on "tribal" lines. Areas of existing states which have developed over time into "regional" homelands, have recently been marked off as new states: Chattisgargh, Jharkhand and Uttaranchal. Under the Indian constitution, the states have the primary authority to legislate in areas closest to their folk's interests: the rural economy, education, the language or languages taught in schools and used in government business, urban development and small business, law and order. The usual political arenas in which sections of the folk contend for the benefits of politics are in their states.

Familiar to Europeans from their own history, a symbiotic relationship grows between the folk and political power. The folk sustain and develop the political unit, the political unit sustains and defines the folk. The homeland-cum-quasi-federal state of the Indian Union becomes, conceptually, a "nation-province." I regret the neology. But I cannot find a concept in use that adequately conveys my meaning. I mean something analogous to the nation-state:[1] a similar, stable relationship of mutual benefit between the homeland's folk and political power. Except that in India the relationship is provincial rather than sovereign. India has become a multi-nation state of nation-provinces, or so it seems. In turn, these nation-provinces have become incubators of bourgeois revolution in the Indian countryside.

To see this, however, to fit it into the picture that we began in previous chapters to piece together upward from little societies at the bottom, we must now – to pursue the metaphor – complete by fitting the pieces together downward from the top. In previous chapters we pieced together pictures of ordinary people doing ordinary things, under changing circumstances. Here, working our way downward, our pieces form pictures of great events and political decisions which changed circumstances for ordinary people.

From homelands to states

The British made positive use of India's ethnic diversity to shape their ideology of empire, and negative use of India's ethnic diversity to draw the empire's provincial borders. Like Europe, India was a geographic term. That, in general, was the prevailing British view. The subcontinent was a vast mélange of people who spoke different languages, had different customs, belonged to different races, were members of different castes and tribes, enjoyed different levels of civilization and worshiped different gods. There was no Indian nation. Indian nationalism was a chimera; worse, it was a self-serving fantasy of the subcontinent's microscopic minority of politically ambitious, English-educated Brahmins and *babus*.[2] From time to time, in its pre-British past, large parts of India had been brought together in the imperium of some dynasty of despots. When imperial despotism lost its effect, the subcontinent fragmented into petty despotisms: its usual condition. The old races of Asia were incapable of putting and keeping in place a political system more sophisticated than personal or, at best, dynastic autocracy. Only British administration, the new race of Asia's genius for "law and system," had built and sustained in India an empire – not a nation, certainly – that was legally, rationally and systematically governed.

So, whate'er the British best administered was best. It was according to this criterion – ostensibly and ideologically, if not in fact – that the captains of empire determined India's provincial borders. The ethnicity of those who lived within these borders was not, in general, an official consideration of the tax-collector's *raj*. For example, consider two British provinces that have since Independence been parcelled out into "linguistic" states. At imperial endgame the British province of Madras contained Tamil- , Malayalam- and Telegu-speakers. Other speakers of these languages lived in other British provinces and in some princely states. Bombay province contained some Kannada-, Marathi- and Gujarati-speaking areas. Others were in the princely state of

Mysore, the British Central Provinces and scores of petty principalities in what is now Gujarat. Only the provincial borders of the United Provinces within the Hindi/Urdu region and Bengal followed language lines.

Bengal had not always been thus. Prior to 1905, Bengal had been a vast sprawling province in which its Bengali-speaking region was bundled together with the Hindi-speaking area of what is now Bihar and the Oriya-speaking area that is now Orissa. Then, for what he said were administrative reasons, that remarkable person, the Viceroy George Nathaniel Curzon, bifurcated the province by drawing a line through its Bengali-speaking region. Thereby he divided Bengalis between two provinces, east and west: a Muslim majority in one and a Hindu majority in the other. This first partition of Bengal, undone seven years later, provided the Indian nationalist movement with its first cause célèbre – and its foreshadowing of Indian nationalism's entanglement in Hindu and Muslim communalism. It also gave a clear indication of the possibilities of bringing nascent Indian nationalism and India's ancient and diverse provincialisms into a mutually supportive opposition to British imperialism.

Even earlier, at the turn of the century, the nationalist firebrand, Bal Gangadhar Tilak, set out to popularize Indian nationalism in his native Maharashtra, among its Marathi-speakers, through the idiom of local Hindu worship and mythology. But it was Mahatma Gandhi who, systematically and for all of India, wedded its provincial diversities to Indian nationalism. In 1920, at its meeting in the central Indian city of Nagpur, the Indian National Congress confirmed Mahatma Gandhi as its supremo. He presented it with a new constitution which, among other things, delineated the Congress's provincial units *not* on the imperial map of India but on an overlay which divided the map into more or less unilingual "linguistic provinces."

Under Gandhi's leadership, the Congress was embarking on a mass non-violent non-cooperation movement whose stated goal was nothing less than the attainment of *swaraj* (self-government). Dividing Congress into "linguistic provinces" was part of turning Indian nationalism into a mass movement. Always the consummate lateral thinker, Gandhi was enlisting long-lived Indian provincialism in the cause of nascent Indian nationalism. In the "linguistic provinces" to which they belonged, the leaders of Pradesh (provincial) Congress Committees – Congress stalwarts and committed nationalists – would be the Mahatma's recruiting sergeants. Connected by caste and community and language to the folk of their homelands, they were native sons made good on the stage of nationalist policies. Their "linguistic provinces" would become Indian nationalism's recruiting grounds. The languages of recruitment would be provincial, but only to better convey messages that were Indian.

I have kept "linguistic provinces" captive in quotation marks to suggest that it is a euphemism for ethnolinguistic provinces. Again, in India, someone's mother tongue is only an important trait in a complex of traits that identify him or her as a Gujarati or Tamil or Bengali or whatever. To be sure, Gandhi organized Indian nationalism from ethnolinguistic clusters. But to say as much would have conceded too much to British – and Indian Muslim – ideologues who denied that there was an Indian nationality. After all, is it not oxymoronic to argue that diverse ethnolinguistic groups can share a common nationality? In ordinary usage, "nationality" was then widely meant as a synonym for what we mean today by "ethnicity." They are the same words from different roots. Indian nationalist ideology avoided the question by readily conceding that Indians speak many different languages. But it insisted that India was their nation. India was a multi-lingual nation. What kept it from becoming a nation-state was not its linguistic diversity but British imperialism and its policy of divide and rule.

Gandhi's reconstitution of his nationalist movement into "linguistic provinces" became a Congress commitment to reorganize the actual provinces of India on "linguistic" lines once *swaraj* was attained. This commitment was reiterated any number of times over the years in various Congress documents, and as late as 1946 in its manifesto for the last Indian election held under British auspices. The Raj was certainly going. *Swaraj*, which the Congress had since defined as "complete independence," was certainly coming. And then the subcontinent exploded. A communal firestorm raged throughout northern India. Hindus and, in Punjab, Sikhs murdered, maimed, brutalized and pillaged Muslims: men, women and children in the hundreds of thousands. Muslims visited the same horrors on Hindus and Sikhs. From what were to become West and East Pakistan, millions of Sikhs and Hindus fled in terror into India. From what were to become the Indian states of Punjab and West Bengal, millions of Muslims fled in terror into Pakistan. Indian and Pakistani troops, only yesterday soldiers of the same British Indian army, fought each other in Kashmir in 1948.

Swaraj came to India in tragedy and violence. Their underlying message, so read by Jawaharlal Nehru and his colleagues, was that the forces, however irrational, that held Indians to their thousands of diverse ethnicities were greater than the sentiments that held them to India. If unchecked, these sentiments were likely to strangle India's nationalism in its cradle and sunder its Union. The fear was this: that the establishment of East and West Pakistan would be the first moves in the subcontinent's balkanization. They had to be the last. The leaders of the new Indian Union were determined to make sure of that. The Dravidian movement in Madras was still secessionist and its goal was nothing less than detaching from the Union all of south India and making it into an independent state of "Dravidinadu" (land of the Dravidians). Tribal groups in the northeast were actively secessionist.

Congress's commitment of 30 years to organize independent India into "linguistic" provinces or states was summarily abrogated by its leaders.

Certainly, they had always known that Tamils were not simply several million Indians who spoke Tamil, nor Bengalis several million who spoke Bengali. After 1947, they were confronted by what they knew, by the ethnolinguistic reality that underlay the ideology of "linguistic provinces." They appointed the appropriate investigative and advisory bodies at the highest levels of government and ruling party. "Nationalism and subnationalism are two emotional experiences which grow at the expense of each other," warned the government commission headed by Judge S. K. Dar. The Congress committee – two of whose three members were the Union's duumvirs, Nehru and Sardar Vallabhai Patel – demanded "the stern discouragement of communalism, provincialism and all other separatist and disruptive tendencies." Both commission and committee recommended against the formation of "linguistic states," at least until a more "opportune time."[3]

For many Indians, however, in the late 1940s and 1950s, the opportune time was then. The Union government had not merely broken its party's long-standing promise, but in so doing it had taken the wrong side on a genuinely popular issue. It had taken a step that seemed to confound the ambitions and expectations of the Congress faithful: ambitions and expectations that had had three decades to incubate. Congress organizations-in-disguise, *praja mandals* (popular groups) had been operating in many princely states from the late 1930s. The caste and communal ties that crossed their borders into neighboring provinces whetted political ambitions for bigger and better "linguistic" states. There was widespread violence and the threat of more to come in the Telegu-speaking parts of the erstwhile Hyderabad principality. The opportune time to carve a Telegu-speaking Andhra Pradesh (state) from Madras province and Hyderabad was hastened to 1953. Two years later, former British provinces and princely states in the rest of South India were merged, and the lot carved up into three more "linguistic" states: Karnataka (formerly Mysore), Kerala and Tamil Nadu (formerly Madras).

Bombay state was not realigned for some more years because of the question of how that might affect Bombay city (now Mumbai). Of that great port and industrial metropolis, Maharashtra is the hinterland and most of the city's ordinary citizens are Maharashtrian. But its capitalists are Gujaratis, Parsis and Marwaris (originally from Rajasthan). There is also a large south Indian population in Mumbai. If, in the 1950s, Bombay had been made the capital of a Maharashtra state, would the city have continued to serve India as its business capital and entrepot on the Arabian Sea? Probably so. It was the goose that lays the golden egg, and Maharashtrian politicians were not about to kill it, however much they wanted a state of their own and railed against Gujarati "colonialism." Would Congress have continued to be the ruling party in western India if Bombay were not made the capital of a Maharashtra state? Probably not. Popular sentiment was overwhelming in favor of a Marathi language state, opposition parties were united in its support, Maharashtrian Congressmen were worried and wavering. In Gujarat, Gandhi's homeland and Congress's stronghold, there was an increasingly strident demand for a Gujarati language state to be hived off from Bombay. Congress hierarchs were confronted with the choice of losing their one-party dominance in western India or dividing Bombay state. In 1960, it was divided into a Gujarati-speaking Gujarat and a Marathi-speaking Maharashtra.

Before Nehru died in 1964, his government had acceded to all major, widely supported demands for "linguistic" states save one; and India had become for the most part a union of homeland states. The exception was the Sikhs' demand for *Punjabi Suba* – Punjabi language state – to be carved from the northern half of the state of Punjab, as it was then. India's first prime minister correctly understood that Sikh politicians were using "linguistic" state as a mask to disguise a trait of ethnicity which to Indians of Nehru's secular persuasion was, and still is, particularly corrosive of Indian national-ism: religious communalism. Pakistan was a product of Muslim com-munalism. *Punjabi Suba* was the demand of Sikh communalists for a state in which the *khalsa* (the Sikh community) would rule. Nehru would not hear of it. But in 1966, ostensibly to acknowledge the loyalty of Sikh soldiers and civilians in India's wars with China and Pakistan, and certainly to help the Congress prepare for a difficult general election in 1967, Nehru's daughter gave way. Punjab was divided: a new, Sikh-majority Punjab in the north, a Hindu-majority Haryana in the south. However, the new Punjab was still in Congress ideology *Punjabi Suba*: another "linguistic" state. "No," was, and still is, the official answer to the question of whether a legitimate demand for a homeland state could be based on religious community.

These demands for homeland states were processed within the Congress Party and settlements were negotiated within the Congress's "syndicate," among its hierarchs who were, at once, leading provincial politicians and guardians of their party's interests at the Centre. These were the days of one-party dominance. Almost invariably, demands for "linguistic" states were accompanied by serious violence in which lives were lost and property destroyed. While such demands were invariably troublesome, they were not all serious. The test for seriousness was whether the demand was accompanied by violence sufficient to forge opposition unity and threaten Congress hegemony. If so, a settlement could be negotiated, if not the demand would be suppressed. That became the precedent, and it was an unfortunate one.

In the last years of Nehru's life, "tribe" was added by the Congress Party to "language" as a trait which legitimated the demands of ethnic groups for homeland states. The establishment in 1963 of Nagaland as a state of the Union was an attempt, as yet unsuccessful, to end the secessionist guerrilla warfare of Naga tribesmen who enjoyed access to Burmese sanctuary and Chinese arms. In India's national ideology, in its constitution and under its laws, there is expressed a special solicitude for those 80 million-or-so Indian citizens who belong to more than 400 "scheduled tribes." They are acknowledged to be the victims not only of British imperialism, but of the venality of their fellow Indians: sedentary cultivators, moneylenders, timber merchants and contractors, corrupt forestry officials. In no small part through armed insurgencies in a strategically sensitive and militarily vulnerable corner of the Union, tribal groups of the northeast have encouraged the government of India to express its solicitude by turning "tribal areas" into homeland states for tribal people. In the 1970s and 1980s, all on India's northeastern borders, the "tribal" states of Arunachal Pradesh, Manipur, Meghalaya, Mizoram and Tripura were created. The total population of these states, including Nagaland, is small: fewer than 12 million people, only about half of whom are tribals.

State borders in quasi-federal India, unlike those in the United States and Australia, are not constitutionally sacrosanct. They can be changed by law. On the initiative of the central government, parliament created India's 26th, 27th and 28th states in 2000. They are the Union's first "regional" states. All were carved from existing "linguistic" states in Hindi-speaking north India. Uttaranchal was created from northern Uttar Pradesh, Jharkhand from southern Bihar and Chattisgargh from eastern Madhya Pradesh. A substantial proportion of the populations of the new states are tribal people. It was they who first marked off the regions' separate identities, and it was in their political movements that the demands for separate statehood originated. The new states have been created not only for them, but for groups of non-tribal people, natives and migrants. Their interests are not necessarily congruent with those of tribal people but either coterminous or contentious: manufacturing, mining and forestry interests in Chattisgargh and Jharkhand, farming interests in Chattisgargh, caste interests in Uttaranchal.

By creating these states, the Centre has probably opened a Pandora's box of claims for separate statehood. There are any number of these, active and inert, based on "region:" one more, at least, in Uttar Pradesh and Bihar, old ones in Maharashtra and Andhra Pradesh. Nepali-speakers want a "Gorkhaland" carved out of West Bengal. Bodos want a new "tribal" state carved out of Assam. Such claims tax the mediatory and arbitrative capabilities of India's parliamentary democracy because they impinge on interests that have over half a century become vested in existing states. But the problem is probably intrinsic to the political environment of the multi-nation Indian Republic: like its monsoonal climate, not something to be solved, but only to be confronted again and again with more or less success. More than less success, certainly in comparison with the explosions of murderous state-destroying, "ethnic cleansing" violence in central and eastern Europe from the late 1980s. More than less success, certainly, when we conclude that nothing has contributed to the vitality of parliamentary democracy in India more than its active presence in the representation of the folk and their provincial interests in homeland states.

Nation-provinces

When does a homeland state, of the "linguistic, "tribal" or "regional" variety, become a nation-province? Unlike nation-state which is a political-cum-legal designation, nation-province is a political designation *only*. It has no legal meaning; and, thus, our question is similar to queries about when to designate a polity as feudal or democratic, or socialist or fascist. We have few precise and consentaneous answers. Mostly, we have indications. India's political history over more than five decades provides a set of relevant indications. These are, in particular, the gradual distintegration in the Indian states of Congress's one-party dominance; and, in general, the declining role in Indian politics of "central" parties and the growing importance of "provincial" parties.

I have already alluded to Congress's one-party dominance. What does that mean? And what do I mean by "central" and "provincial" parties? During the first two decades of India's independence, Congress was India's dominant party. Through three general elections, until 1967, Congress was the governing party in all states of the Union, with one brief interval in Kerala. Until 1977, through five general elections, Congress ruled without interruption at the Centre. There was no shortage of opposition parties and independent opposition candidates in all these elections, and they were free and fair by ordinary parliamentary democratic standards. But the Congress Party always won enough seats – usually with less than a majority of votes – to form ministries in state legislative assemblies and parliament.

This one-party dominance, about which I have more to say in chapter 6, was India's major variation on the parliamentary democratic theme. Then in the 1967 general elections, two things of relevance to our discussion here occurred. First, in several states, the Congress Party was voted out of power and non-Congress ministries were formed. Second, for the first time since she had been made prime minister by her party hierarchs, Indira Gandhi led Congress to election victory. It was anything but a resounding triumph, but it was enough. Soon afterward, Congress became, in fact and then in name, Congress (I): (I) for Indira. In her pursuit of power for herself and her sons, Indira turned Congress into her shadow and, finally, into a shadow of what it had once been.

With regard to my categories of "central" and "provincial" parties: we must first disentangle these from the Indian Election Commission's form-ulaic categorization of parties. According to the commission, parties are "national," "state," and "registered unrecognized." A party becomes "national" when it meets the minimal criteria for a "state party" in four states: in each, by having won a minimum of 6 percent of the valid vote in the last election and 3 percent of the seats in the legislative assembly. Other than the Congress and the BJP, the remaining five of the commission's "national parties," are, like the Bhujan Samaj Party, serious players only in their home states: the states in which they have their basic, sustaining constituencies. Even "national parties" which have the same name and organizational ties across state borders – most famously, in Kerala and West Bengal, the Communist Party of India–Marxist – operate as separate parties in their separate home states. "State parties," too, may operate in more than one state; but, generally, they are serious players only at home. There, they may do better than "national parties," as did the Samajwadi (socialist) Party and the BSP in elections for the Uttar Pradesh Legislative Assembly in 2002. The commission's categories impose themselves on political reality and have serious consequences for the categorized parties – in the allocation of election symbols, for example. But for our purposes the formula is not particularly meaningful.

In my meaning, a "central" party is one with enough electoral support across India to lead a coalition government at the Centre. Nowadays, only the BJP and Congress qualify. Neither, however, is able on its own to form a government in New Delhi, nor is there any likelihood of either being able to do so in the foreseeable future. Other than the BJP and Congress, all other parties are "provincial." They are rooted in the provincial concerns of their homeland states. Generally, they claim to represent the interests of their folk, in such matters as the use of their official languages and the promotion of their state's particular interests vis-à-vis other states and the Centre. But within their home states, provincial parties almost invariably compete with one another. They compete as representatives of the interests of some group or groups particular to their states' populations: castes or quasi castes or tribes or their fragments and factions, or coalitions of any of these.

Provincial parties virtually monopolize politics in Tamil Nadu. It is probably the best developed nation-province in India. It used to be Madras. It was renamed by the Dravida Munnetra Kazhagam (DMK) which first came to power in 1967. The DMK was then the most recent manifestation as a political party of the long-lived Dravidian movement. Its first modern appearance was as the Justice Party, organized in the years between the world wars: a period of great political activity all over India. The *weltanschauung* of the Dravidian movement was that Dravidians, the folk of south India, were systematically expropriated and enslaved by Brahmins and their ideology of Brahminical superiority, which they – originally migrants from north India –

derived from the Sanskrit texts of north Indian Hindu injunctive scripture. The Dravidian movement was anti-Brahmin; anti-Sanskrit, the language of Brahminism; anti-north India, the homeland of Brahmins and Brahminism; and anti-Hindi, the Sanskrit-derived language of north India. For the first decade or so of Indian independence, the Dravidian movement was secessionist. Then, it became the most vociferous and active opponent of any attempts by the government of Jawaharlal Nehru – a north Indian Brahmin – and his successors to enforce the constitutional provision that made Hindi the official language of the Indian Union.

After 1967, there was a schism in the DMK and it was succeeded in government by the breakaway AIADMK (All-India Anna Dravida Munnetra Kazhagam), which claimed to be the True Church of the Dravidian movement. For a decade until he died in 1987, the AIADMK chief minister of Tamil Nadu – indeed, his party's one of one – was Maruthur Gopala Ramachandran: MGR to his fans, the all-time superstar of the Tamil silver screen. After his death, the AIADMK schismed. The Congress government in New Delhi used the occasion to vie for government in Tamil Nadu by mounting one of the most expensive and apparently well-orchestrated political campaigns in India's electoral history. It failed miserably. In the elections of 1989, the DMK, led by a former film writer and director, was returned to power after thirteen years in opposition. In 1991, the DMK was succeeded in government by the AIADMK, under the chief ministership of MGR's most famous protégée, Jayalalitha. A film ingenue in her youth, she is a formidable politician in her middle years. Her party was defeated by the DMK in the elections of 1996. The erstwhile Dravidian movement further fragmented into a half-dozen-or-so splinter parties which represent the interests of castes and caste clusters and throw their weight in alliances led by the two major provincial parties. In 2000, Jayalalitha was tried and convicted of corruption. Undaunted, she led the alliance headed by her party to victory in the state elections of 2001, assumed Tamil Nadu's chief ministership, was disqualified as a convicted felon from doing so by the Supreme Court, was subsequently cleared of her conviction and returned in triumph to the *gaddi.* Cut and print!

Congress and the BJP are, at best, minor players in Tamil Nadu's politics. Neither won a seat in the 1996 elections for the state's legislative assembly. Their combined tally was eleven out of 234 seats in the 2001 assembly elections. The serious players in Tamil Nadu's politics are provincial parties. They have not been secessionist for almost half a century. As a multi-nation state of nation-provinces, India has come good for Tamil Nadu. Anti-Brahminism was yesterday's politics. Today's politics are the usual tussle between provincial castes and communities for sandwiches and candles. Outside of the Tamil-speaking south,[4] the fragments of the Dravidian movement compete for power nowhere. The center of their political world is Tamil

Nadu's legislative assembly. In Parliament and even abroad – in India's relations with Sri Lanka, and in vying for foreign investment – Tamil Nadu's provincial parties represent the interests of Tamil Nadu and Tamils within the Indian Union. They have become the parliamentary democratic parties of Tamil nation-provincialism.

Nowhere in India had Congress been more secure in its one-party dominance than in Tamil Nadu's northern neighbor, Andhra Pradesh. In no Congress government or organization in any state had Indira Gandhi placed and replaced her *chamchas* (tools; literally, spoons) with greater frequency or less regard to their standing in provincial politics than in Andhra Pradesh. She reduced the Andhra Pradesh Congress to no more than a satrapy of the *Dilli Durbar*. It had no place for a local hero. He was to be found instead, larger than life and however flickeringly, on the Telegu silver screen. In 1983, in spite of "Indiramma's" (mother Indira's) relentless personal campaigning in Andhra Pradesh and her best efforts to mobilize government and party resources to win state elections, her Congress was defeated. And almost single-handedly by Nandamuri Taraka Rama Rao. NTR, to his fans. He was the all-time super-star of the Telegu cinema. Like MGR, he personified the provincial ethos in its most popular medium. It is in this way, and not only in India, that movie stars are not merely actors and actresses who portray heroes and heroines, but heroic performers in their own rights.

Before 1983, NTR had never appeared in an election. To carry him to victory he fashioned en route and largely from his fan clubs a political party which he called Telegu Desam – the Telegu nation – and proclaimed it to be the defender of the "3,000-year-old history of the Telegu people." Alas, NTR proved to be less durable as a politician than he was as a movie idol. In 1989, the voters of Andhra Pradesh turned his Telegu Desam out. He was deposed from its leadership in 1995 and died in 1996.

The post-mortem tussle for succession to the Telegu Desam's leadership was between NTR's second wife and the children of his first marriage. Thus, life paid its final tribute to the great actor by imitating the movies. The battle was won by the party's general secretary and NTR's son-in-law, Chandrababu Naidu: at once, a leading light on India's path to the age of information technology and an adroit provincial politician. He became Andhra Pradesh's chief minister in 1995, won a second five-year term in 1999 and is apparently well on the way to establishing the Telegu Desam as Andhra Pradesh's party of nation-provincialism. By neutralizing the BJP with an electoral alliance in 1999 and confronting Congress at the polls, the Telegu Desam won more than twice the number of parliamentary seats and almost eight times the number of legislative assembly seats than the combined totals of seats won by the two central parties.

The Communist Party of India–Marxist (CPI–M) separated from the Indian Communist Party in the mid-1960s to pursue a career as an revolutionary, ideologically sophisticated, nation-wide party with a Marxian world view. But instead, quipped Arun Shourie, a leading journalist and now a minister in the Vajpayee government, the CPI–M became "the DMK of West Bengal."[5] The quip is not quite fair. But it is fair enough. To be sure, a branch of the CPI–M is one of Kerala's major provincial parties, in and out of government; and candidates of the party's other state branches compete here and there for parliamentary and legislative assembly seats. To the Indian Election Commission, the CPI–M is a "national party." But, really, it is most at home in West Bengal, and there it enjoys a one-party dominance equal to Congress's anywhere at any time.

Without interruption, the CPI–M has been the ruling party in Kolkata (Calcutta) since 1977. In 2000, Jyoti Basu, the party's octogenerian leader, retired as India's longest serving chief minister. His successor led the party to victory in legislative assembly elections in 2001. Its major opposition was from another provincial party, the Trinamool Congress. The BJP won no seats and the Congress took fewer than one in ten. In West Bengal, the CPI–M is a provincial, parliamentary democratic party of the moderate left. Its greatest strength is in the countryside, among the *chhotolok*: the "little people" – ordinary farmers and sharecroppers, of ordinary caste. The CPI–M's leadership, however, belongs to the *bhadralok*: the "gentle folk" of upper-caste, middle-class, urban residence and white-collar inclination. In no other provincial party have people like the *bhadralok* been so successful in holding on to power.

The Akali Dal, the party of the godly, flourishes among the Sikhs of Punjab. The Dal is both a communal and a provincial party, and one of the sub-continent's oldest and most durable. It survived Punjab's partition in 1947, a brief merger into the Congress in the early 1950s, the movement for an independent "Khalistan" in the 1980s, the invasion in 1984 by Indian troops of the Sikh's holy of holies in Amritsar – the Golden Temple – and the sub-sequent assassination of Indira Gandhi by Sikh members of her bodyguard. In Punjab's state assembly elections in 1997, the Akali Dal won 75 of 117 seats. The junior partner in its coalition, the BJP, took 18 seats. Congress took 14. In defeats across the board for the BJP in four state elections in 2002, the Akali Dal–BJP coalition government in Punjab was unseated. Congress was returned to power: largely, it would seem, by defections from the BJP's Hindu constituency. No one imagines that Congress has replaced the Akali Dal as the Sikh political party.

Khalsa raj karega – the *khalsa* (Sikh community) will rule! That battle cry sums up the community's belief in the critical importance to it of political power. A leitmotiv throughout the community's history has been the efforts of its leading members to emplace political barriers to the demonstrated capacity of Hinduism to be religiously absorbent, to reabsorb Sikhism –

either in the drift of things or by design. At the temple town of Anandpur Sahib in 1973, the Akali Dal called upon the Union government to limit its powers constitutionally to India's defense, foreign relations, interstate communications and transportation, and the provision of its currency. All other government powers would be reallocated to the states. In effect, the Anandpur Sahib Resolution demanded a constitutional framework for a multi-nation *confederation* of nation-provinces.

In terms that were not markedly different from those of the Anandpur Sahib Resolution, other provincial parties demanded autonomy for their states during the 1980s. Much of this was in response to Congress's lingering one-party dominance at the Centre. Not only did it afford Mrs Gandhi the means to rule state Congress parties from New Delhi, it also provided her with tools to wreck the state governments of opposition parties. Her instrument was "President's Rule." The number of times she used it exceeds the combined number of times that it was used by all her predecessors and successors. President's Rule entails the temporary dismissal of a state's government and the assumption of its administration by the Centre when the President of India accepts the advice of that state's governor that it is unable to govern itself "in accordance with the provisions of [the] Constitution."[6]

As an instrument for toppling the state governments of opposition parties, prime minister Gandhi supplemented President's Rule by employing state governors as her political agents and using her retainers as agents provocateurs in provincial politics. Her persistent attempts to subvert the regimes of provincial parties, however, did more to discredit the Union government and increase disruptive and defensive provincialism than to recapture the states for the Indira Congress. Under her regime at the Centre, the danger to India's efficient and humane functioning was less in what used to be called the "fissiparous tendencies" of provincialism than in the "relentless centralization and ruthless, unprincipled intervention" into state politics by the Congress.[7] The last use of President's Rule by a Congress government was in 1992. Prime Minister P. V. Narasimha Rao dismissed four BJP state governments after the destruction of the Babri Masjid in Ayodhya.

As a consequence of Congress's demise at the Centre, President's Rule no longer worries state governments as it once did, and their calls for provincial autonomy have become less frequent and strident. A renegotiation of the constitutional relationship between the Centre and the states in favor of increasing their autonomy is still on the agenda, but there is no great urgency to bring it to a vote. In recent years, National Democratic Alliance constituents from West Bengal and Tamil Nadu have pressed the BJP's prime minister to dismiss the state governments of their enemies. But he did not do so. Given the transience and volitility of political alliances and their lack of any ideological coherence, the wrong party today may well be the right party tomorrow. President's Rule has become a risky business. Even in state capitals, coalition governments have become commonplace, sometimes with central parties as the dog and sometimes as its tail.

Hindi-speaking northern India, and Uttar Pradesh, in particular, the home state of the Nehru-Gandhi dynasty, used to be the Congress's heartland. No more. The first blows were struck by such Jat luminaries as Charan Singh and Devi Lal. In the 1989 and 1990 elections in north India, Congress was routed by parties whose underlying ideology was folkishness. They were the parties of the "real people": the Hindi-speaking sons and daughters of the soil, and not the bureaucrats and plutocrats and politicians of New Delhi who mimic English and work in air-conditioned offices and go home to foreign wives and keep their money in Swiss bank accounts and cannot tell a paddy field from a field of wheat.[8]

The next blows came, first from *mandir*, and then from *mandal*. Nowadays, these are the catchwords of Indian politics. *Mandir*, referring to the temple-mosque controversy in Ayodhya, is more or less synonymous with *Hindutva*. *Mandal*, again, is shorthand for the OBC wave that followed government implementation of the Mandal Commission's recommendations. In Uttar Pradesh, *mandir* brought the BJP to power in the 90s. But nowadays, as I suggested earlier, even the BJP recognizes *mandal* as the game. In most of north India's "cow belt," outside of Madhya Pradesh, Rajasthan and, possibly, Uttaranchal, the parties to beat are provincial parties. In Uttar Pradesh, Bihar and Haryana, parliamentary elections in 1999 yielded for Congress and the BJP a combined total of seats no more than half the number won by provincial parties. About 70 percent of India's Hindi-speaking populations lived in these three states. In legislative assembly elections, where constituencies are smaller, often more homogeneous and less expensive to contest, the two central parties do even more poorly. In the 1996 assembly elections in Uttar Pradesh, the BJP, with 32 percent of the seats, formed a government in coalition with its provincial allies. Congress was decimated. In the 2000 assembly elections, provincial parties and independents won more than 75 percent of the seats in Haryana and Bihar.

Most recently, in the 2002 state elections in Uttar Pradesh, the winner of the most seats was the provincial, *mandal*, OBC-based Samajwadi Party. The runner-up, its enemy, the provincial, *mandal*-leaning, Dalit-based Bhujan Samaj Party increased its tally of seats to 98, up from 67 in 1996. A collection of mostly provincial "one-caste" parties won two more seats than Congress (26 to 24) and a positively disproportionate vote share. The BJP's conversion from *mandir* to *mandal* was apparently unconvincing, and/or too little too late. It came third and its state government was unseated.

The Asom Gana Parishad (Assam people's organization) is unabashedly a party of "Assam for the Assamese." Popular hostility to the growing population of Bengalis in Assam brought the AGP to power in 1985. Particularly

unpopular are Bangladeshis, whose illegal immigration was allegedly unchecked because they were part of Congress's vote bank in the northeast. In
the 1996 elections to the state legislative assembly, the AGP emerged as the
largest single party by far. Five years later, however, the AGP was beaten at
the polls by Congress. This was not the result of any flagging in Assamese
provincialism, but rather of the AGP being flanked on the left. The National
Liberation Front of Asom (NLFA) wants its Assamese state for the Assamese
to be independent of India, and the front is not loath to make its case through
the barrel of a gun.

It will certainly fail in this, as did the "Khalistani" secessionists in Punjab. However, like other militant provincial movements, the NLFA may be
successful in using violence and the threat of secession to press their
demands in India, to shore up their bargaining position with the Centre.
New Delhi forgives repentant secessionists and negotiates even with ultras
who have only stacked their arms, but it will put down secessionism:
whatever the cost in property destroyed or lives lost and damaged. India
has not lost a square centimeter to secession. Its capacity to marshall its
resources against the occasional secessionist movement is, at least in part,
a reflection of its having had so few of them. By the conferral of statehood in
the Indian Union, the Centre has succeeded in meeting most provincial
claims, and all the major ones. Every major tribal group that shares both the
northeast with the Assamese and their hostility to the influx of Bengalis/
Bangladeshis is represented by a variety of provincial parties: parliamentary
democratic and/or revolutionary, Indian loyalist and/or secessionist. Never
ceasing, only moving from Nagas to Mizos to Bodos to Kukis and on and
on, tribal insurgencies have become regular – predictable and manageable –
events in the northeast.

If not the most long-lived, certainly the most vexing, dangerous and tragic
secessionist movement in India is in Kashmir. The "Kashmir issue" is an
appropriate subject for chapter 6, and readers may follow it there. Here, we
note only this: abetted by Pakistan and its sponsored *mujahidin*, parliamentary democracy in India has failed to reach the state of Jammu and
Kashmir. It has failed to generate parties there that are both rooted in the
interests of the state's Muslim majority and loyal to the Union. New Delhi has
failed to meet the provincial demands of that community by the conferral
of statehood in the Indian Union.

Bourgeois revolution and the cultivating middle classes

What has all this, the growth of nation-provincialism, to do with bourgeois
revolution in India? In provincial India, bourgeois revolution has been both
a cause and an effect of nation-provincialism's development. The development together of capitalism and parliamentary democracy in provincial India

has encouraged provincial embourgeoisement, and particularly the establishment of cultivating middle classes. Who are they and what is their relationship to nation-provincialism and to India? In the last chapter I nominated somewhere between a fifth and a quarter of cultivating households as middle class. There are regional variations, of course. A household farm with fewer hectares in Punjab, where there is a well developed infrastructure for commercial agriculture, may be more paradigmatically middle class, as well as doing better, than a larger household farm in Bihar.

The cultivating middle classes first marked their turf in the 1950s and 1960s, by supporting the formation of "linguistic" states in anticipation, correctly, of being its beneficiaries. More recently, the creation of "regional" states has been supported by the same classes for the same reasons. The aggregation of cultivating middle-class interests is facilitated by concentrating the castes of their families in the same provincial parliamentary arenas. Nowadays, on their turf, the cultivating middle classes have become capitalist or at least quasi or proto-capitalist producers. They sell most or much of what they produce. The Green Revolution's spread in India over the past three decades gives us some measure of agriculture's commercialization.

About 90 percent of India's wheat and 75 percent of its rice is grown from high-yielding seed varieties produced by Green Revolution technology. The technology needs an infrastructure and that, too, has spread: irrigation and storage facilities, supplies of pesticides and credit, markets and village-to-market roads, agro-industries, price supports. Land reforms that favored tenants-in-chief and small-holders, parliamentary democracy at the state level, *panchayati raj* and the Green Revolution: these have been the events in India's passage from subsistence to commercial agriculture, and to the establishment of cultivating middle classes. The Green Revolution, particularly, and the related phenomena of the mandalization and provincializing of Indian politics have produced the second wave of *embourgeoisés*: OBC small-holders.

The Green Revolution was gifted knowingly to the cultivating middle classes by a Congress government which had hitherto failed to foster India's self-sufficiency in food grains. By its failure to do so, India had become dependent on soft loans from the United States to buy its wheat and, thus, uncomfortably vulnerable to Washington's Cold War pressures. Then, in the late 1960s, the line that demarcated the cultivating middle classes may have been at half the upper quintile-to-quartile of farm families. Tomorrow's line may demarcate them at an upper quartile-to-half. The demarcation line is being pushed steadily downward by the power of OBCs in state politics, the trend since at least the 1970s of a decrease in the average size of family farms, the scale-neutrality of Green Revolution technology and the spread of its infrastructure. Nowadays, rural embourgeoisement's only foreseeable floor is between families with some land and families with none – the poorest of the rural poor.

They have not been benefited by the events that established cultivating middle classes. Rural reform legislation which was supposedly meant by urban reformers to benefit rural society, in general, and particularly the poor, has been either appropriated by the cultivating middle classes for their own benefit or evaded by them. They have appropriated *panchayati raj* and even various anti-poverty programs, for example. They have evaded such rural reform measures as land ceilings, minimum wages for agricultural laborers and special protection for the holdings of Dalit households. Predictably, the hectares of useable land redistributed to the landless over the years by state legislative assemblies controlled by the landed have been few and far between. The considerable powers allocated by the constitution to the states and fastened on to by the cultivating middle classes have been used by them consistently and with notable success to serve their interests. They established universities to train their sons for white-collar employment and bureaucracies and public sector enterprises to employ them. They have kept outsiders out by legislating monopolies on the use of their languages for public business and even on street signs. They established state and co-operative financial institutions and public utilities which meet their demands for credit and for forgiveness in the collection of their debts. They have made the levying by any state of a tax on agricultural income politically unthinkable.

Although divided by caste and community, the cultivating middle classes have been able to aggregate their interests in order to serve them. They are aggregated, automatically, as it were, in the calculations of politicians who know, for example, that cultivating middle-class households of whatever caste will respond in the same punitive way to any government that enhances their irrigation charges. They are aggregated in ministries, in the councils of parties and in *panchayati raj* institutions by representatives of different castes who share the same cultivating middle-class interests. In the late 80s, those interests were aggregated in the various farmers' movements

Their protests were buoyed with folkishness. India does not live in New Delhi's palaces and mansions, built on the toil of farmers, but in its villages. Never Indira, but they, the sons of its soil, are India. In 1988, the farmers' movements held a monster rally in New Delhi in protest against the Union government's alleged discrimination in favor of urban interests. It was an extraordinary event. For weeks, farmers occupied a spacious lawn planted by the Raj to imperial proportions and turned it into their camping grounds. Here they cooked their food on *chulhas* (clay hearths); bathed from plastic buckets, washed their clothing, slept on bales of hay, chatted, played cards, read under the shade of tarpaulins stretched from their tractors, and half-listened to the amplified harangues of their leaders and sympathetic politicians. Wandering into the scene from one of the capital city's broad avenues the visitor entered what was apparently the enclave of another country. So little did its inhabitants resemble those of their temporary surrounds.

The scene seemed to illustrate the juxtaposition that we have already encountered of "Bharat" and "India," of the expropriated provinces and the expropriating Centre. But appearances and epigrams may deceive. The usual horizons of cultivating middle classes are certainly provincial. They are, after all, classes of village-based small-holders. Usually circumscribed by state borders, their castes and quasi castes are their primary organizations and their interests are aggregated in state legislative assemblies and *panchayati raj* institutions. In the Indian constitution's division of powers, most of what closely and immediately concerns cultivating middle classes is allocated to the states. Of course, the farmers' movements made their demands in the name of the eternal countryside. Like that of any sophisticated interest group, their rhetoric elevated their cause above mere self-interest. But their demands and to whom they were addressed told their own story. Propelled by the commercialization of agriculture, in general, and the Green Revolution, in particular, they were the demands of Indian cultivating middle classes directed toward their national government. The sectorial conflict that was growing in the 80s was not between "Bharat" and "India," but between Indian middle classes.

The cultivating middle classes have become, more and more, parts of wider Indian middle classes. Bourgeois revolution connected cultivating middle classes to their urban counterparts of the provincial city. Through their investments and participation in local small businesses – bus companies and cinemas, for example – and their employment in the provincial white-collar salariat, the cultivating middle classes have become increasingly attached to the provincial city. Bourgeois revolution in India and, more recently, the "globalization" of capitalism have drawn the provinces into India and India into the world. The cultivating middle classes which established their dominance in state politics almost from their inception, must have power at the Centre to maintain their dominance there and to protect their interests everywhere. Their Green Revolution produce would, of course, be useless to them without markets in which to sell it. The markets for commercialized agriculture are national and international, and the Centre is there to protect them for India's cultivating middle classes.

From the mid-1990s the Centre's two-steps-forward-and-one-step-backward progress to liberalization of the Indian economy has come up against a general deceleration in the rates of agricultural growth. This has prompted re-examinations of Indian agricultural policy in such matters as: public investment in rural infrastucture, the regulation of agricultural markets by the Centre and the states and their procurement policies for farm produce, the adequacy of credit for farmers and its availability to small-holders, the costs and benefits to agricultural productivity and social equity of explicit and implicit subsidies, wide variations between states in their agricultural productivity and the welfare of their rural populations, sustainable development in the face of an increase in water-logging and soil salinity.[9] Wherever this re-examination leads, it cannot ignore the interests of the cultivating middle classes. Perhaps we need say no more than this: in the Green Revolution's fourth decade and post-*mandal*, neither Congress nor the BJP, nor any other central party that might appear on the political horizon, will be able to take government at the Centre and keep it without the alliance of the cultivating middle classes' provincial parties.

Selling their produce and educating their sons, and more recently their daughters, are the cultivating middle classes' priorities. Educated sons, like our hypothetical medical doctor, produce prestige and remittance income for farm households. Educated daughters ally the household to well-employed, prestigious and useful in-laws. The education that best serves these purposes is a university education. The relationship in India between university education and university-educated employment is not dissimilar to that between agricultural production and marketing: a relationship of symbiosis, in which the states produce the graduates and the Union provides them with a national market for their university-acquired skills.

When India became an independent state, there were 19 universities with a total enrollment of about 300,000 students. By 1970, more than 2 million students were enrolled in 60 universities. Nowadays, there are more than 235 institutions in India that are officially recognized as universities, and they are attended by more than 6 million students. So, over the past 30 years, while the population of India has less than doubled, the number of university students has more than trebled. This percentage increase in university enrollments also exceeded the increase in primary and secondary school enrollments. About one-third of India's university students are women.[10]

Fewer than 20 Indian universities are governed and directly funded under laws of the national parliament. All the others are state universities. State budgets provide 90 percent of university funding, and much of it goes to subsidize student fees. These are low and affordable by middle-class families. In the best of Indian state universities, the best colleges, departments, institutes and so forth are comparable to the best in most places. Unfortunately, they are exceptions. The rule is a poor-to-mediocre standard of education, often further vitiated by improper and meddlesome interference from politicians and bureaucrats, administrative incompetence, nepotism, caste-ism, communalism and corruption. If Indian state universities are not celebrated for their educational standards, however, they are nonetheless noteworthy for their contributions to contemporary Indian society.

They have broken the monopoly on university-educated employment that was enjoyed under the Raj by a tiny, largely self-perpetuating, largely urban elite of English-language proficients. In British India, English was not only the sole medium of university instruction, English-language proficiency was the sine qua non of professional career advancement: from university matriculation to Indian Civil Service promotion. The state universities of independent India have not so much put an end to all this, but rather pushed it to the top of a national career ladder which, at the same time, they have pulled downward into the realm of the largely Indian-languages-proficient provincial middle classes.

For ordinary secondary school students who have completed a two-year university preparatory course, state university admission is not particularly difficult into other-than professional, technological and science courses. In courses other than these, most undergraduate education in northern India is in Hindi; and many undergraduates in other states have the option of studying in their state's official language in preference to English. In those courses in ordinary state universities where English is the formal language of instruction, a relevant reading knowledge of it is necessary. Otherwise English is frequently mixed for instructional purposes, informally, in greater or lesser measure, with the state's official language. In sum, university education is available to middle-class village and town households' children who have virtually no English or only some English as a second language. Concomitantly, the states have made not English but their languages the languages of university-educated employment in their bureaucracies and public sector enterprises. In India, the public sector employs more than twice the number of people employed by the organized private sector; and state governments and their public sector enterprises employ more than twice the number of people employed by the Union government and its public sector enterprises. Again, for "scheduled tribes and castes" these doors have been opened by compensatory discrimination; and for an OBC catch-up, by *mandal*.

State university graduates may, of course, seek and possibly find rewarding and remunerative employment in their own states and in their own state language. And most of them do, but they need not. By virtue of their Indian citizenship, they have privileged access to an India-wide university-educated employment market. In order to enter and compete in it, however, state university graduates must themselves enter into the symbiotic relationship between the states and the Indian Union. They cannot, in their working lives at least, remain provincial. They must become Indians. They must be able to work in languages of India other than those of their states. In particular, they must be able to work in either or both of the Indian Union's official languages: Hindi and English.

The Hindi-speaking states – of which the Union capital is, after all, but a cutout – have assiduously cultivated Hindi as their language of official business. In effect, job aspirants who do not have some proficiency in Hindi nowadays, at least as a second language, have closed off about 40 percent of their opportunities for university-educated employment in India. More than 40 percent of India is governed by states whose principal language is Hindi. This has been the primary incentive to increased Hindi-language learning all over India: not the constitutional provision that makes it the Union's first official language nor any revision of the ideological or regional objections to it being so. The BJP/NDA government at the Centre is more encouraging of the use of Hindi than were its predecessors, and this is bound to be of some effect.

The first official language de facto of the Indian Union, certainly at its higher public and private reaches, is still English. It is still the language of India's university-educated upper middle classes. But it does not exclude as it once did. Nowadays, there is a ladder down, and its bottom rung for provincials who are bright, lucky, enterprising, ambitious, well-connected is an undergraduate degree from a state university. They learn English on the way up. With a postgraduate degree from the Delhi School of Economics or the All India Institute of Medical Sciences or an Indian Institute of Technology, for example, their skills are marketable nationally and internationally.

In sum, then, congruence has characterized bourgeois revolutions at India's Centre and in its provinces. With leads and lags, to be sure, capitalism and parliamentary democracy have developed *together* in India, and *together* in national and provincial India in such ways as to complement and supplement each other. Capitalist agriculture which developed under the patronage of parliamentary democracy in the states (albeit with New Delhi's encouragement) increasingly turns for its further development to parliamentary democracy at the Centre. Parliamentary democracy at the Centre serves the aspirations of provincial university graduates. My guess is that the multi-nation Indian Union is in no danger of being balkanized by its nation-provinces as long as it meets the growing demands of India's growing middle classes in ways in which its nation-provinces cannot.

3 *The British empire in India, c.1900*

Part II

Change from above

There are six essays in part II. The underlying argument of the first two essays in chapter 5 is this: Bourgeois revolution in Indian society was initiated in its experiences of British imperialism. It was domesticated, particularly, by the Indian National Congress which evolved in response to British imperialism; became an India-wide, mass nationalist movement under the leadership of Mahatma Gandhi; and finally succeeded the Raj in 1947. Because of its relevance here and to my earlier discussions of subcontinental Islam, I have added an essay on Muslim separatism

In the first two essays in chapter 6, I pick up the thread of bourgeois revolution in the Indian Union and trace its course. Through its policies of political and economic development, the Union has promoted and institutionalized the growth in tandem of capitalism and parliamentary democracy. Unrelated to this argument, but certainly related to development in India, the final essay of chapter 6 deals with New Delhi's international politics.

Following both a suggestion of Barrington Moore, Jr. and what seems to me self-evident, I accept the following proposition: A major contribution to the development of bourgeois revolution in India lay in the composition of the dominant classes in the Indian National Congress's pre-Independence alliance.[1] The allies were English-educated professional people, landed peasants and, with some reluctance until the late 1930s, modern industrial entrepreneurs. Certainly, there were other contributions, without which bourgeois revolution might well have aborted or died long before the Union's fifty-fifth birthday. Some of these were related, however tangentially, to one another and/or to the Congress's alliance. The bureaucratic efficiency and relatively benign political nature of British imperialism made a contribution,

as did Mahatma Gandhi's *satyagraha* strategy of conflict and conflict resolution, the swift and virtually bloodless integration of the princely states into
the Indian Union, Jawaharlal Nehru's commitments to parliamentary democracy and a planned and mixed economy, Congress's post-Independence
one-party dominance.

Britain's "transfer of power" – an apt expression – to the Indian Union
did not disarray the Congress's alliance of dominant classes. Since 1947,
bourgeois revolution has turned landed peasants into farmers. The alliance
has become solidly middle class. The middle classes have increased dramatically in size and diversity and come to dominate Indian politics at the Centre
and in the states. In independent India, the middle classes are the primary
beneficiaries of the development together of capitalism and parliamentary
democracy.

My use of "class" in these essays is consistent with my earlier use. Classes
are groups which share a similar "market situation," whether or not they are
conscious of it. It is to the middle classes that I have addressed most of my
discussion: in form, for the sake of economy, expository order, congruence
with my argument and because they are essays rather than summary tours
of the horizon; and in substance, because I believe that India's development
is best understood, not entirely but mostly, as the product of, by and for its
middle classes. Again, they are comprised of groups whose family incomes
are derived from ownership of sufficient business capital to provide for a
middle-class standard of living and from cultivating-proprietorship of medium
size to large family farms; from employment in the educated professions,
including politics, and in higher salaried positions in government bureaucracies, modern industry and commerce. In addition, there are millions of
families which have the appropriate values and reasonable aspirations to
middle-class status, but have not yet made it.

Chapter 5

British imperialism, Indian nationalism and Muslim separatism

To argue that bourgeois revolution in India was the consequence of British imperialism and Indian nationalism is really one argument of related parts, certainly from the last decades of the nineteenth century. From then and for the next half-century or so until Independence, India's history unfolded largely in response to the intricate interplay between and within the forces of imperialism and nationalism. One consequence, in part, of the exchange, now marked by Pakistan and Bangladesh on the map of the subcontinent and on the consciousness of its inhabitants, was Muslim separatism.

British imperialism

Nowadays, students of modern Indian history are routinely cautioned against regarding the British imperial enterprise in India as a monolith. And indeed it was not a monolith. There was Her Majesty's Government in London under whose ultimate authority India was governed. But of its concerns, governing India was only one, and rarely a major one. The secretary of state for India was the concerned minister. But his concerns had to contend with those of other ministers and correspond with the interests, electoral and otherwise, of the government. There was a British government of India in Calcutta until 1911 when it shifted to Delhi. It was headed by a titled British politician, the Viceroy and Governor-General. In organizational theory, he was the Secretary of State's man in India. In practice, relationships between the two men and their governments were negotiated.

The British government in India was run by bureaucrats. The Raj was a bureaucratic empire. At the imperial and provincial levels of empire and between them, between bureaucrats who were department heads and bureaucrats in the districts, there were competing concerns, conflicting interests, divergent views, personal friendships and animosities. Sometimes, decisions made at the top evaporated as they filtered down. Decisions made at the bottom sometimes percolated up as faits accomplis. There was a Political Department that exercised the Indian government's "paramountly" – its protectorate – over princely India. It occupied about one-third of the subcontinent and was, in effect, a parallel imperium. There was the Indian Army which was part of both the Raj and the British military establishment. There were British companies in India and companies in Britain with major business interests in India. There were British planters. There were churchmen and missionaries. There were British families.

While not a monolith, the British empire was nonetheless a purposive undertaking. It was a British state enterprise which used Indian resources to serve British economic and political interests. That was not all that it did, certainly. But that was its raison d'être. That it served British interests well, there is little doubt. The doubts, expressed with increasing persuasiveness in the revisions of economic historians, are about the disservices of the British Raj to Indian interests. About the "exploitation" of the subcontinent by British imperialism.

India best served British interests as an approximation of a "colonial open economy." Its relevance to the establishment and maintenance of modern urban industry and to an imperial army and the resources that sustained it are our concerns here. On terms largely dictated by British governments, India became, from the nineteenth century, a major supplier of raw materials to British factories, of raw materials and textile goods to various parts of the world and a major market for British manufactured products. India was also a major market for British investments of capital: particularly in railways, mining and such major export industries as tea and jute production. These enterprises were largely British-owned and managed, and British financial investments in Indian enterprises were almost entirely in them. Their major financial arrangements were managed by British banks. Rates of exchange, between rupees and pounds, were determined by British authorities to British advantage. British ships carried most of India's exports and imports. On these, tariffs and other charges were determined by British governments. Thus, from the late nineteenth century, India enabled Britain to make good between two-fifths and one-third of her deficit with other industrialized nations, and to continue to perform as an economy with a world-wide balance of payments surplus long after her trading position had declined.[2]

The British Indian Army protected British India by suppressing "domestic unrest" and was otherwise used to fight Britain's battles all over the world: in the Crimea, Afghanistan, Africa, China, Persia, Turkey, Southeast Asia, North Africa, Europe. In peacetime, the costs of the Indian Army's maintenance were borne almost entirely out of Indian revenues. These paid, directly and indirectly, for most of the army's expenses in wartime. Ordinarily, the army accounted for about 40 percent of the Government of India's budget: by far its largest single item. Would Britain have been a great power from the middle of the nineteenth century through the early decades of the twentieth without an Indian Army sustained by Indian revenues? It seems unlikely. The army fielded a million-and-a-half troops during the First World War and two-and-a-half million during the Second. Of such value was the Indian Army to Britain that, even from 1917 when British governments began talking about "dominion status" for India and greater control for the (British) Indian government over its tariff and monetary policies, the plan for the Indian Army was to bring it under the direct command of the Imperial General Staff.

These services to Britain's interests performed by its Indian empire imply costs to it, certainly. But economic historians now question whether these implications have been accurately drawn and whether and in what ways British "exploitation" of the subcontinent actually disserviced Indian interests. So, for example, in spite of British unwillingness to protect it with tariffs, a cotton textile industry developed in nineteenth-century India to become one of the world's largest. And it was overwhelmingly owned and operated by Indians. It seems unlikely, as the demonology of imperialism would have it, that imports of British cloth "deindustrialized" India and devastated Indian handloom weavers. Insofar as they were devastated by power looms, it is more likely that these were owned by Indian producers of coarse cloth.[3] In spite of a general British policy of discouraging Indian industrialization, the Parsi entrepreneur J. N. Tata received "extensive official assistance" in his efforts to establish the Tata Iron and Steel Company more than a decade before the First World War. Under imperial patronage, Tata's mill at Jamshedpur in Bihar would grow to become one of the largest steel works in Asia.[4] Tata's shareholders were almost all Indian. British governments insisted on collecting their "home charges" from India. These were the cost to it, in pounds, of servicing its public debt to Britain and enjoying Britain's military protection and the administration of its bureaucrats. It was a "drain" on India's resources. But its extent has probably been exaggerated.[5]

To better understand India's introduction to economic modernity under British rule, some shift in emphasis may be helpful: *away* from what the Raj *was*, an "exploitative" imperial regime, and toward what it *was not*. It *was not* a national government. The shift does not mitigate the British imperial government's defects as an industrializer of India. Rather, it emphasizes imperialism's inherent, structural weakness as a system for the economic development of its colonies. Doubtlessly, some British officials were keen to develop Indian industries, particularly after the First World War. Many were dedicated to the service of Indian interests, farsighted and intelligent. But ultimately British Indian officials were the servants of a foreign country's government. They were the representatives of a government in India that was indirectly responsive to the interests of a British and not an Indian electorate. As such, the British government of India was disabled from the vigorous pursuit of any industrialization strategy whose primary concern was India's "national interests," and that demanded in their service some sacrifices from sectorial interests "at home." Incapable of singular purpose and deficient in legitimacy, the British government of India could not have done what the Japanese government of Japan did from the late nineteenth century. Much less, for better or worse, could the Raj have pursued for 40 years until the 1990s the Indian Republic's consistent import-substitution strategy of industrialization.

Under the Raj, India industrialized in bits and pieces: in "enclaves"[6] of industrialization in an unindustrialized subcontinent. So, not only were the Indian railways built to facilitate agriculture, commerce and troop mobility *rather* than industry, but their effects on furthering industrialization were limited. The railways purchased their locomotives and other complex machinery from Britain. They employed Britons in the railways' higher managerial and technical positions. The heavy machinery used in India's highly developed cotton textile industry was bought from Britain. It was not manufactured in India. India's foreign trade was mostly in the hands of British companies. Most foreign investments in India were arranged in London, and the development of share markets and a modern banking industry in India was thereby retarded. During the Great Depression of the 1930s, British authorities maintained an over-valued rupee: in British interests and to the disaffection of Bombay's mill-owners. But fearful of the political consequences of further disaffecting them, British authorities were loath to tax mill-owners to support India's industrial development. Where its own interests were not immediately concerned, imperial government, as many historians now contend, was timid. The imperial policy of laissez-faire was doubtlessly an ideology that rationalized the use of India's resources by Britain in its interests. But it was also an excuse for leaving well enough alone. For not rocking the Indian boat. To supplement India's industrialization in enclaves, there were other bits and pieces of enclave modernization. A university system was created by the British whose medium of instruction was English in an India whose population was overwhelmingly non-English speaking and illiterate

Cumulated, these bits and pieces of industrialization and modernization melded into a bureaucratic regime that shaped modern India. Their combined institutional effects were at least these: an administrative and political integration of the subcontinent that was unprecedented and sustained by subcontinental systems of law and administration, a near-monopoly by government of coercion and repression, forums for the interplay of imperialist and nationalist politics, nascent capitalism in industry and agriculture, facilities for tertiary education and professional training, modern means of transportation and communications.

In consequence of these events, bourgeois revolution was initiated on the subcontinent. The foundations and some of the superstructure was constructed on which the Indian Union would be built. British-initiated bourgeois revolution did not produce general welfare in India and may have reduced it. After more than a century and a half in Britain's possession, its erstwhile "jewel in the crown" was possibly the largest aggregate of impoverished, unhealthy and illiterate people in the world. But the Raj did produce middle classes. Modern educated and business middle classes developed under the British Raj and in response to it. Their development was the human aspect of the institutional consequences to India of British imperialism. In 1947, when the Raj was succeeded by the Congress *raj*, these middle classes were the senior partners in its alliance of dominant classes. The cultivating middle classes were conceived as a consequence of bourgeois revolution's initiation in British India. But they remained embryonic until land reforms of the 1950s in the states of the Indian Union. The Raj's contribution to the shaping of modern Indian middle classes is the story of the rest of this section and it is organized accordingly.

The development of English-educated middle classes in India paralleled and was in the first instance a consequence of the deposal and debilitation by the British of the warrior-landlord classes of post-Mughal India. During the decades before the Mutiny in 1857, the British ended the regimes of *rajas* and *nawabs* in over two-thirds of the subcontinent. Many of these Indian princes, their barons and courtiers, retained their landholdings, albeit under a new, imperially dictated form of land ownership. They kept their titles, too, power over their tenants and dependants and local influence. But they ceased being rulers, and became subjects of the Raj.

Some of the Mutiny's lessons for the British were that imperialism was as much a matter of politics as it was of administration, and that in imperial politics it is useful to have allies. The princes, by and large, had served the British as "breakwaters in the storm" of 1857. It seemed politic to encourage them to perform that same service in the event of storms to come and, in general, to think of themselves as the Raj's "subordinate allies." After the Mutiny, the British government ended its policy of deposing princely regimes and aggrandizing their territories into British India. To those princes who were still sitting on their *gaddis* went British guarantees to this effect: that they and their heirs would be permitted to continue to rule their principalities as clients of the British government. As such, many princes prospered and increased the power of their *durbars* in their domestic politics. But their prosperity and, particularly, their power became increasingly dependent on their clienthood. In 1947, the British political system, on whose patronage the princes depended, was taken over by a bourgeois Congress government that wanted no princes as clients or otherwise. They were allowed to retain their titles and chattels and pensioned off with generous "privy purses." But their *durbars* were liquidated and their territories merged into the states of the Indian Union – all done in a year or so, with no great fuss and the show of armed force in only three instances.

The Raj's preservation in clientage of 500-odd princely *durbars*, pushed them to the empire's political margin. Its political arenas were in British India. Politics had become the game less of warrior-landlords than of the English-educated middle classes. The British tended to regard them with suspicion. "Sedition" had its home in the particularly Hindu, particularly Bengali, middle classes. As a matter of "balance and rule," Peter Hardy's variation on the theme,[7] the Raj post-Mutiny tried to enlist the warrior-landlord classes, individually and collectively, in imperial maintenance. Four "chiefs' colleges" were opened in the 1870s to educate sons of India's "natural leaders" to noblesse oblige and imperial loyalty. A Statutory Civil Service was inaugurated to employ them and, later, an Imperial Cadet Corps was formed to stimulate them to manly pursuits and to symbolize viceregal concern for the Indian aristocracy. Princes were invited to invest in the Indian railway system and to hold government of India securities. In their otherwise ceremonial armies, princes were encouraged to maintain British-trained crack units which could and would be used under British command to defend the empire. Tied into the 1919 and 1935 packages of British constitutional reforms for India were provisions for incorporating into the structure of the Raj a collective representation of the princes' interests.

Imperial solicitude for India's "natural leaders" did not have the intended result of relieving the Raj's daily dependence for its business on the English-educated middle classes. In the very nature of bureaucracy, a handful of British bureaucrats spread over a vast, populous and exotic terrain had little choice but to depend for their regime on a much larger group of locally recruited and trained subordinate bureaucrats and professionals. The Raj's subordinate bureaucrats and the Indian professional men who provided the bureaucracy with its ancillary services were overwhelmingly from the middle classes. They had to be Indians. In their tens of thousands, they could not be supplied from Britain. That would have been prohibitively costly and, per-haps, unwise politically. Indians of the ancien régime's educated castes and classes were keen and readily available. They worked cheaply and India was not exotic and orientally inexplicable to them. They spoke the language, and their employment by the British Raj opened the possibility of their becoming its collaborators.

In the nineteenth century, India's English-educated middle classes came disproportionately from places in which the British regime was earliest and best established: from the three coastal "presidency" towns of Calcutta, Bombay, Madras and their environs. They were mostly Hindus from twice-born castes, or castes that aspired to that status, in which the skills of literacy and numeracy and their supporting values are cultivated. There were educated middle-class Muslims, too, primarily in the cities of the Gangetic Plain and from families that had served or claimed to have served Muslim courts. The families of the educated middle classes, Hindu and Muslim, tended to be relatively well-to-do rather than rich. They were families that wanted careers for their sons and were willing, often at some sacrifice, to pay for their education. From the latter half of the nineteenth century, their formal education was in English and they were most likely to be educated at a university that had been established in India by the British to train subordinate bureaucrats and professionals.

The Indian National Congress began as their organization. It was founded in 1885, largely as an interest group of the English-educated middle classes. Increasingly aware of the empire's dependence on their services, they used the Congress platform to couple declarations of unswerving loyalty to Her Majesty with assertions of their demands on her government in India. They wanted employment in *superior* bureaucracies and bureaucratic positions. They wanted representation on deliberative, quasi-legislative bodies at the empire's Centre and in its provinces and cities. Meeting these demands *to some extent* would have meant for the British only some additional costs for the use of India's resources. *To some extent*, the imperial enterprise would have been able to absorb these additional costs. They would have been *to some extent* investments in Indian human capital that might have increased the Raj's political dividends. But to what extent? That was the question. I can only indicate the answer: *not* to the extent that these additional costs would have impinged upon India's rule by British officers.

With regard to their employment as superior bureaucrats, the educated middle classes of India might have hoped, mistakenly but not for long, for the fulfillment of the promise in Queen Victoria's post-Mutiny proclamation of 1858:

> So far as may be, our subjects of whatever race or creed, [shall] be freely and impartially admitted to offices in our service, the duties of which they may be qualified by their education, ability and integrity duly to discharge.[8]

That promise was never fulfilled. Given the underlying purpose and structure of the British superior bureaucracy in India, it probably could not have been fulfilled. From the middle of the nineteenth century, the rationale for it not being fulfilled was, increasingly, racist.

The purpose of the superior bureaucracy in India was not simply to govern it, but to govern it in British interests: to facilitate Britain's use of India's resources. Now, if after 1858, Indians had been impartially admitted to the elite Indian Civil Service (ICS) and impartially employed by it, it seems likely that this governing bureaucracy would have – sooner rather than later – drawn the large majority of its officers from the subcontinent's English-educated middle classes. Could they have been relied on to govern India in Britain's interests? The captains of empire thought not. The English-educated middle classes, for example, had through their Congress, from its earliest meetings, objected in India's interests to two of the empire' s crucial services to British interests: the use of Indian manpower to fight Britain's wars and of Indian revenues to pay for them.

But the Indian English-educated middle classes were not simply men who had Indian interests. They were *Indians*. In his 1835 "minute on education" in India, Thomas Babington Macauley averred that, "a single shelf of a good European library was worth the whole native literature of India ..." There was no British argument with that. But Macauley also believed that an introduction to that library, a good European education, would produce in India "a class of persons Indian in blood and color, but English in taste, in opinion, in morals and intellect."[9] In this he was certainly mistaken. Presumably because his "minute" antedated the last half of the century's flowering of "scientific" racism, Macauley did not understand that Indians were also racially inferior.

To what Edward Said has named "orientalism,"[10] that cumulation of inferiorities that define the "oriental other" – religion, language, culture and so forth – "science" added race. Blood and color would out. The educated middle classes were men of Indian *races*. All different: the feline Bengali, the non-Aryan Tamil, the martial Punjabi. And all *inherently* inferior to the British in their capacity to rule according to "law and system." Bureaucracy was a genius of Europeans. One of the empire's nineteenth-century guardians, scholar and hierarch, Sir Alfred C. Lyall, considered seriously the affirmation of Joseph Arthur de Gobineau that "the civilization of Europe has never taken and will never take root among the old races of Asia."[11] Gobineau was an originator of modern European "scientific" racism. Self-evidently superior to the civilizations of India in general, and particularly in its capacity for systematic government, European civilization could take root on the subcontinent only in that new race of Asia: the Anglo-Indians.

The Anglo-lndians were the core of British society in India. Orientalism was the ideological barrier that protected them from India. Like other ideologies, orientalism served the real interests of those who subscribed to it. More Indians in Her Majesty's superior services were readily translatable into fewer positions in India for the sons and nephews of Anglo-Indian families and fewer prospective husbands for their daughters and nieces. Of more general imperial concern, what effects would such translations have on Anglo-Indian rule in India? The Anglo-Indians were a ruling aristocracy of (largely middle class) British families in India. No less, they were a community of British families. They were not a landed aristocracy. They were an aristocratic meritocracy that ruled from positions of superior employment in the bureaucratic empire. Informally, but no less, they ruled from their place as an aristocratic community. The Anglo-Indians spoke each other's language and knew each other's secrets, joined in each other's games, tipped each other off and helped each other out, let their hair down in each other's company and didn't let the side down in the company of Indians, dined in each other's bungalows and married each other's children, referred to the same distant island as "home," were each other's kind: "us." The *daftar* (office) and the club were connecting rooms in the house of British imperialism.

From the latter half of the nineteenth century, access to both were impeded for Indians by the addition of "scientific" racism to Anglo-Indian orientalism. Thus, like Macauley's "minute," Queen Victoria's promise to India's educated middle classes was uninformed by Gobineau's "science" and could not be kept, ought not to be kept. Informed by "science," her ministers, their successors and her Anglo-Indian aristocracy would have to negate her promise in the interests of her empire. Examinations for the ICS were so structured as to make it exceedingly difficult for any young man to take and pass them if he did not have: a first-language competency in English, an English "public school" and university education and a residence in Britain. The Indian group that was most successful in competing on their intellectual merits for places in the empire's bureaucracies and professions, the Bengali *bhadralok*, were made an object of imperial scorn and ridicule. *Babus*, Kipling's *banderlog* (monkey people), "competition-wallahs," Lyall's "half-civilized *avocasserie*, that bane of all British India" who excelled at swotting up for examination, but lacked both the depth of knowledge and the soundness of character that distinguished British officers.

A landmark in the development of anti-imperialism among the English-educated middle classes was the successful campaign by the Anglo-Indian community in 1883 to pressure the viceroy to withdraw what was known as the Ilbert Bill. It would have made Europeans in India subject to trial, as were Indians, by Indian judges of British district courts. Membership in the best clubs of British India was for Europeans only. The Anglo-Indian community tabooed marriages between Europeans and Indians and closed its doors to their offspring.

Orientalism, in general, and racism, in particular, served the end of securing the empire under Anglo-Indian rule. The Indian English-educated middle classes were denied the prerequisite cultural depth and racial merit for membership in a European superior meritocracy and the fundamental human equality that Anglo-Indians recognized in those of their own. For the

Indian English-educated middle classes, orientalism and racism were the added insult to the injury of professional discrimination. Both were felt more keenly as educated unemployment grew from the twentieth century.

With regard to the English-educated middle classes' other major demand, for representation on municipal and provincial councils: the question for the British was, again, *to what extent* could such a demand have been absorbed into the cost structure of their enterprise? *To some extent*, the demand could be put to its political use, to the service of the Raj. After the Mutiny, the British began to use Indian landlords and haute bourgeoisie as municipal councilors. The anticipated benefits, to the British government, from Indian participation on such councils were these: they would raise municipal revenues and in the process relieve the British government of some of the onus of collecting taxes, provide a source of political information for British officers and help to recruit collaborators by making the prestige and boodle of municipal administration available to local notables.

During the remaining decades of British rule in India, and largely in reaction to demands of the English-educated middle classes, the imperial government allowed more and more Indian representation at higher and higher political levels: from municipal corporations to provincial councils to the governor-general's council. Certainly, from the inter-war years of political ferment in India and Mahatma Gandhi's rise to power in the Congress, imperial hierarchs could no longer safely (however accurately) continue to dismiss the English-educated middle classes as a "microscopic minority." Their so-called nationalist movements were self-serving and essentially in-authentic, to be sure; but troublesome nonetheless, and increasingly so.

Originally appointed by the British government of India, Indian members of provincial representative councils were from 1909 elected by Indian constituencies. The franchise in British India was always subject to economic and educational qualifications, but these became less and less restrictive over the decades and the proportions of Indians entitled to vote increased. Their elected representatives were granted more and more legislative and gov-ernmental power under a succession of British laws. From 1917 British politicians began to talk about responsible government and eventual self-rule in India. Was that really the eventuality, the inevitable course of British Indian constitutional reforms, ended forever by the Second World War? From hindsight, some historians have tended to think so, but Indian politicians at the time were more skeptical. In the course of constitutional reforms, they discerned – I think, correctly – a persistent British unwillingness to part with the substance of power. Periodically, the British government delivered pack-ages of constitutional reforms in which ostensible concessions to nationalist aspirations were wrapped together with insidious schemes to protect British power from what it conceded.

We can identify the schemes, simply, as *divide and rule*, and *retain the prerogative*. Both were present in the India Act of 1935. It is instructive to consider it. The 1935 act provides a tally at endgame of the costs that Britain was willing to incur, the extent to which it was willing to go, to meet the Indian middle classes' political aspirations. The act and the elections held under it in 1937 represent, in effect, Britain's last chance to negotiate a continuation of empire by conceding Indian middle-class demands for self-government. The extent of the concessions was great enough to outrage dyed-in-the-wool imperialists like Winston Churchill. It was endgame, nonetheless. With Churchill's government after 1939, and later Attlee's, the Indian middle classes were willing to negotiate only a termination of empire. The 1935 act and the elections of 1937 were landmarks in the course of bourgeois revolution in India.

The centerpiece of the 1935 act was responsible parliamentary self-government in the provinces of British India. Popular elections were to be held. From among the elected, British governors were to choose ministries which enjoyed the confidence of a majority in the legislatures. This was a considerable advance over the omnibus India Act of 1919. Under its ill-fated system of "dyarchy," some minor portfolios had been "transferred" to elected Indian politicians who served as the governor's ministers: at his pleasure and often under the de facto supervision of their ICS department secretaries. Under the authority of the 1919 act, about 6 percent of India's adult population had been enfranchised. This percentage was increased about fourfold for the 1937 elections.

Under neither the act of 1919 nor 1935, was the electorate enfranchised to vote in general, geographical constituencies. The constituencies were communal and "special interest." Muslims, Sikhs, Eurasians, Indian Christians and Europeans had their separate constituencies. Where these communities were minorities, they were enfranchised to elect provincial councilors whose numbers were "weighted" in positive disproportion to the communities' share of the general population. Again, the British government's "communal award" of 1932 would have introduced yet another separate electorate, for "scheduled castes," had Gandhi not opposed it by embarking on a "fast unto death." The "special interest" constituencies were for commerce and industry, universities, landlords and organized labor. "General constituencies" in these elections were, in effect, Hindu constituencies. They were increased by weightage in those provinces – most notably, Punjab and Bengal – where Hindus were a minority. Otherwise, Hindu voters elected numbers of representatives in negative disproportion to the Hindu population.

The provision of separate electorates and weighted representation to non-Hindu religious communities invested them with political interests secured by British power: interests in keeping their political lots apart from the Congress's and from those of its dominant Hindu middle classes. The British position was that they were only protecting minorities in response to their demands for protection – from Hindus. Congressmen believed that the British were playing the "communal card" to divide and rule. They readily acceded to minority demands because it suited British interests to do so. They were trying to reduce the Congress to an organization of some twice-born and touchable Hindus, discredit Indian nationalism, proliferate and politicize communal divisions within the Indian middle classes in order to oppose them one to another and fragment their opposition to British rule. In a sub-continent of myriad ethnic diversities, the communal card could be played over and over again.

It did not win in the 1937 elections, however. Congress did. In eight of British India's eleven provinces, Congress was able to form ministries. But it withheld them from taking office until it received assurance from the British government that the overwhelming power conferred on provincial governors by the act would be "restricted to the narrowest limits possible."[12] Under the act, governors had almost complete control over the budgets of their province. They had the power to enact legislation entirely on their own authority. By refusing their assent, governors could nullify with finality any act passed by their provincial assemblies. Governors had the power to prorogue their assemblies and dissolve their lower houses.

The power of the viceroy and governor-general was unreformed by the 1935 act and absolute. He was responsible only to the government in London. There was a scheme in the 1935 act for a bicameral central legislature. It and its ministers would have been completely subservient to the viceroy. But the scheme never came into being. It was misnamed Federation. In effect, it was meant to bring the Indian princes, Britain's most dependable and dependent collaborators, into the structure of empire by giving them collective representation at its Centre. A Chamber of Princes had been tied into the 1919 package of constitutional reforms. Though only consultative, the Chamber had embodied for the first time a British invitation to the princes to act collectively in support of their privileges and of the empire that provided them.

Federation was the second invitation. It provided for a weighted princely contribution to imperial legislation. Although the population of the princely states was about one-quarter of the empire's, the princes, *not their subjects*, were empowered by the act to appoint one-third of the representatives to one of the central legislature's houses and two-fifths to the other. Congress opposed federation, of course. And the princes, for a variety of reasons, not least their shortsightedness, balked at "federating." Once again, the British played their princely card. And once again, it lost. It was never a winning card. Federation failed, as did every other British attempt to use the princes, individually or collectively, to diminish either the political importance of the English-educated middle classes in British India or the empire's dependence on them to staff and operate its bureaucracies and provide their ancillary professional services. Like the communal card, the princely card diminished the credibility of the British players and British constitutional reforms.

Indirectly, but decisively, the viceroy, Lord Linlithgow provided the most succinct contemporary evaluation, in spirit and deed, of the 1935 act and the 1937 elections. He simply ignored them when in 1939 they got in the way of imperial interests. Acting entirely on his own authority and without even pretending to consult Indian representatives, His Excellency declared India to be at war. The Indian Army was a major military asset for the embattled empire. Constitutional reforms could be postponed to another day. But not for the Indian National Congress. Its "high command" ordered Congress's provincial ministries to resign in protest, and they did. In hindsight, the chance of a united Indian state succeeding the Indian Empire may well have been sacrificed by their resignations. By precipitating their resignations, the British government sacrificed its last serious attempt to hold India to the empire.

The act and the elections advanced significantly India's bourgeois revolution. The basic Congress alliance – of urban, educated Hindu professionals and Hindu landed peasants – held and triumphed at the polls. For reasons that I have yet to discuss, the reluctance of Hindu and Parsi "merchant princes" to join the Congress alliance diminished considerably through the 1930s, and they became Congress's financial angels and the recipients of its quid pro quo. The 1937 elections were the precursor of parliamentary democracy in India. Congress became what it was to become: a moderate, reformist party that played to the accompaniment of radical, leftist rhetoric. Its most popular rhetorician, Jawaharlal Nehru, made his debut as Congress's prize vote-getter in 1937, and remained so for the next 25 years. Congress began its career as a party of vote-getting in 1937. It became what Judith M. Brown calls "a political environment,"[13] to which all who were interested in the exercise of power or its rewards or its protection gravitated. Upper-caste local politicians became Congressmen, as did "dominant" caste faction leaders, "Harijans," ideologues of almost all varieties, mill-owners, trade union leaders, intellectuals. Increasingly, Congress came to depend for its sustenance on Hindu landed peasants at its base and Hindu and Parsi *crorepatis* at its summit. In consequence, moderation in all things, save rhetoric, became Congress's modus operandi. In a word, the "Congress system" which guided India to parliamentary democracy and held it there for two decades made its electoral debut in 1937.

The 1937 elections were also a landmark in the Indian National Congress's failure to rally Muslims to its banner. There were a handful of "nationalist Muslims" at the Congress's top, but outside of the Northwest Province – a special case – there was nowhere a constituency of Muslims at the party's grass roots. Certainly, that did not make the 1947 partition of the sub-continent inevitable, nor the creation of Pakistan, nor the stillbirth of bourgeois revolution there. But it increased the possibility of these things happening. Insofar as there was an India-wide political organization of Muslims in the 1930s, it was the Muslim League. It was, in comparison to the Congress, poorly organized, undisciplined and thin on the ground. It did very badly in the 1937 elections: winning only 5 percent of the votes and less than a quarter of the seats in constituencies reserved for Muslims. But it did better than the Congress in its campaign for Muslim votes. In the Muslim-majority provinces of Bengal, Punjab and Sind, the Congress was defeated outright. In the United Provinces, Congress seized defeat from the jaws of victory by reneging on its pre-election commitment to take League leaders into its ministry. For the League and its intended constituency here was evidence yet again of the central contention of Muslim nationalism on the subcontinent: a Congress *raj* would be a Hindu *raj*. After the elections, the League commissioned reports which accused Congress's provincial ministries of being explicitly Hindu in their style and, in their substance, insensitive to Muslim sentiments and interests. In 1939, the League's Quaid-i-Azam, its Great Leader, Mohammad Ali Jinnah, called upon Muslims to celebrate as Deliverance Day the resignations of Congress's provincial ministries. A year later, at Lahore, the League passed its enigmatic and portentous "Pakistan Resolution."

Founded in 1906, the Muslim League barely existed, even as an organi-zation of Muslim notables, until the 1920s. From then, it existed largely in factions of Muslim landlords and urban gentry. Only after its 1937 debacle and under Jinnah's leadership did the League become a disciplined party with some hold over a constituency of northern India's ordinary Muslims. What it claimed to be before 1937 – "the only authoritative and representative political organization of Musalmans in India"[14] – the League became only afterwards. "Pakistan" did the trick. It was no more than a slogan and rallying cry in 1940, but it mobilized support for the League among Muslim villagers. Its appeal was to Muslim religious and communitarian sentiments. That had worked before, in the Khilafat movement most recently, and it worked again. After 1937, political time was short. The League recruited Muslim peasants and artisans as adherents of its "Pakistan" rather than as members of its alliance of landlords and prosperous professionals and businessmen. In alliance with generals, these were to become Pakistan's dominant classes.[15] The League's legacy to the failure of parliamentary democracy in Pakistan was this subcontinental variant of the "marriage of iron and rye:"[16] the archetypical anti-democratic alliance between aspiring capitalists and an established class of landlords in a country whose majority are peasants.

By refusing to federate and thereby establish their corporate presence as Britain's loyal ally at the center of its Indian empire, the princes may well have disserved their own interests by thwarting the possible arrangement in India of an anti-democratic "marriage" similar to the one that was being consummated in Pakistan. Certainly, with imperial sponsorship, such an alliance in India was at least possible. Though ultimately unsuccessful, the British were interested in conciliating India's industrialists, not least to close their coffers to the Congress. The patresfamilias of India's great industrial houses were better known for their fear of "labor unrest" and the Congress left than for their fondness of parliamentary democracy. In the 1930s, there was an increase, "not altogether negligible," of industrial investment in the princely states, where there were no trade unions and hardly any labor legislation. And princely investments in Indian industry in British provinces were probably "constant and significant."[17] In Rajasthan, for example, there were close familial and business connections between Marwari business families and the families of Rajput noblemen and princes.[18]

The 1935 act prefaced the inclusion of India's "merchant princes" as a major partner in the Congress coalition of dominant classes. As the English-educated middle classes were largely of families and castes that had long cultivated the skills of literacy and numeracy, so the modern business classes were largely of families and castes that had long cultivated the skills of commerce. There had been Indian traders, bankers and brokers who facilitated trade throughout the subcontinent and beyond for more than a millennium before the British East India Company established its "factories." Even more than the educated middle classes, the business middle classes were Hindu. Exceptions, more notable for their success than their numbers were business families of Jains and Parsis: followers of an ancient and well-articulated variation of Hinduism and descendants of Zoroastrian migrants from Persia. There were some Muslim quasi castes in Gujarat, Sind and Kashmir whose families cultivated the skills of commerce. There were a few Muslim merchant princes. But apart from these, Muslims in commerce were few and far between, except as petty traders.

The Indian business classes began their modernization in the seaport "presidency" towns of British India. Some business families were locals. Many were migrants. Most notably, Gujarati traders migrated down the coast of the Arabian Sea to Bombay and Marwari traders traveled from Rajasthan across the subcontinent to Calcutta. Typically, they began their modern careers by performing a variety of comprador services for British businesses in India: money changing, labor contracting, arranging for the supply of Indian raw materials and the distribution of British manufactured goods. Their heirs were to become India's great families of industrialists. In Claude Markovits' group portrait of them in the 1930s, on the eve of their country's independence, they appear as men confident in their business and hesitant in their politics.[19] If they suffered economically, it was not from having too little, but rather from having not enough. Their political dilemma was this: On the one side, there was a known imperial regime in which the safety of their enterprises was apparently assured but their opportunities limited. On the other, there was an unknown Indian national state in which their opportunities would be less limited – far less, perhaps – but only if the safety of their enterprises could be assured.

In Bombay and Ahmedabad, India's cotton textile industry, one of the world's largest, was owned and managed almost entirely by Indian investors and entrepreneurs. The Raj's business capital, across the subcontinent, was in Calcutta. Here, Indian firms had entered successfully into the erstwhile British monopolies of jute manufacturing and external trade during the First World War's boom time for Indian industry. Existing Indian industries profited from restrictions on imports that wartime imposed on the subcontinent. Other industries, such as munitions and cement, had their beginnings. The Tatas were making steel at Jamshedpur. There was the potential for Indian heavy manufacturing in the railways. Through combinations of circumstances and efforts, Indian industry had grown in spite of the unwillingness of the British government to protect it.

Britain's commitment to a policy of "free trade" had, in effect, maintained in India a minimally industrialized colonial open economy dominated by British interests. In form if not in substance, there were to be some changes in this after the Great War. The British government of India was to be allowed to impose tariffs to protect Indian industry. The relative decline of British naval power during the war had convinced London that in defense of the empire, its Barracks in the East would need the logistical support of an Indian workshop. Indian events, particularly the quickening of nationalist activity before and during the war, and Gandhi's elevation to the Congress's *gaddi* in 1920 and its call for *swaraj*,[20] inclined the British to conciliate Indian industrialists. Their unheeded calls for protective tariffs were long-standing, persistent and wound into the mythology of imperial "exploitation." Between the Mahatma and two of India's major business groups, Gujarati *baniyas* (castes whose traditional business is business) and Marwaris, there were caste and Hindu affinities. Increased access to their purses would have been (and was) of considerable benefit to the Congress.

In the end, imperial assuredness, the offer of protective tariffs and even the tariffs themselves, which were in some cases substantial, were insufficient to reconcile Indian industrialists to the Raj's perpetuation. We may understand this, I think, as Indian industrialists came face to face with what the Raj was *not*. Again, it was *not* a national government to which millionaires had the privileged access that money buys. At best, the government of India was a semi-autonomous branch of a foreign government. In its interests, the constitutional reforms of 1935 *did not* transfer India's finances from the viceroy's control. Despite the protests of Indian industrialists throughout the 1930s, an overvalued rupee was retained because it was in British interests to retain it. The government of India preferred Indian industrialists to negotiate their tariff protection within the framework of "imperial preferences" and to take the consequences. For protection against the importation of Japanese cloth, for example, Bombay had to come to terms with Lancashire to Ahmedabad's disadvantage. To circumvent India's new tariff barriers, British firms opened subsidiaries on the subcontinent: a British-owned Lever Bros. subsidiary replaced an Indian-owned company as India's leading soap manufacturer. The competition was unwelcome to Indian businessmen. They could reasonably anticipate from their own experiences that British business managers in India would enjoy, if not the outright favor, at least the sympathetic ties of countrymen with the British officers who enforced the Raj's rules and did its purchasing. The boardroom of British firms, after all, adjoined the club and the *daftar*.

Indian businessmen with imperial interests were distressed by Burma's separation from the Indian empire in 1935, and by the apparent disinclination of British officers in Africa to protect, as they had in the past, Indian business interests there from local hostility and competition. Indian businessmen who wanted a share of India's coastal shipping were distressed by the unwillingness of the Indian government to support their ambitions. Indian businessmen, in general, were distressed by Sir James Grigg, who was the government of India's finance member from 1934 to 1939. It was not only this British bureaucrat's outspoken advocacy of agriculture's primacy in India's economy and laissez-faire in its industrial economy, nor his particular hostility to leading Indian businessmen and his insensitivity to their concerns in general, that distressed them. It was his personification of their powerlessness.

In the 1930s, India's industrialists probably had no clear consciousness of themselves as a modern business class, no shared vision of their country as an industrialized nation, no ideological or programmatic unity and not a few competing interests: industrial, regional, associational, political, familial, personal. They did, however, share a "market situation" as modern business classes, and there was a set of stimuli to which they could, and would, share a negative response: their powerlessness under the Raj to make or take their opportunities. The elements of their "common situation," according to Markovits, were "... their integration within the framework of a colonial economy over which they had no control but which still offered them some scope for expansion, and ... their radical separation from political power."²¹

This political powerlessness pushed them toward the Congress. They were pulled by Congress conservatives, most notably Gandhi and Sardar Vallabhbhai Patel. But there were crosscurrents. The government of India was a big customer: its railways for Tata's iron and steel, for example. Some industrialists were imperial loyalists. Almost all were distressed by the apparent growth and growing prominence within the Congress of its left wing. Particularly distressing was talk about "socialism" from the Mahatma's anointed and the Congress's rising star, Jawaharlal Nehru. Gandhi himself was a source of some distress. His vision of independent India inclined toward *dehati* (local) politics and village handicrafts. Businessmen were troubled by the emphasis on rural reform in the Congress's pronouncements: a consequence of Gandhian ideology and the Congress's alliances with landed peasantries. Congress's "civil disobedience" was a form of opposition that distressed businessmen. It was immediately disruptive. In the long run, perhaps corrosive of the law and order which protected property and on which the business of business depends.

Over these crosscurrents, push and pull finally brought the modern business classes to Congress *in power*. In provincial power, from 1937 to 1939, Congress governments were moderate and reformist. They were financially responsible, defensive of bureaucratic order, protective of property in the countryside, discouraging of labor union militance and strikes in the cities, responsive to the money-power of industrialists and sympathetic to their interests, purchasers of *swadeshi* (Indian manufactured) goods. In their moderation, Congress's provincial governments were supported not only by the big business friends of its "high command," but by Jawaharlal Nehru. If one discounted Nehru's left-wing rhetoric, and one could, he was no enemy of Indian business or of political order. In contrast to Gandhi and other Congress conservatives, Nehru was an unequivocal advocate of Indian industrialization. A leading light of Congress's National Planning Committee, founded in 1938, Nehru shared with Indian businessmen their enthusiasm for planned industrialization.

Here was the point of convergence between the Congress and modern big business, and the beginning of a mutually beneficial industrializing design. India could industrialize and Indian industrialists could make their opportunities only with the active assistance of a national state. A national state governed by Congress could industrialize only with the active assistance of India's modern business classes. The safety of their enterprises would be assured in a Congress *raj*. In 1944, the Bombay Plan, signed by the patres-familias of almost every major Indian industrial house, was their proposal for the development of an industrial economy in India through the cooperation of Indian government and Indian big business. During the 1930s' depression,

Indian industry had grown, if not at the expense of its British competitors, in relation to them, certainly. The Second World War was another boom time for Indian industry. By 1944, the Tatas and the Birlas, the Singhanias and the Goenkas, had outgrown the Raj.

The cultivating middle classes grew from the seeds of capitalist land ownership, sown over the subcontinent by various British "settlement" schemes. To facilitate and enhance its collections of land revenue, the British government at various times and places in India "settled" land ownership on families that were in some way involved with cultivation. The earliest, most infamous and ruinous settlements were on the so-called *zamindars* of northeastern India. They had been, for the most part, revenue-collecting intermediaries. They were made land-owners by imperial fiat. In other parts of India, British Indian governments settled land ownership on families of chief cultivators, usually, or groups of such families. All settlements, however, departed from the usual Indian conception of landholding in this crucial regard: under British law, agricultural land became property that was *owned*. A commodity. It could be sold or otherwise alienated. It could be mortgaged and legally forfeited to the mortgagor in default of payment. It could be taken from its owner by government for non-payment of taxes and sold at auction.

In class terms, the settlements were noteworthy for producing non-cultivating landlords and land-owning cultivators. Of these, the landlords were far more important in British India. Some of India's richest and most powerful families were landlords. The British courted landlords as the countryside's "natural leaders" and as counterbalances to the middle classes. At the same time, because under the British dispensation land was something whose ownership could be lost,[22] and often was, the social composition of landlord classes become more varied. Simply, families of warrior and *gens de la robe* landlords lost portions of their holdings to English-educated and modern business middle-class families that invested their money in land and became absentee, rentier landlords. Appropriately, their organization, the Indian National Congress, was not notable for its concern with the plight of India's peasantries (or industrial work forces) until it started to become a mass, nationalist movement in the twentieth century, particularly under the leadership of Mahatma Gandhi.

The legality of land ownership in British India also created families of land-owning cultivators. They were, thus, sharply differentiated, as they had not been before, from families of landless cultivators. As we have noted, state governments in the Indian Union have retained that differentiation, and it has become crucial to those class relationships that determine the political and economic realities of agricultural and rural reform. In a word, by turning agricultural land into private property, the British laid the foundation for capitalism in agriculture and for class relationships appropriate to it. But under the Raj, capitalism and parliamentary democracy *did not* develop together in the Indian countryside. The latter lagged. Before they had their state legislative assemblies and *panchayati raj* institutions in independent India, families of land-owning cultivators, however well-to-do, were still peasants: subject cultivators. They were subjects of foreign bureaucrats in an imperial *raj*.

Mahatma Gandhi and Indian nationalism

Mahatma Gandhi, London-trained barrister-cum-Hindu saint-politician, domesticated India's bourgeois revolution. In no small part, he did so by attaching to his charisma a strategy of conflict and conflict resolution with the Raj which did this, at least: first, it fostered within the Congress the tripartite coalition alliance that facilitated the development together of capitalism and parliamentary democracy. Second, Gandhi's strategy pre-served for the Congress's use those institutions of British India in which this development had begun and would continue. Significantly, perhaps critic-ally, Gandhi's domestication of bourgeois revolution was in an idiom that resonated in and to his vast following of ordinary Indians, or at least, of their Hindu majority.

Gandhi became the Congress's supremo in 1920. He directed its final pre-Independence transformation from an interest group of the English-educated middle classes to a nationalist movement. Over two-and-a-half decades, his supremacy in the Congress was from time to time obliquely or directly challenged. From time to time he exited from the center of the political stage: of his own volition, to strategic withdrawal or social work, involuntarily (but not always inconveniently) to jail. But he always re-entered: by compromising with his challengers or besting them, and by knowing intuitively how, when and with what. He dominated Congress affairs until, not he, but his trusted lieutenants, Jawaharlal Nehru and Vallabhbhai Patel, finally negotiated India's independence with its last viceroy, Mountbatten. So, for all but the last few years of India's final quarter-century as a British colony, Gandhi reigned over India's dominant nationalist movement. He also articulated and per-sonified Gandhianism, the dominant ideology of the pre-Independence Congress and of Indian nationalism.

Certainly, there were other movements, other organizations and other ideologies. There was the Hindu Mahasabha and its belief that, with *swaraj*, India should become Bharat: a Hindu nation in which non-Hindus, particularly Muslims, would be citizens on Hindu sufferance.[23] There was the Muslim League and a Muslim nationalism that denied any common nationhood with Hindus. There was a "scheduled caste" movement led by Ambedkar, who understood the underlying relationship between touchable and untouchable Hindus as one of contempt and hatred. The Dravidian movement in Tamil Nadu wanted its own state, apart from an Indian Union ruled by north Indian Brahmins. There were communists who shared Gandhi's solicitude for the poor and his belief that their misery was a consequence of Britain's capitalist imperialism. But the remedies that communists offered were as repugnant to the Mahatma as his remedies were obscurantist to them. Poor peasants and dispossessed tribal people rose from time to time in localized and more or less self-generated jacqueries and "subaltern" movements.[24] They marched under the banners of caste and tribe, varieties of religious faith, millenarianism, Gandhianism. They produced their own leadership or took it from others: free-lancers, social workers, communists, *'ulama, sadhus*. But so central to Indian politics before Independence were the Congress, Gandhi and Gandhianism, that all these other movements and organizations and ideologies had ultimately to come to terms, or be forced to terms with them. They are, appropriately, the focus of this brief discussion of the Indian nationalist movement. In particular, I want to pinpoint the consequences of Gandhianism and its central tenet, *satyagraha*, for bourgeois revolution in India.

For *satyagraha*, non-violent non-cooperation is the usual English translation. It is not at all literal, neither is it satisfactory. But to begin the discussion, it will do. It was the ideology of a charismatic politician. Now, the ideologies of charismatic politicians may not be very important in the apparently literal meaning of their words. Charismatic leaders often personify as well as articulate their ideologies. Like Gandhi, their ideological articulation may be unsystematic and sometimes inconsistent. But charismatic leaders invariably come with ideologies, or messages which their disciples and successors articulate into ideologies. It is difficult to imagine a mute Christ. He came with a message. In essence, He may have been the message, but He had to say it out in words. The words may be ignored in practice, distorted, misused; but they are still important in a symbolic way as a bond between the charismatic leader and his followers. Followers who accept their leader's charisma can claim to be faithful to his or her ideology. The faithful appropriate their leader's charisma and ideology as their resources. Resources are only things that can be used: publicly, privately; selfishly, selflessly; intelligently, foolishly; honestly, dishonestly; constructively, destructively; and so on and so forth. Amongst users of these resources, there are likely to be great differences in why, when, where, how and for what purposes they are used. One need only reflect on the myriad uses to which Christians have put Christ and Christianity over the ages.

Amongst politicians like Nehru and Sardar Patel, who were in the inner circle of Gandhi's lieutenants and drew their political sustenance from him, there was not one who accepted the Mahatma's gospel that non-violence was a moral absolute in politics. Nor did they share his aspirations for Congress to become a social service organization after *swaraj* and for political authority and industrial production to devolve to India's villages. There were local and provincial politicians who identified themselves as Congressmen and Gandhians, thereby gaining access to Congress's material, organizational and reputational resources. These they used to fight their local and provincial battles, which sometimes had little or nothing to do with Indian nationalism. Cotton mill-owners sometimes supported the Congress, although Gandhi made the wearing of hand-loomed cloth a nationalist virtue. Mill-workers sometimes turned to Gandhi and the Congress to support them in their industrial conflicts with mill-owners. Touchable Hindu farmers used the resources of Congress to defy the empire's tax collectors. Untouchable landless laborers looked to the Mahatma for some hope of ending their exploitation by touchable Hindu farmers.

Kisan movements linked Gandhi's name to their local rebellions, although these were often violent. Non-violent *satyagrahis* went down under police batons shouting "*Mahatma Gandhi ki jai*," although they may have had only the most rudimentary notions about what on reflection academics have defined and politicians celebrated as Gandhianism. At Congress's call and in Gandhi's name, but not without some calculation of profit and loss, merchants observed *hartal*, closed their shops. In their battles against Indian timber merchants and British forestry officers, tribesmen were known to don "Gandhi caps" as amulets to protect them from police bullets. A charismatic leader and his ideology can be used as resources by different and sometimes mutually antagonistic followers, for different and sometimes mutually antagonistic purposes. Such varied use is likely to produce consequences unintended by the leader: paradoxical, ironical, but nonetheless significant. In his "Story of the Grand Inquisitor," a chapter in *The Brothers Karamazov*, Dostoevski treats this phenomenon with literary genius.

So, however Gandhi intended *satyagraha* to be used and used it himself, our concern is with the consequences of its varied use as a resource. As a resource of Indian nationalism, *satyagraha* was at once strategies of conflict, conflict resolution and reassurance to the Indian middle classes. *Satyagraha* was devised by Gandhi during his long apprenticeship between 1893 and 1914 as a leading Indian politician in South Africa. Like most of his political inventions, *satyagraha* was a product of Gandhi's genius for revaluing the commonplace. The commonplace here is a technique of conflict and conflict resolution that has enjoyed for ages both wide familiarity and social acceptability in India. It is called offering *dharna*. It is a strategy for that party to a conflict who is too weak to fight with physical violence, economic coercion, harassing litigation.

Typically, *dharna* will be offered as a fast on the doorstep of their antagonist by aggrieved tenants or disaffected workers. Unable to punish their
antagonist, they punish themselves in order to give public witness to the
rightness of their cause and to shame their antagonist into its reconsid-
eration. *Dharna* is only incidentally non-violent. It is the weapon of self-
sacrifice for those whose weakness precludes them from using violence
successfully. Congruent with Indian inegalitarianism, is a non-belief in
Marquess of Queensbury rules: a belief that in conflict, as in all things,
unequal people are unequal. The weapons of the strong cannot be the
weapons of the weak.

Gandhi ideologically revalued *dharna* from a weapon of the weak to the
weapon of the strong, from a weapon of those who have no choice to the
weapon of those who make moral choices. The revaluing, too, was in familiar
terms: *satya* and *ahimsa. Satyagraha* was Gandhi's neology. He compounded
it from two nouns: truth and insistence. *Satya*, Truth, is the crucial noun. A
central tenet of Hinduism and its offshoots is that God is Truth. *"Ram ka nam
Satya hai, Hari ka nam Satya hai"* is the familiar chant that accompanies
Hindu funeral processions. By whatever epithet He is called, God's name is
Truth. Hindu scripture provides the constitutionally secular Republic of India
with its motto: *Satyameva Jayate* – Truth alone triumphs. Appropriate to the
Hinduism from which their faith emerged, Sikhs greet each other with *Sat
Shri Akal.* God is Truth. God is the essence, the Truth in all things. Through
study, good works, devotion, we strive to realize the Truth that is God. Those
who succeed become powerful beyond human measure: repositories of holy
power. The power ultimately to transcend not merely victory and defeat, but
life and death.

The *satyagrahi*, the one who insists upon the truth, is a moral actor in
conflict and a powerful one. Ironically, because Gandhi was in a long line
of Hindu reformers who abhorred and condemned the practice of wives
immolating themselves on their husbands' funeral pyres, the *sati* – literally,
the woman of Truth – was probably the *satyagrahi*'s best known ideological
model in the Indian countryside. In one extraordinary act of conscious self-
sacrifice in realization of the Truth, that she has no life apart from her
husband's, in one act of the most extraordinary moral and physical courage,
the *sati* transcends life and death. That is the ideology, anyway. The
satyagrahi's self-sacrifice, like that of the *sati* and unlike that of the *dharna*
offerer, is meant to be a choice derived from great strength and productive
of strength greater still.

Ahimsa or non-violence, is a major ethical precept of Hinduism (also
of Buddhism and Jainism). It enjoins the doing of injury to any sentient
being, and particularly its killing. Vegetarianism is *ahimsa*'s most conspicuous application in practice. Otherwise, there is a disconcerting, inhumane,

ritualistic formality about it. Hindus who will not eat animals treat them with cruelty and abandon. Hindus who will eat animals treat the slaughterer as a pariah. Jain moneylenders who take ruinous interest from their debtors protect themselves from the responsibility of killing moths by enclosing their light globes in gauze sachets. One of *ahimsa's* supporting beliefs is that non-violence is spiritually rewarding to those who practice it. In practice, this belief seems to dominate the precept: the best reason for not doing physical violence to others is that it will vitiate one's own *karma*. Gandhi returned to the precept. He interpreted the concept of *ahimsa* in humane, moral terms: an injunction against violence in its myriad forms. He extended the injunction to conflict. Unlike the powerless villager who has no choice but to offer *dharna*, the *satyagrahi* chooses *ahimsa* because it is morally *and effectively* superior to *himsa* (violence).

The *satyagrahi* chooses non-violent non-cooperation not merely to give witness to the rightness of his cause but to triumph in it. We need not be concerned with such questions as to whom among Gandhi's *satyagrahis*, and how many of them, believed in *satyagraha* or even understood it as he meant it to be understood. That it was morally different to *dharna*. *Satyagraha* was a resource: an ideological extension of the Mahatma. From the 1920s, there were any number of campaigns of protest which were called *satyagrahas* by their organizers. A few were national or of national significance, like the Salt Satyagraha of 1930. Many were local. The best remembered were directed against the British government or British interests in India, but there were others against industrial exploitation and untouchability. Some were led by Gandhi or his lieutenants, others were disapproved or censured by him. But again, our primary concern is with *satyagraha's* consequences. It was a resource whose use mobilized for the nationalist movement a far greater number of Indians than had ever been mobilized before: at one time or another, men and women, in virtually every part of British India. *Satyagraha* facilitated the development of the Congress's basic tripartite alliance. It gave the alliance a strategy of conflict that made a moral and political virtue of its Indian-ness and its incapacity and fear of violent confrontation with imperialism – the force of order and overwhelming, after all.

As distinguished from its serving as a stimulus to charisma-induced responses, *satyagraha* as a strategy of conflict served the middle classes. As to why this was so, I can only repeat the usual suggestions. Gandhi hated *adharma*, disorder; and while he may never have read Euripides, I suspect he knew intuitively that middle classes save states. His biases, and those of his closest lieutenants, were conservative. Their nightmare was of India's nationalist struggle against the British turning into a class struggle amongst Indians. They directed their mobilizing efforts toward the ideological and social middle. The most enthusiastic audience for movements that redis-cover the folk and its virtues are often at society's middle. There also are middle-class interests in property and propriety. Congress politicians, in general, were men of the middle, disproportionately of the urban, upper caste, upper middle class. At the rural middle of Hindu society, the Hinduism inherent in *satyagraha* and the Mahatma resonated. It may be, as Eric Wolfe suggests,[25] that peasants who are most amenable to mobilization come from the middle of rural society. At the top there are vested interests in the status quo. At the bottom, poverty and debility preclude any organized and sustained movement – only rebellion born of despair. The middle classes also make states.

Might it have been otherwise in India? Did Gandhianism, in effect, preempt the possibility of subaltern – poor peasant and/or proletarian – revolution in India. I doubt it. I doubt that revolution-from-the-bottom was any more possible in British India than it has been in the Indian Union. In the 1960s, the hope, if not the expectation, of many Indian revolutionaries was that localized communist-led conflagrations in West Bengal and Andhra Pradesh would spread into "prairie fires" engulfing India. Instead, the local fires reached the local fire-breaks of caste, tribe, religious community; and they were readily and finally extinguished by armed force. Why would the "prairie fire" that failed to ignite after Independence have ignited before? Why would the primordial fire-breaks in Indian rural societies that function now not have functioned then? Why would British Indian police have been any less successful in firefighting than the Republic's paramilitary police? The peasant rebellions and revolutionary movements of the nineteenth and twentieth centuries were invariably localized and easily suppressed. In India's cities before Independence, the potential for subaltern revolution was even less than it was in the countryside. The industrial working class was tiny, and only a proportion of it was organized in unions that were revolutionary. The Communist Party was small, its strength in some labor unions and rural pockets, but neither it nor any other party offered creditable, national revolutionary leadership.

Unaffected by Gandhi's charisma, there were imperialists, Winston Churchill for one, who rejected *satyagraha* as a strategy of conflict resolution and regarded it only as a nasty form of political blackmail: pitting unarmed volunteers, many of them women, against armed police. But a more thoughtful British view was that *satyagraha* presented an opportunity to negotiate. It was meant, of course, to increase the negotiating advantage of Congress, but there were advantages in it for the government of India as well. Gandhi was a negotiator. He and his lieutenants sought *swaraj* always through a negotiated settlement with the British. When Congress mobilized tens of thousands of *satyagrahis*, its message to the British was not that it wanted to fight but that it wanted to negotiate, and that it negotiated on behalf of a mass movement.

It is true that *satyagraha* imposed some limits that might not otherwise have been there on the government of India's ability to meet Indian nationalism with violent suppression. But I do not think that these limits disadvantaged the British. Dean Inge's observation that no government can sit comfortably or for long on a throne of bayonets, is well-known and generally true. Even before the Raj's first constitutional reforms at the beginning of the twentieth century, and certainly from then, captains of empire understood that their enterprise in India was a matter for political negotiations, no less – and perhaps more – than for bureaucratic fiat. Moreover, the Raj had a home front to contend with. Across the wire, there were politicians, journalists, writers, scholars, churchmen and other public figures who consistently made speeches, asked questions in the House, filed reports, wrote articles and editorials, sent letters to *The Times*, and preached sermons that were critical, and often very knowledgeably so, of the ways in which Indians were treated by their British government.

There were occasions, certainly, and usually during "emergencies," when the government of India suppressed nationalist agitation with a very heavy hand. On its heavy-handedness, however, there were limitations imposed from Britain's free society, of which its Indophile minority was a very small but vocal, informed and well-placed part. *Satyagraha*, illuminated by Gandhi's aura and his considerable public relations skills, used those limitations in the cause of Indian nationalism. We need not be concerned here with arguments about the universal applicability or non-applicability of non-violent non-cooperation to situations of conflict. *Satyagraha* was a strategy of *Indian* conflict, and any good strategist makes use of his opponent's vulnerabilities. The Mahatma was a very good strategist. Like *dharna*, *satyagraha* assumes that those against whom it is directed are shameable. The British government of India was shameable. For almost two centuries, it had been telling itself, its countrymen and the world, and I think generally believing that there was a moral purpose to British imperialism .

The most infamous single incident of British heavy-handedness in suppressing Indian nationalism occurred in the Punjabi city of Amritsar in 1919. At a place in the city called Jallianwallahbagh, British troops opened fire on an assembly of unarmed civilians; and in the months that followed this horrible incident, the British provincial government compounded the horror by imposing humiliating punishments on the citizens of Amritsar. The Jallianwallahbagh massacre is *the* British atrocity in the epic history of the struggle for Indian independence. More than 300 people were killed, and about treble that number were injured. An atrocity, to be sure. But a small atrocity, really, in a century that measured its atrocities in the tens of millions: victims in some *lagar, gulag*, detention center, free-fire zone, killing field, ethnic-cleansing round-up in which the murder of 300 uncomprehending, tormented, tortured innocents was less than a day's day-to-day work. The British government appointed a special commission to inquire into the Amritsar atrocities and allowed a Congress committee to investigate them and publish its condemnatory findings. The British military officer who was responsible for the massacre, Brigadier General Reginald Dyer, from an Anglo-lndian family of brewers, was forced to resign from the Indian Army: although he enjoyed the support of the governor of Punjab and of vocal groups of his countrymen in Britain and India.

In a word, the limitations on the British government's freedom to use violence to suppress the nationalist movement were certainly greater than the limitations on the viceroy's freedom to negotiate with Gandhi. And the viceroy was not at a negotiating disadvantage. It was his government, after all, that had the power. The power that Congress wanted and could only negotiate for. Of the government's great negotiating advantage, some measure can be taken from my discussion of the 1935 India Act. As a strategy of conflict resolution, *satyagraha* was basically an invitation to negotiate: pressed by the weaker party on the stronger, acceptable to the stronger because of its negotiating advantage and the advantages to it of negotiating with the Congress rather than relying on violence to suppress it. Or of suppressing Congress, only to deliver Indian nationalism to a leadership less disposed than Gandhi's to negotiate.

Finally, *satyagraha* was a strategy of reassurance for the Indian middle classes. Congress would not allow the struggle against British imperialism to be turned into a class war among Indians. *Satyagraha*, of course, proscribed violence: the modus operandi, by everyone's definition, of class war. *Swaraj* would not be followed by the expropriation of property. Yes, Gandhi's ideal was a classless society. But no, it was not to be reached by force. Rather, the propertied would voluntarily convert themselves into trustees of their wealth: if need be, pressured to do so by the non-violent non-cooperation of the propertyless. The state would not interfere to bring about a classless society. "The violence of private ownership is less injurious than the violence of the state."[26] Classlessness in India would be a product of class cooperation rather than conflict. A product of negotiations between the haves and the have-nots. In the words of one of his critics: "Gandhi recognized and renounced in burning words the barbarities of capitalist exploitation, but could not transcend his essential bourgeois outlook."[27] And would not!

This outlook was reflected time and again, not only in Gandhi's glosses on *satyagraha* but in his leadership of the Congress. He courted and readily accepted the support of Indian industrialists. He was loath to extend Congress activity into the princely states. Among peasant families, it was generally the landed whom Congress sought to recruit to its banner and who rallied to its banner. Dalits responded to Gandhi's charisma. He abhorred untouchability but would "fast unto death" rather than allow the possibility of his Harijans attaining autonomous political power. Within the Congress organization, the men who consistently supported Gandhi and whom he consistently supported were those who shared his faith in negotiated settlements and his bourgeois outlook. The only partial exception to this was Jawaharlal Nehru,

but Gandhi knew that Nehru's allegiance was less to socialism than to a
united Congress and Indian independence.

India was not freed by *satyagraha*. Rather, it set in train and kept on course
an ongoing process of negotiations between Congress and the Raj that was
occasionally interrupted but never terminated. As a strategy of conflict and
conflict resolution, *satyagraha* helped to ensure that Congress would inherit
from the empire the foundation and skeletal superstructure, more or less
intact, on which a bourgeois democratic state could be built. The civil
bureaucracies, police forces and military were passed over virtually intact.
There were no purges. Industry and infrastructure for further industrialization – the railways and postal services, for example – had been established
and were intact. There were no expropriations of private property. The
political infrastructure – electorates, legislative assemblies, a legal system,
ministries – on which a parliamentary democracy could be built was embryonic but intact. There were no serious second thoughts about the
appropriateness of bourgeois democracy for India.

As it was personified, enunciated, glossed and put into political practice by
Gandhi, *satyagraha* affirmed and reaffirmed his Congress's commitment to
class cooperation rather than class conflict as its modus operandi. It has been
affirmed and reaffirmed by the Mahatma's successors in post-Independence
India. Without such affirmations, it seems unlikely that Gandhi and the
Congress could have effected and maintained the alliance of middle classes
that was the Congress nationalist movement and that became the Congress
Party. Without Gandhi it seems unlikely that Congress would have survived
intact to become independent India's ruling party. Partition tore the Indian
fabric at its edges, but otherwise left it intact. Gandhi, we know, did not want
India to become a bourgeois, democratic, capitalist, industrialized country.
But he is rightly, if ironically, honored as the Father of the Nation.

Muslim separatism

With tragic consequences, the middle classes that Gandhi was least successful
in bringing into his Congress movement for an Indian nation were those
whose members were Muslim. The ugly divorce that separated the Indian
empire into the republics of India and Pakistan in 1947 was largely the
consequence of a half-century-old political triangle whose principals were
the Indian National Congress, various groups of wise, wealthy and well-born
Muslims and British officers of the imperial government. Like all triangles,
this one had a context. Its genesis long antedated the beginnings of bourgeois
revolution anywhere. And to its substance, British imperialism's contribution
was significant, certainly, but not determinant.

"Islam has a fundamental political orientation ...," writes Ishtiaq Husain Qureshi. That was an element in the context. "The Muslim community is, ideally, an association of believers organized for the purpose of leading their lives in accordance with the teachings of their faith."[28] Yet another ideal! And while it too – in Indian history, certainly – affects rather than reflects reality, for Muslims it affects reality *because* it reflects it. It reflects reality particularly in and from the *shari'ah* and the history of Islam's brief and glorious golden age.

Islam is more than the *shari'ah*, but the *shari'ah* is fundamental to Islam. It is the Law: God's law, Islamic sacred law. It is based on the Qu'ran, God's revelations to the Prophet, and what are generally regarded by Muslims to be authentic compilations of the Prophet's words and deeds as they were recorded by his Companions 14 centuries ago. Through exegeses on these texts, generations of Muslim legists have elaborated sophisticated systems of Islamic jurisprudence, legal training, juridical practices, comprehensive penal codes and bodies of law. These are meant to govern every aspect of the lives of believers: the minutiae of their ablutions, their diet, their personal and family relations, their behavior to coreligionists and others, their commercial and financial dealings, their worship and rituals of worship, their obligations to their rulers, and their rulers' obligations to God. In a word, for Muslims, the teachings of their faith are incorporated in sacred law. Their teachers are not clerics nor even theologians, as they are in different guises for Christians and Jews, but *'ulama*, legists: interpreters and pronouncers of God's law.

In the *shari'ah* and from it are reflected the theocratic ideal of Islam: an international government that rules according to God's law and is instructed in its governance by men who are learned in God's law. Most Muslims believe, however, that this theocratic ideal of Islam was only realized before the *shari'ah* was elaborated. For four decades from the first year of the Muslim era (622 CE), the Prophet and, in turn, four of his Companions – the "pious *khalifahs*" (successors) – ruled the faithful according to their intimate knowledge of God's law and conquered an empire for Islam. Islam emerges into history not as the belief of those who were martyred by pagan rulers but as the faith of warriors who through God's will conquered pagan rulers, smashed their idols – most memorably in Mecca – converted their subjects to Islam and ruled them according to sacred law.

But, from the end of this golden age, in India as elsewhere, the political reality for Muslims has been more or less the same separation of Church and State – with more or less the same variations in cordiality and ideological consensus between them – as Christians have experienced in Christendom. Nonetheless, the Islamic ideal persists of itself. The Christian injunction to "render ... unto Caesar the things which are Caesar's; and unto God the things that are God's" is blasphemous (however apposite) preaching to Muslims. The ideal persists in the *shari'ah* and its continuous use by *'ulama* to proclaim God's law, even to the chastening of kings. It persists in the hagiography of the Prophet and his Companions. It persisted, at least symbolically – not everywhere, to be sure, nor at all times – in the survival until 1924 of the office of the Prophet's successor, the *khalifah*, wherever located in the Muslim world and however titular for most Muslims.

For Muslims, the effect of the theocratic ideal on their political reality has been to produce a second-best. The ideal is a boundless and politically undefined Islamic polity. Second-best is a Muslim state. If we understand that "second" includes higher and lower levels of acceptability – as in the divisions and gradations of second-class honors degrees, for example – second-best is how we might describe Muslim governments in India before they were succeeded by the Raj. A Muslim government is a government of Muslim rulers. They may barely recognize any Islamic restraints on themselves. Still, they more or less foster Islamic worship and patronize Islamic institutions, cater particularly for the interests of their Muslim subjects and apply the *shari'ah* to the regulation of their personal and family affairs.

In the century or so before the Mutiny, second-best political systems for Muslims began to disappear on the subcontinent as Muslim governments were dismantled by the British East India Company. The Company *raj* was a government of Christian rulers whose allegiance was to a Christian monarch. They brought their own legal system with them. They were, in general, no less contemptuous of Islam's "fanaticism" than of Hinduism's "superstitions." Most of the Company's subjects in India, including most of its collaborators and compradors, were Hindu. Most of the Company's Muslim subjects, who were poor farmers and artisans, were of no particular concern to the Company's officers. Indian Muslims, as I have already said, were and are as socially heterogeneous as Indian Hindus, and it is not at all surprising that the reactions to the Company *raj* should have varied from Muslim community to community.

The most hostile reactions came from Indian Islam's lower rather than higher strata. They came not long after the Company had established itself as the subcontinent's dominant power: almost four decades before the Mutiny. The best organized of these hostile reactions were the *fara'izis* of Bengal and an Islamic chiliastic movement centered in northern India, led and inspired by one Saiyid Ahmad Bareilly. His movement is best-known in Anglo-Indian literature as "Wahhabi," imprecisely after its Arabian counterpart. Though they differed in their modus operandi, both *fara'izi* and Wahhabi movements in India were Islamic and Islamizing. They imposed on British India the Islamic stigma of *dar al-harb*: literally, the "abode of war," a polity un-acceptable as second-best. In opposition to its rulers, the faithful must either fight – as did the *mujahidin* of Saiyad Ahmad – or take flight or, at the very least, withhold their allegiance and services. Thousands of ordinary Muslims became *fara'izis* and Wahhabis. From their movements' *mullahs* (legists) and *sheikhs* (Sufi leaders) they learned about the theocratic ideal of Islam, about the *shari'ah* and about how they would have to cut away the vestiges of their Hindu origins in order to be bona fide Muslims.

The highest strata Indian Muslim community, combining landed wealth and the claim, at least, to aristocratic lineage, the best of Muslim "good families," the most illustrious and influential were the Urdu-speaking Ashraf (literally, nobility) of the Gangetic Plain. It was the geographic and political center of the Muslim dynasties that ruled northern India, from the beginning of the thirteenth century to the collapse more then 500 years later of the Mughal empire. The United Provinces in British India – now centered in Delhi and Uttar Pradesh – were the heartland of Indian Islam's high culture. The Ashraf were its guardians. As distinguished from their quasi Hindu, peasant and artisan coreligionists, the Ashraf were, or were assumed to be, bona fide Muslims in their religious observances. The origins of many Ashraf family landholdings were in court services. They or their ancestors served Muslim courts in various military-cum-civil capacities and were remunerated for their services – as were their medieval European counterparts – with service tenements, land grants. In sum, among landholding Ashraf families there was the tradition of court service and the cultivation of the appropriate values and skills of literacy and numeracy. New Ashraf families who succeeded old Ashraf families on the land emulated their traditions, values and skills.

Muslim courts disappeared as the Company *raj* advanced. Few Ashraf families fell so far into ruin as those who had served Muslim courts in less exalted capacities – musicians, artisans, menials, ordinary soldiers – but the Ashraf fell from greater heights. When the mighty are fallen, the poignancy, felt most keenly by themselves and their rhapsodists, lies in where they have fallen from rather than fallen to. Quite comfortable obscurity, oftentimes. To be sure, some Ashraf families lost their holdings as a consequence of British land settlements. But not because they were Muslim, and probably in no greater proportion than Hindu landholders. The Ashrafs' greatest loss was their *izzat*, their social honor, as noble families of Muslim courtiers. One of their poets grieved:

> The master is turned slave, such is the will of fate:
> The owner of the palace is now keeper of the gate.[29]

Unreconciled to the will of fate, saddened, some Ashraf families withdrew into landed obscurity rather than serve the palace's new owners. But many did not. Many were applicants for gatekeepers' positions. Like that Christian empress, Maria Theresa, they wept and took. In the United Provinces, they were the Company *raj*'s most conspicuous collaborators. They took the benefits of the Company's laws as landlords. In positive disproportion to their numbers, they took positions in the Company's subordinate bureaucracies and they schooled their sons to succeed them. In Punjab, too, families of Muslim landlords and urban gentry were not under-represented in the Company's subordinate services or in educational institutions that prepared their sons for such service. No more than the United Province's Ashraf were Punjabi Muslim good families – in Anglo-Indian parlance – "backward." "Backward," that is, in filling the ranks of the Company's subordinate bureaucracy.

Bengal was the only place in India in which there was a large concentration of Muslims – the largest on the subcontinent, two-thirds of the province's population – whose good families were markedly "backward." But for a handful of Muslims, Bengalis in Company service and in educational institutions that prepared candidates for Company service were almost all Hindu *bhadralok*. For this situation, various explanations are offered. Good families of Bengali Muslims had a particular preference for placing their sons in traditional Muslim educational institutions that neither prepared these boys for Company service nor inclined them to it. Good families were a tiny minority of Bengali Muslim families. The vast majority were overwhelmingly poor, illiterate and converts from the lowest strata of Hindu, Buddhist and tribal societies. Good families of Bengali Muslims could not compete successfully against *bhadralok* families for places in modern colleges and in Company service because these Bengali Hindus got there first and entrenched themselves. Whatever the validity of these and other explanations, it is certainly true that within large ethnically and linguistically defined Muslim populations, Bengali Muslims of good family were "backward." But among such Muslim families in India, "backwardness" was peculiar to Bengalis.

It was generalized into a myth of *Indian* Muslim "backwardness" by the British in the decades after the Mutiny, and even after it was shown to be no more than a myth in 1882 by an education commission of the British Indian government. From their immediate indictment of Muslim "fanaticism" as the Mutiny's primary cause, the British in post-Mutiny India soon came to the judgment that Muslim "separateness" from Hindus offered the Raj a political opportunity. The opportunity was to use religious divisions among Indians to rule them. The myth of Indian Muslim "backwardness" was perpetuated and patronized by the British government. In the myth's elaboration, the British enjoyed the collaboration of one of the extraordinary men of his age, the leading Muslim modernist reformer of the nineteenth century: Sir Saiyid Ahmad Khan. The British and Sir Saiyid had complementary interests in the perpetuation of the myth of Muslim "backwardness."

The British quite correctly perceived the *'ulama* as a generally unfriendly elite. The myth of Muslim backwardness could be used to patronize an alternative elite, the "natural leaders" of almost one-quarter of their Indian subjects: Muslim landlords.[30] The myth could be used to tie together with the interests of Muslim landlords the interests of the English-educated Muslim middle classes and thus divide them from the empire's most potentially "seditious" subjects, the English-educated Hindu middle classes. For Sir Saiyid the myth could be used to gain imperial patronage for Muslims in the non-Muslim regime under which they were fated to live. It could be used to secure against the encroachments of Hindus the positions of power and trust occupied by Muslims in an empire whose operations depended and would depend increasingly on the collaboration of its subjects from good families.

Sir Saiyid was born in 1817 into a very good family: an Ashraf family of Delhi with a Pathan pedigree, landholders and Mughal court servants. But as the Mughal empire declined, so did the family's fortunes. In 1839, Sir Saiyid entered the British government's subordinate service. Here he established a distinguished career as a judicial officer and a personal reputation through his written work and lectures as a leading advocate of the reconciliation of Indian Muslims to British imperialism. He was conspicuously loyal during the Mutiny, and was awarded a knighthood in 1869. Only after his retirement in 1876, however, did he build his monuments to Anglo-Muslim reconciliation. A few, associations to promote the interests of Muslim good families and publicize their loyalty to the Queen Empress, did not endure. His enduring monument was the Muhammadan Anglo-Oriental College which prospered under imperial patronage to become in 1920 the Aligarh Muslim University.

Between his British patrons and Sir Saiyid, the agreed-upon remedy for his coreligionists' "backwardness" was a special position for Muslims under the Raj. Its markers came to be known as "reservations" and "weightage." Thus: in order for Muslim good families to shed their "backwardness" – indeed, to keep them from falling further "backward" – it would be necessary to reserve for Muslim candidates a proportion of places in imperial service and relevant training institutions. In the municipal and provincial councils which the British began to establish in India after the Mutiny, Muslim "backwardness" would necessitate the reservation of a proportion of separate constituencies for Muslim politicians and Muslims enfranchised to vote by virtue of their wealth or educational status.

Moreover, these reservations ought to be "weighted" in positive disproportion to the Muslim population. Sir Saiyid argued this case ideologically, and in a way that was compatible with the ideology of empire. No more to Sir Saiyid's thinking than to the captains of empire's was India a nation. Rather, it was a congeries of nations. Among these the largest and most inclusive groups, defined by what is most important about them and fundamentally different between them, were Hindus and Muslims. Muslims were not a minority of the Indian population. As such, there was no Indian population.

The British Empire in India had a population, but it was of two nations which inhabited the same Indian space. To be sure, the Muslim nation was the smaller. But the importance of nations is properly judged qualitatively: in terms of their history, culture, political and economic significance. Nations are not measured in the mere quantities of their populations. More, could one even say that the Hindu nation was the larger or even a nation? On the basic criterion of nationhood, religion, Hindus divide themselves into multitudes of sects and castes. About one-fifth of these, the "scheduled castes," are placed by Hinduism outside its nation. The Muslims were a nation.

Sir Saiyid certainly knew that the Ashraf were *not* "backward" in northern India, but rather advantaged in professional and administrative imperial employment. But without the protection of reservations and weightage, the Ashraf might become "backward" in the post-Mutiny empire, if only to the point of losing or having to share their advantages. This seems to have been Sir Saiyid's apprehension. Queen Victoria's promise of 1858 that Indians would be "freely and impartially admitted to offices in our service" was not welcomed by Sir Saiyid. It implied the admission to the empire's superior services of Indian candidates who were educated in British or British-model universities and performed well in competitive examinations in English. It implied to Sir Saiyid the domination of the superior services by Hindu *bhadralok*: the empire's "competition-wallahs" par excellence. In comparison to them, the Ashraf were under-represented in university enrollments and comparatively disadvantaged in English-language education.

Sir Saiyid's language of employment had been Urdu. The language for employment in which his Muhammadan Anglo-Oriental College students were being trained was English. Although the College taught some Islamic studies, its curricula were modeled on those of British institutions. More than providing a modern, English-language education for a handful of Muslim boys, the College was meant to encourage them in substantial numbers to aspire to such an education, wherever it was offered. To Sir Saiyid, modern, English-language education was, for Muslim good families, the way out of their "backwardness." But the way would have to be lit by British favor. Of what value, after all, would such an education be to Muslim families if on the battlefields of competitive examinations for professional and bureaucratic employment battalions of their sons were pitted against regiments of more experienced and better prepped *babu* and Brahmin boys. The interests of Muslim good families would be served *not* by free and impartial competitive examinations, but by their sons' official nominations in weighted numbers to British service by officers of the Raj.

On the battlefields of local politics, in the post-Mutiny empire's municipal and provincial councils, *babu* and Brahmin contingents would be joined in their Hindu regiments by detachments of *zamindars* (landholders) and *baniyas* (businessmen). Together, they would outnumber and overwhelm

Muslim forces. Other than in Sindh, Punjab and Bengal, Muslims were a minority of the population. In Bengal the *enfranchised* majority, by virtue of wealth and education, would be Hindu. Only if special positions were created for Muslims in every elected assembly would their interests be protected. For Muslim candidates and voters, there needed to be reserved and separate constituencies, their numbers weighted in positive disproportion to the Muslim minority in that assembly's jurisdiction.

Although Sir Saiyid wanted the political advantages of British favor, he advised Muslims to eschew political activity as a way of getting it. Only the British could create a special position for Muslims in their empire, and they did not like political activity. The agglomeration of Sir Saiyid's coreligionists, the fragments of his imagined "nation," the jumbled mass of its real communities and quasi castes was probably incapable of organizing a political demand for reservations and weightage. Moreover, to the vast majority of Indian Muslim families, poor and illiterate, there would be little to gain from reservations and weightage. A special position for Muslim good families in the empire could only be the self-interested gift of the Raj. In return for British gifts, what Muslim good families could offer was "loyalty." Their own, of course, and because they were the imperially ordained "natural leaders" of ordinary Muslims, their loyalty as well. Political inactivity was a demonstration of "loyalty." Sir Saiyid demonstrated his by advising Muslims not to join the Indian National Congress. It was a political organization. Behind its make-believe of Indian nationalism, it represented only the interests of *babus* and Brahmins. It was in their interests, and contrary to Muslims', that Congress supported an examination procedure in which Indians could really compete for positions in the Indian Civil Service. Congress was an organization of India's Hindu nation; or more accurately, of its twice-born middle classes.

Saiyid Ahmad's efforts to produce a modernist interpretation of Islam, an Islam reconcilable to modernity, although intellectually impressive, had no great effect, even on Muslims of his "Aligarh school." A warmer reception was accorded by Muslim good families to his ideological arguments in favor of Muslim reconciliation to the realities of British rule. The Raj did not interfere with Islamic worship, Saiyid Ahmad argued. It was sufficiently respectful of Islamic institutions. It supported the *shari'ah*'s application to the regulation of Muslims' personal and family affairs. It was sensitive to the interests of its Muslim subjects. And last but not least, it protected Muslims from the crueler fate of a Hindu *raj*. Although its rulers were not Muslims, the Raj was for Muslims an acceptable second-best, albeit not of the first division.

In 1906, some years after Sir Saiyid's death, in one of the most fateful of such meetings in modern Indian history, the viceroy, Lord Minto, was presented with an "address" by a delegation of Muslim notables. Most of them were great landlords and they were led by one of the greatest, the Aga Khan.[31] In its address, the delegation expressed its appreciation of "the incalculable benefits conferred by British rule" on India and pledged the "unswerving loyalty [of Muslims] to the Throne." In return, the delegation asked for reservations and weightage for Muslims: in government service and on representative bodies from district boards to the viceroy's council.

The British were playing the Muslim card. The Punjab Alienation of Land Act of 1900 favored Muslims, in general, and disfavored urban Hindus. In 1905, Curzon partitioned Bengal. Not all Muslim good families supported it, but most did. British officials, including Curzon, told them that they should. Liberated from the domination of Calcutta's Hindu *bhadralok*, the Muslims of East Bengal would enjoy unprecedented opportunities for English-language education and political representation. Muslim good families would finally shed their "backwardness." "Muslims in East Bengal," writes Peter Hardy, "were coming closer to Muslims in the upper provinces, in that they were slowly acquiring something to lose."[32] It was not their "backwardness." Bengal was reunited in 1911.

Reservations and weightage endured, however. Minto and his Secretary of State for India, John Morley, were pleased to accede to the "prayer" of the Aga Khan's delegation. Recruitment practice in many provincial bureaucracies inclined toward reservations and weightage. They became the rule in British India's provincial assemblies in the Indian Councils Act of 1909, and were subsequently perpetuated by Parliament's omnibus India acts of 1919 and 1935. Over almost four decades, until 1947, Muslims of good family had the opportunity to develop a vested interest in being Muslim. What endured less well among them was "loyalty." The reunification of Bengal tested and dismayed the "loyal." Apart from frustrating the expectations of upper- and middle-class Bengali Muslims, the reunification gave all the appearances of a British retreat: a rout of the Muslim's mighty patron by the Hindu *babus* and Brahmins of the Indian National Congress.

While ordinary Muslim families of farmers and townspeople were little concerned with reservations and weightage, they were apparently very concerned with a matter no closer than these to their immediate, material interests: the fate of the Ottoman *khalifah*, the Prophet's last successor. It was for him, their ruler, and not for the British monarch, for whom Muslims in mosques all over India, Friday after Friday, offered a prayer. It was in defense of his empire, and not of Britain's, that ordinary Muslims rallied. And they rallied against Britain. They rallied against Britain's role as the *khalifah*'s enemy in the Great War and its part in the dismantling of the Ottoman empire after the war, in the Treaty of Sèvres. The Khilafat Movement of

1920–22 had as its ally the Hindu Non-Cooperation Movement led by
Mahatma Gandhi. The alliance proceeded from the Lucknow Pact of 1916
which gave Congress's sanction to reservations and weightage for Muslims
and, in effect, recognized Hindus and Muslims as separate communities in a
negotiated, inter-communal Indian nationalism.

Like the *fara'izi* and Wahhabi movements before it and the "Pakistan"
movement afterward, the Khilafat Movement was Islamic and Islamizing
in this sense: its rallying cry, the sentiment that called it into being and
energized it, was drawn from the political ideals of Islam. Among its followers
were thousands of ordinary Muslims. Among its leaders, there were *'ulama*
as well as Muslims from good families – but rarely from the best. Even before
the Khilafat Movement, the aged Sir Saiyid Ahmad Khan, who had initiated
the trade of Muslim "loyalty" for British favor, was embarrassed by the
attachment of ordinary Muslims to the Ottoman *khalifah*. Jinnah, who would
have no part of mass movements until he came to lead one, stayed away from
the Khilafat Movement.

The Khilafat-Non-Cooperation alliance foundered and failed. Its partners'
interests in opposition to British imperialism were at best complementary
and often contrary. Gandhi insisted on non-violent opposition, but *khilafatists*
had no more interest in *ahimsa* than Hindu Congressmen had in the Ottoman
khalifah. Muslims were fearful of the growing influence in Congress and on
it of Hindu qua Hindu politicians, and of the Congress tail wagging the
khilafatist dog. The mobilization of Hindus and Muslims for political action
had as its denouement their turning on one another. In the 1920s, even before
the alliance collapsed, there was a marked increase in the number of localized
clashes, "riots," between groups of Hindus and Muslims. The anticlimax
came in 1924, when not the British but the Turkish republic abolished the
khalifah.

In 1927, the British government sent a commission to India led by Sir John
Simon to recommend constitutional reforms further to those of 1919 and
further toward responsible government at the provincial level. To the Simon
Commission, no Indian member was appointed. That was a blunder. It
prompted hostile demonstrations all over India. It offended Hindu and
Muslim elites who had come to think of themselves as stakeholders in the
empire as well as subjects of it. It inspired an All-Parties Conference which
produced in 1928 its own recommendations for constitutional reforms
which would further India on the path to self-government.

The Muslim League, or a faction thereof, was represented at the conference
by Mohammad Ali Jinnah. Apparently, as he saw it, the problem was to adjust
the special position of the Muslim elite in British India to a political situation

in which there was likely to be considerable devolution of power to provincial Indian politicians. His proposed solution was to treat reservations and weightage as negotiable, in part, and in favor of the constitution of an Indian federation or confederation. In it, the numerical majority of Muslims in Muslim-majority provinces would become an electoral majority. The constitutional balance of power between Centre and provinces would be tipped in favor of the provinces. They would be tipped to protect Muslim interests. A Hindu majority at the Centre would be wary of Muslim majorities in Punjab and Bengal. Punjab was on India's frontier, its major agricultural province and recruiting grounds for the Indian Army. India's major industrial city, Calcutta, was Bengal's metropolis and its great industrialists were non-Bengali Hindus. There was no particular reason to take the League very seriously in 1920s. And the conference didn't. All of Jinnah's "fourteen points" were rejected. The Lucknow Pact was abrogated. For Jinnah, the conference marked "the parting of the ways." It would never again be joined. Although it might have been: even after 1928, even after the 1937 elections.

The Muslim League's "Pakistan Resolution" of 1940 makes no mention of "Pakistan," much less does it demand the creation of a separate state of "Pakistan." The convoluted language of the resolution seems calculated to obscure rather than make clear what it does demand. Thus, a "constitutional plan" for India would be acceptable to the League only if it were "designed on the following basic principles":

> ... that geographically contiguous units are demarcated into regions which should be so constituted with such territorial adjustments as may be necessary, that the areas in which the Muslims are numerically in a majority should be grouped to constitute "independent states" in which the constituent units should be autonomous and sovereign.[33]

The idea of a Muslim-majority state in northwest India separate from "Hindustan," Hindu India, was certainly not new. The leading Indian Muslim poet and philosopher, Muhammad Iqbal, revived it in 1930. A few years later it was dubbed "Pakistan" by a group of Indian Muslim students at Cambridge. But was the "Pakistan Resolution" really about what was to become Pakistan? It seems more likely, in 1940 at least, to have been Jinnah's elaborate negotiating juggle, whose favored outcome would be an Indian federation or confederation on the lines of his proposal of 1928. At once, Jinnah was threatening a "Pakistan" that he did not want in his negotiations with the Congress and the British, and juggling that threat against the

League's mobilization of ordinary Muslims in support of a concretized *dar al-Islam* apart from Hindu India and called "Pakistan." At once, Jinnah was promising provincial autonomy to Muslim leaders in Punjab, where the League was virtually non-existent, and in Bengal, where it was out of his control. That promise he juggled against his insistence on being recognized as the "sole spokesman" for India's Muslims in their negotiations with Congress and the British government.

In 1946, India held its last elections under British auspices. The Muslim League and its "Pakistan" swept the field of Muslim constituencies. Jinnah established himself as the Quaid-i-Azam of Indian Muslims, their great leader, an equal in negotiations with Congress and the British. In 1946, too, the British government sent a Cabinet Mission which followed the Cripps Mission of 1942 in recommending a federal or confederal constitutional settlement for independent India. The British had at least these interests complementary with Jinnah's. They wanted India as a market for British goods and the Indian Army intact. Jinnah accepted the Cabinet Mission's plan. Nehru finally rejected it for the Congress. Jinnah, his negotiating time at an end – the British were to leave in a year – declared August 15, 1946 to be "Direct Action Day" for Muslims. The horror began. The subcontinent was partitioned, Punjab and Bengal were divided, and Pakistan was born in a whirlwind of death and destruction.

Who was responsible for the tragedy of Partition and for what Jinnah himself called a "moth-eaten" Pakistan? There is enough responsibility to go around. Ayesha Jalal, in particular, has questioned the conventional opinion that Congress was the party of Indian unity and the Muslim League of Partition and Pakistan.[34] Rather, she argues that, given the choice between Jinnah's acceptance of a united subcontinent of autonomous provinces, an Indian federation or confederation, on the one hand, and, on the other, a partitioned subcontinent with an Indian Union strong at its Centre, the Congress duumvirs, Jawaharlal Nehru and Vallabhbhai Patel, chose partition. Denying the reality of Muslim communalism, of the League's claim to represent the interests of ordinary Muslims and of Pakistan's viability as a separate state, Congress leaders expected or hoped that it would be reabsorbed into India before long. But Congress's complicity in Partition does not absolve Jinnah of his responsibility. He was too clever by half. Apparently, he assumed that in his negotiations with viceroys and the Congress's "high command," Jinnah could, at once, fight a barrister's war of words with "Pakistan," keep its meaning ambiguous and negotiable, while at the same time, rousing ordinary Muslims with a Quaid-i-Azam's call to throw off the Hindu yoke in a "Pakistan" that to them came increasingly to mean only Pakistan.

British imperialism did not create Pakistan, certainly, but it did help to develop the context in which it was created. Simply by ruling the subcontinent, the Raj – unalterably foreign, neither of Hindus nor Muslims – bred its own opposition from them and prompted their opposition to each other. The bureaucratic empire reified and concretized often fluid and contextual distinctions among people by putting them into categories for its censuses and gazetteers. By acceding to the pleas of Muslim good families for a special position under the Raj, it vested them with political and economic interests in being Muslim, gave them something to lose in an Indian Union that was either "secular" or "Hindu." In the related context of bourgeois revolution, British imperialism facilitated the diversion of most of the sub-continent's Muslim good families from the Indian middle-class mainstream in which capitalism and parliamentary democracy had begun to develop together.

Chapter 6

The Indian Union in a changing India

In general terms, and with variable consistency and success, Indian governments have pursued two major policy goals: political and economic development. "Democracy" and "secularism" are at once the officially designated means of political development and its desired ends. Democratic and secular political development is meant to produce a democratic and secular political culture. Corruption is not meant to be there at all. But it is. With parliamentary democratic development and Indian secularism, it is a subject of this chapter's first section. My discussion of industrial development and the educated and modern business middle classes follows in the second section. As the once-officially designated means to industrial development, "socialism" was never much more than a slogan. Nothing much remains of it today other than a large and varied public sector menagarie of industrial white elephants. Not socialism, but private and state capitalism have developed together with parliamentary democracy in India. Together they have produced an officially sponsored, subcontinental variant of bourgeois revolution.

My third section deals with India's international politics. These are connected to bourgeois revolution in India: partially and as elsewhere, an external manifestation of things domestic. But to approach India's international politics by way of bourgeois revolution would probably strain the concept beyond its limits.

Political change: parliamentary democracy, political corruption and India as a secular state

Led for all but three of the Union's 42 years to 1989 by three generations of the Nehru-Gandhi dynasty, India's governing party from its independence was Congress. It was defeated in the elections of 1977 and 1989 and it moved to the opposition benches. Thus, under the Congress prime ministerships of Indira and Rajiv Gandhi, India twice passed my acid test for parliamentary democracy. A government defeated at the polls surrendered power. In 1991, India's parliamentary democracy passed yet another test. Rajiv was assassinated in May: after voting had begun in India's tenth parliamentary elections, but before they were completed. Parliamentary elections are held over a period of days in India because of the logistical problems in holding them among so large and widely dispersed an electorate. The bomb blast that stopped (or paused) the reign of the Nehru-Gandhi dynasty delayed the elections' completion by only a fortnight. In a process similar to that which takes place in parliamentary democratic parties the world over, Congress hierarchs chose the dead leader's successor: one of their number, P. V. Narasimha Rao. He led the central government until 1996, when Congress was again defeated and again surrendered power.

The eleventh, twelfth and thirteenth parliamentary elections of 1996, 1998 and 1999 posed two new problems for India's parliamentary democracy. At this writing, they are unresolved, but, I believe, on their way to resolution. These are: first, the emergence of the BJP as a central party organizationally connected to a *sangh pariwar* (organization family) of Hindu revivalist organizations and theoretically committed to some undefined *Hindutva*. Second, one-party dominance's succession at the Centre and in many of the states by some assortment of ideologically and programatically disparate parties bundled together in coalition governments. But before we come to these problems, we must acount for parliamentary democracy's achievements in dealing with problems that it has already encountered and its failure to deal with some others.

The most remarkable achievement of parliamentary democracy in India is that it has survived so well in so apparently unpromising a social environment. In five-and-a-half decades, one of the world's few stable parliamentary democracies has been produced by a society that is more populous and diverse in every way than Europe's, scattered over more than half-a-million localities in a vast and varied subcontinent, largely parochial and illiterate and fundamentally anti-democratic in its traditional institutions and cultural biases. In attempting to explain this, we can only rely on informed speculation. In general, it seems possible for parliamentary democracy to enjoy reasonably wide acceptance not as an ideology nor even as a set of immutable "rules of the game," but only as a currently workable modus operandi for resolving conflicts over distributions of power and pelf.

Parliamentary democracy is likely to provide such a modus operandi under these circumstances: first, if it is acceptable to those social groups which enjoy and can aspire to power, wealth and status. Second, if the imposition of an alternative system is clearly beyond the capacity of those groups which do not enjoy power, wealth and status. And, finally, if no one group or alliance of groups can reasonably aspire to a monopoly of political power – if political majorities are only transient coalitions of minorities. In India, these circumstances prevail.

The largest group of aspirants to power, wealth and status and the greatest beneficiaries of parliamentary democracy in India, we have already encountered: landed cultivators. They were freed from imperial bureaucratic direction by Independence, and from the direction of landlords, initially, by land reforms. These were, of course, opposed by great landlords. But their opposition counted for little with the Congress. In its pre-Independence coalition of classes, the countryside was represented not by landlords but by landed peasants. Land reforms either transformed them into cultivating proprietors or confirmed their status as such. Then, legislative assemblies with substantial powers at the state and local level gave these farmers governments of, by and for themselves: in their own languages, empowered to create their own bureaucracies, public sector enterprises and universities. Embourgeoisement, once in train, wended its way downward. "Dominant" and twice-born castes were joined and sometimes succeeded in political power by OBCs. Groups of large farmers have been joined and sometimes succeeded in political power by larger groups of smaller farmers. Now outrun by mandalization, Congress set the parliamentary democractic pace. It mobilized "pressures from subordinate classes for democratization" and balanced them with effective protection for "dominant class interests."[1]

At various times and places Naxalite militias have led the poor and oppressed in violent protest against their poverty and oppression. But while these protests have sometimes affected parliamentary politics at the state and local level, they offer no alternative to parliamentary democracy. Really, it is the only political game in India. Violence brings fragments of have-nots into futile confrontations with the coercive power of the haves and the overwhelming forces of the state. Making the best of parliamentary democracy is the real alternative for the coutryside's poor and oppressed. For the minority of their best and brightest, compensatory discrimination and *mandal* have opened opportunities for remunerative and prestigious urban employment. And this has fed back – economically, politically, psychologically – into the countryside. In recent years, MBCs – Most Backward Classes – have become a new category in Indian politics, and made themselves and been made by enterprising politicians into castes to be reckoned with in state politics. Dalits have become effective participants in state legislative assemblies and *panchayati raj* institutions. The Dalit-based Bhujan Samaj Party (BSP) has become a major player in Uttar Pradesh politics and a political inspiration to Dalits elsewhere.

Common to those groups that are relatively powerful in state parliamentary arenas and at the Centre, to those that aspire to power in these arenas and to those that are relatively powerless are such multiplicities of cross-cutting diversities – class across caste, caste across faction, faction across class – that no group nor even alliance of groups can reasonably aspire to gain or hold a monopoly of power. In the early 90s, there was some concern that this might change, and to the detriment of parliamentary democracy. After the Mandir-Masjid crisis in Ayodhya, there was some apprehension that *Hindutva* might mobilize Hindus qua Hindus into persistent political majorities. But that has not happened. As of now, *mandal* has triumphed over *mandir*. The embedded social differences and antagonisms of caste have overcome a sectarian rally. Politics have trumped ideology. Given the vast diversities – caste, class, language and ethnicity, province – along every social axis within the ideologue's Hindu "community," *mandir* is most likely to be something that passes in and out of political focus. Only when Hindus see, or are made to see, Muslims as "them" do Hindus become "us."

Violence has accompanied both *mandal* and *mandir*. Indeed, violence is ordinary in Indian politics. Sometimes, as in communal riots, it is simply the violence of blind or one-eyed hatred. When it is used politically, however, it is less often meant to achieve some end directly than to achieve it indirectly by forcing a government audience for the user or establishing the user's negotiating credentials. In sum, then, parliamentary democracy has become *the* modus operandi of group conflict and conflict resolution in India. It has demonstrated its workability over the past five decades: the political lifetime of almost two generations.

In a society whose social ideologies are fundamentally anti-democratic, the workability of parliamentary democracy may be explicable in part because its acceptance is not as an ideology but as a means sufficient to the day's political business. A paradox, it may owe something to the British Raj. Perhaps because so much of modernity in India was originally and is still exogenous, the consequences of imperialist and urban importations, Indians seem particularly adept at fitting rules to suit their contexts. So, it may be recalled, the rules of purity/pollution which villagers are expected to observe in their villages, they are not expected to observe outside their villages. In like manner, there are old rules of social inequality which define access to village wells and new rules of social equality which define access to polling booths.

The paradox may owe something to parliamentary democracy's adaptability to non-democratic Indian society. For example, the myth that democracy's fundamental right, the franchise, is exercised individually, in substance as in form, is only more palpably a fiction in India than it is elsewhere. Everywhere, people exercise their franchise socially, as members of social groups. In India, this produces, as the late Ravinder Kumar suggested, a conservative irony: many people exercise their democratic right to vote according to instructions they receive from customary, non-democratic authorities.[2] Patrons issue voting directions, for example, as do preceptors of one sort or another, communal or caste elders, lineage or family heads. Parliamentary democracy has certainly challenged some non-democratic relationships in India, as between castes, for example. But it has also reaffirmed other non-democratic relationships, as within patron–client relationships. It provides new and important opportunities for the exercise of customary hierarchical authority.

Parliamentary democracy has been adaptable both to traditional Indian beliefs in familialism, of which dynasticism is a manifestation, and to beliefs about the quality of breed or blood. One thinks immediately of the Nehru–Gandhi dynasty. Here parliamentary democracy adapted to virtually all the elements combined of traditional political authority. The founder of the line, Jawaharlal Nehru, established his right to rule through his charisma, the manifestation of his innate ruling capabilities. Not the first Brahmin to do this, certainly! There is to Kshatriya-hood an achievement criterion. Who rules successfully demonstrates that he or she was meant to rule. To his daughter and grandson, Nehru passed on his rule because they were his heirs, albeit of lineal irregularity. His capabilities passed to them through his blood. Lions come from lions' dens. His grandson's widow, Sonia, is the mother of Jawaharlal's great grandchildren. To be sure, this is not the whole story of her journey from reclusive domesticity and her childrens' regency to leadership of the Congress Party, but it is the beginning of it.

Dynasties abound in India's parliamentary democracy. To name only the most prominent: the present chief ministers of Haryana and Orissa inherited their *gaddis* from their fathers. Farookh Abdullah inherited the chief ministership of Jammu and Kashmir from his father, Sheikh Abdullah, the Lion of Kashmir, whose grandson is next in line. The chief minister of Andhra Pradesh inherited his position from his father-in-law. The leader of the AIADMK in Tamil Nadu was her predecessor's protégée. The leader-elect of the DMK is the son of the present incumbent. When he was jailed for corruption, the irrepressible Laloo Prasad Yadav passed on the chief ministership of Bihar to his wife, and is apparently grooming an adolescent son to succeed her. In Punjab, pre-selection of candidates for elections in 2002 was a family affair for both Congress and Akali Dal hierarchs.[3]

Among Indian dynasts, in the long history to the present of Indian dynasties, Jawaharlal Nehru was a giant. He was the founding father of parliamentary democracy in India and, concomitantly, he was the guardian of Congress's one-party dominance. He took the role of parliamentary democracy's preceptor to the Indian electorate. Preceptor is an ordinary politician's role in India, adopted by ordinary politicians, particularly in their discourses to villagers. In Nehru's case, the role was credible. Although he was the towering figure of post-Independence Indian politics, Nehru was a democratic ideologue: truer than most bourgeois politicians, certainly, to his ideology. He might have succumbed easily, as did many of his contemporaries in Asia and Africa, to the self-serving revelation that parliamentary democracy is for any number of reasons inappropriate to a third world country and declared himself chief guide in a "guided democracy," first person in a "people's democracy," president-for-life, great helmsman. But he did not. Instead, he led his party in India's first three democratic elections and tutored its electorate in parliamentary democracy. He tolerated dissent within Congress and suffered the rivalry of opposition parties. He bore the restraints that parliamentary democracy imposes on executive power: by cabinet and party colleagues, a lively parliament, an articulate opposition, a free press, an independent judiciary and an unpoliticized civil service. Rare among politicians, Nehru was a preceptor in practice.

He was also the champion of Congress's one-party dominance. It was a legacy from the Indian National Congress's movement for independence. The Congress Party is a post-Independence manifestation of the Indian National Congress. It was a bourgeois nationalist movement-cum-party and its progenitor was a bourgeois nationalist party. From its pre-Independence ancestor, the Congress Party inherited its goal-orientation. Not the affirmation of some ideology, but winning has always been the goal. Like its ancestor, the Congress Party accommodates different ideological positions and social classes under its umbrella. But like most umbrella organizations, Congress is most comfortable to those in the middle. Its base is in the middle classes. In a proper parliamentary democracy, the Congress is a proper centrist party. And now, a shadow of its former self, it still is. Its ideological explications notwithstanding, the underlying inclinations of the Congress is primarily to middle-class welfare: to the discouragement of class conflict, the maintenance of law and order, the protection of property, the encouragement of upward social mobility and the patronage of increasing agricultural and industrial production. In 1947, it was the beneficiary of Mahatma Gandhi's charisma and Jawaharlal Nehru's leadership. Britain's transfer of power had been to the Congress. It was the best and most widely organized political party in India. The party of demonstrated "responsibility" in provincial government. For two or three decades after Independence, it was the party most likely to win elections and deliver the goods.

Measured against what actually happens in most elections in most parliamentary democracies most of the time, elections in independent India have usually fallen within the range of "free and fair." But for the first two decades of Indian independence, Congress won them all almost all the time: in the states until 1967 and until 1977 at the Centre. The more elections it won, the more Congress became a party of, by and for election winners: for those who wanted to exercise political power and those who wanted to profit from its exercise. The more the Congress became a party of, by and for election winners, the less explicitly ideological it became. Or more exactly, the less its concoctions of Gandhian and socialist rhetoric described Congress's policies, and the more they came to be determined by the interests that they served. These were, primarily, of the middle classes, rural and urban. One-party dominance depended on them. But its success compelled the support of others. It was William Faulkner, I think, who observed that the world's wisdom is summarized in a dozen-or-so cliches: "nothing succeeds like success."

However much they opposed land reform and decried Nehru's "socialist pattern of society," landlords and great industrialists understood that in order to serve their interests they had no better alternative than to support, if only from their purses, Congress and Congressmen. Officials were not slow to appreciate that, election after election, whoever their political masters, of whatever family, caste, community and class backgrounds, they were almost certain to be Congressmen. Groups of the weak and despised, Dalits and Muslims, for example, sought the Congress's protection by becoming their vote banks. Although they gained little from their support of the ruling party, they feared to gain even less by impeding its way to certain electoral victories.

On the Congress's periphery, in virtually ceaseless fission and fusion, were parties of opposition. Some were more or less ideological, like the communists and socialists on the left and the short-lived, "free enterprise" Swatantra Party on the right. *Hindutva* has always had its parties. Other opposition parties were provincial and usually dominated by a particular caste or community: the Akali Dal of Punjab by Sikhs, the Republican Party of Maharashtra by Mahars, the Lok Dals of northern India by Jats, Andhra Pradesh's Telegu Desam by Kammas, the Dravidian parties of Tamil Nadu by non-Brahmin castes, and so forth. Factionalism was rife and party loyalty weak in most opposition parties. They fissured between and within their constituent factions, between their local units and within them, between and within the personal followings of their leaders and on the lines of individual opportunism and fearfulness. The general failure of opposition parties to hold themselves together, much less to ally with one another, crippled their capacity to oppose and contributed crucially to one-party dominance. When, in reaction to Indira Gandhi's "emergency," opposition parties allied to fight and win parliamentary elections in 1977, their failure to remain allied as a government brought Congress back for its Indian summer of 1980 to 1989.

No less than most opposition parties was Congress, even in the heyday of one-party dominance, profuse in its factions and insecure in the loyalties of its members. The results of this, however, were ambiguous: at once to facilitate one-party dominance and to undermine it. A party of factions, unburdened by ideological commitment, inclined to promote middle-class welfare, purposeful primarily in winning elections and positioned to deliver the goods to its voters, the Congress patched together its pluralities and majorities from India's vast heterogeneity. Here from one village faction, there from another. Here from one caste or caste fragment, there from their rivals. From a constituency alliance here that included a particular community, from another there that excluded it. From a state coalition here that depended on the support of "dominant" and twice-born castes, from another there dependent on the support of backward classes. The myriad, separate cost-benefit calculations that held the Congress together in fragments and factions could, however, undo it in fragments and factions. Factions wanted to know what was in it for them. If Congress was likely to lose here or there, how could they avoid the loss or, better still, by a switch in time, gain from it?

So, Congress's dominance was always tenuous. Where it was most long-lived, at the Centre, Congress never won a majority of the popular vote in any parliamentary elections. During the heyday of the Nehru-Gandhi dynasty, Congress governments commanded majorities of 70 to 80 percent of the seats in the Lok Sabha. But these were the magnifications by a first-past-the-post electoral system of popular vote pluralities of 40 to 49 percent. When opposition parties came together and the Congress's alliance patchworks came unstitched – invariably related events of intersecting and complementary cost-benefit analyses – one-party dominance was vulnerable. Opposition parties came together to win elections. And, generally, for no other purpose. They allocated constituencies amongst themselves in such ways as to confront the Congress in straight fights. The programmatic unity of anti-Congress opposition fronts was of their lowest common denominator or largely decorative. In the Congress's defeats, dissidence within the party was as crucial as opposition from without.

Unlike all six of his non-Congress prime ministerial predecessors, Atal Bihari Vajpayee has the distinction of never having been a Congressman. Morarji Desai was prime minster for 28 months between 1977 and 1979. V. P. Singh was prime minister for 11 months between 1989 and 1990. Both led stitched-together, non-Congress coalition governments that came unstitched. They were the two leading opposition figures to hold prime ministerial office until Vajpayee came to it in 1998. They had both been Congress chief ministers and cabinet colleagues of Congress prime ministers.

Morarji Desai had also been a member of the Congress Party's "syndicate." It was one of Jawaharlal Nehru's instruments for establishing and maintaining a parliamentary democracy that was dominated by one party. The syndicate was the nickname given to the collectivity of Congress's senior state and regional bosses. Nehru acknowledged and accommodated their power. They, in turn, from their bases in local and state politics, produced the patchwork whose sum was Congress's dominance. Under Nehru's guidance, one-party dominance served as a system of tutelage in democratic conflict resolution for a society in which parliamentary democracy was culturally and experientially foreign and in which conflicts were many, inveterate and multiplex.

Thus, peasants learned that through caste and factional alliances they could turn ballot papers into wealth, status and power. They could turn themselves into farmers. That they would not in the learning process turn Congress out of office was the syndicate's job to ensure: by its members' separate and collective knowledge of provincial politics, their positions as leading provincial politicians, their demonstrated political abilities and their common interests in keeping Congress in power. When, for example, popular agitation in the 1950s for "linguistic" states threatened Congress's dominance in various parts of India, it was largely within the syndicate that the matter was negotiated and successfully resolved. One-party dominance was maintained. Congress's dominance allowed democratic competition but limited its consequences. My guess is that one-party dominance served to maintain parliamentary democracy by providing it with a cut-off mechanism that kept it from being worked beyond its capacity.

Would Nehru's faith in parliamentary democracy have withstood creditable and widespread challenges to Congress's one-party dominance? We don't know. No less than his Congress contemporaries and successors, India's first prime minister believed that the real alternative to Congress rule in India was chaos. Under the constitutional cover of President's Rule, Nehru sanctioned the removal from office in 1959 of the duly elected Communist Party government of Kerala. We know that, and we know that among his confidants none advised Nehru more strongly in favor of dismissing the Kerala Communists than his daughter. As prime minister, Indira Gandhi established her personal preeminence within Congress, and used one-party dominance and President's Rule as her instruments for centralizing in herself political power in India. In this she was assisted by her sons and annointed heirs: first Sanjay, who was killed in an airplane crash in 1981, then Rajiv.

Mother and sons worked to establish their political hegemony: to reduce to submission or subservience to them, institutions that generate political power and people who exercise it. The syndicate was dismantled. Congress chief ministers and Pradesh Congress Committee chairmen were appointed by the Gandhis and served at their pleasure. Governors were appointed as Congress point men to meddle in the internal politics of opposition parties and to find and create pretexts for the imposition of President's Rule in states governed by them. Within the Congress, the rewards of the Gandhis' regimes went to those who professed loyalty to them, however self-serving the profession or incompetent and dishonest the professor. "Indira is India," proclaimed one of her toadies, "and India is Indira."

The Gandhis' autocratic rule of Congress's state parties may well have increased, rather than reduced, factionalism and opportunism in them. I suggested earlier, in chapter 4, that for their efforts to rule India's states from New Delhi the Gandhis may have decreased the capacities of state Congress parties to reconcile within themselves their factional conflicts. Instead, these were pushed out into opposition, and provided opposition parties with a rallying cry: the *Dilli Durbar* versus "us." In any case, from Indira's first electoral victory in 1967 to Rajiv's defeat in 1989, Congress dominance was disappearing from state politics. By 1992, it had all but disappeared. Now it is nowhere to be found. In several states Congress governs, often in coalition with other parties. In several states Congress is a minor player. Wherever there is a Congress government, it can be defeated. But no European-like system of stable parties, stable multi-party competition and stable coalition governments has emerged to succeed one-party dominance. The factionalism that characterized it survives it.

Post-*mandal*, it is frequently said that politics in India have become caste politics. More accurately, they have become the politics of caste factions. Castes and communities of any size and political importance are invariably factionalized. The faction is the basic unit of political competition and cooperation, even within caste and communal lines. Central and successful provincial parties are largely aggregations of caste factions. The proliferation of provincial parties in recent years is largely the proliferation of caste factions striking out on their own. Parties enable factions to compete for political power, to attain it and its benefits. Through their affiliation with parties, factions compete for dominance within their castes, arrange the delivery of power and status, electricity and esteem to their members. In an economy of real and perceived scarcity, where political power decides so much of who gets what, getting the goods and winning in politics are inextricably connected. If one party can't or won't deliver, then perhaps another can and will. Parties that are basically uncertain and shifting alliances of factions produce government and opposition coalitions that are basically uncertain and shifting alliances of parties.

The pervasiveness of localism in Indian politics is one explanation for its factionalism. Caste factions are usually local. Parties tend to choose candidates for state legislative assembly seats who are local faction leaders or enjoy their support and/or who match the particular caste and communal configurations within the parties and their local vote banks. Legislative assembly factions are midpoint, so to speak, in factional networks: factions of factions that connect village *panchayats* to the Lok Sabha. There, at India's Centre, a vestige, at least, of Congress's dominance was present in 1992. No longer. No party is dominant. No party, neither Congress nor the BJP, can reasonably aspire to rule in New Delhi except at the head of a multi-party coalition. As of today, the stability of such governments is largely determined by factionalism and fortuity.

Specifically: Does political factionalism at home incline to defection any of the provincial parties in a governing coalition at the Centre? If so, does any such party hold a sufficient number of seats in the Lok Sabha so that its defection will end the governing coalition's majority and bring down its government? The representation of provincial parties is largely determined in state politics; so, too, are their defections or threatened defections from coalitions at the Centre. In 1998, the AIADMK of Tamil Nadu defected from the BJP-led coalition government at the Centre because the BJP would not use central government powers to oust the state government led by the DMK. The AIADMK had the numbers in the Lok Sabha, and the BJP-led government fell. In 2001, the Trinamool Congress of West Bengal defected from the BJP-led coalition at the Centre because the BJP would not use central government powers to oust the state government led by the CPI–M. The Trinamool Congress did not have the numbers in the Lok Sabha, and the BJP-led government survived. In neither instance was there any real issue of national politics.

No less than provincial parties and over a wider geographical spread are central parties afflicted with factionalism. During its heyday, Congress kept its factions in place by winning. Nowadays, winning only occasionally, here and there, but on an upswing lately, the party and its state units are more factionalized than ever. Before the BJP started winning, its commitment to *Hindutva* and its membership in good standing of the *sangh pariwar* tended to keep the party's factions in line. Now that the BJP is winning, its factions have booty and power to fight over. In Gujarat and Uttar Pradesh, most notably, the party has been fractured by its factions. Everywhere, the party's true believers are met on parish pump battlefields by factions of johnnies-come-lately who are in the battle only to win it.

Only somewhat less than factionalism does corruption pervade India's parliamentary democracy. The "folklore of corruption," as Gunnar Myrdal calls it,[4] is pervasive in India. It is generally held to be true that political transactions are routinely tainted with corruption. The public servant acts

according to how and by whom he is bribed or intimidated. The businessman uses black money to buy favors from politicians and bureaucrats. The
politician sells his loyalty and pays for votes.

The folklore, it would seem, is supported by the facts. Peons and clerks in
government office routinely demand *bakshish* from Indian citizens to access
their ordinary citizens' entitlements. Customs and excise officials at Indian
ports are notoriously corrupt. In 2001, their boss, the chairman of the Central
Board of Excise and Customs, India's premier revenue-collecting agency, was
arrested on charges of massive corruption. It is well known that in many
states officials can and do bribe their way to greener fields for boodle from
postings where the pickings are slim. In 2002, the chairman of the Punjab
Public Service Commission was arrested on charges of massive corruption. It
is alleged that over a period of six years in office he made himself a very rich
man by selling public service jobs. The Bofors scandal which first broke in
1990 is as yet unresolved and hangs like a dark cloud over Rajiv Gandhi's
memory. Indian agents, including a resident Italian businessman who had no
business being an Indian agent, except that he was a close friend of the prime
minister's family, are accused of taking millions of dollars in illegal kickbacks
to faciliate the purchase of Swedish artillery pieces for the Indian army.
More recently, the chief ministers of Tamil Nadu and Bihar have been im-
plicated in various illegal money-making enterprises. In a sting operation in
2001, a group of Indian internet journalists video-taped the president of the
BJP taking a bribe, and forced the resignation of the government's defense
minister.

The ordinary fuel of corruption in India is unreported income, black
money. Chief Vigilance Commissioner, N. Vittal, the head of India's central
corruption-fighting agency, estimates that black money accounts for 40
percent of India's GDP. Black money's base is in the political system. It pays
political parties' bills and is a major source of election campaign funding. It
is in no small measure responsible for the politicization of the bureaucracy,
the entry of known criminals and their thugs into politics and the nexus
between them and outright criminal activity: smuggling, for example. "The
film industry, a substantial part of the construction industry and a large
number of small industries are run on the basis of corruption."[5] It is common
knowledge that black money pays for 40 to 60 percent of the price of urban
real estate: including its most salubrious black money laundries, the peri-
urban farms of the gentry.

Transparency International was not yet in business in 1992. Its first
annual Corruption Perception Index was published in 1995. Since then, TI
has become the leading international non-governmental organization dedicated to the comparative, cross-national study and exposure of corruption.
Its annual Corruption Perception Index is Transparency International's best
known work. It is a "poll of polls": a composite of surveys conducted

Table 2 India's Position on Transparency International's Corruption ✓
Perception Indexes

Year	India's rank	No. of countries surveyed	Countries ranked with India
2001	71	91	Honduras, Kazakhstan, Uzbekistan
2000	69	90	Philippines
1999	72	99	Colombia
1998	66	85	Bulgaria, Egypt
1997	45	52	none
1996	46	54	none
1995	35	41	none

around the world by such organizations as the World Bank, the Economist Intelligence Unit, the Political and Economic Risk Consultancy. The surveys record experiences and perceptions "of the degree of corruption [in the countries surveyed] by business people, academics and risk analysts."[6] The 2001 index is a composite of 14 such surveys. India's place in each of the seven annual indexes appears in Table 2.

In sum: year after year, in survey after survey, India's place has been in the quartile of the most corrupt and in the company of the most corrupt. What explanations can we offer for this? One-party dominance, I have argued, was probably a vital period of tutelage for parliamentary democracy. There is no doubt, however, that black money was the treasure trove of one-party dominance. One of its legacies may be the perpetuation of corruption. There is some evidence, in Eastern Europe certainly, to suggest that corruption once entrenched may well survive the political power that protected it. India's pattern of democratic development provides some explanation. However well or ill India was served by four decades of a government-controlled economy, the legal requirements on businessmen to secure various licenses and permits from bureaucrats in order to carry on their businesses was a standing invitation to corruption. A legacy of this "license-permit *raj*" has been the perpetuation of corruption. Today, politicians and bureaucrats are still entrenched in the business of business. It need hardly be said, and again we may learn from Eastern Europe's recent history, that after decades of government control, economic liberalization – India's path for more than a decade – issues its own invitations to corruption.

We are certainly aware of the argument that corruption is socially defined: what is corrupt in one society is not corrupt in others, ends that are served by corruption in one society are served by legitimate means in others. What is familial duty and praiseworthy here is nepotism there. The tax evasion which is illegal and widespread in India and produces great hoards of black money is elsewhere managed by estimable firms of chartered accountants and produces green money accounts in foreign tax havens. In India, there are widespread patterns of socially approved behaviour – routinely, the use of public office to serve family interests – that help to explain corruption. Increasing demands on middle-class salary earners employed in the public sector – for children's school fees, holidays, consumer goods, keeping up with the Jains of the private sector – explains some corruption. And doubtless there are other explanations as well.

There is, however, a less tolerant perspective on it, and it is this: India's commitment to democratic, secular development has as its corollary a commitment to universalist public values. And within these, there is a definition of corruption. Thus, succinctly put by Transparency International: "The abuse of public office for private gain" is corruption – here, there, everywhere, under any circumstance, however rationalized and socially defined. Corruption is corruption. While it facilitates parliamentary democratic politics by helping to pay for them, corruption also discredits them. The poor are the particular sufferers. Corruption is inflationary, depleting poverty and emergency alleviation programs through "leakages," conducive to the production and consumption of luxury goods, a weight on the deficit side of the balance of international trade, and in general, an obstacle to economic development.

Before Independence and immediately afterward, India was torn by sectarian violence. Jinnah's "Muslim nation" seceded. India's Mahatma was assassinated by a Hindu fanatic. The subcontinent was enveloped in a communal holocaust. India's new Congress government responded by projecting India's commitment to secular statehood. The Republic would be politically indifferent to its citizens' religions and equally respectful of them. Secularism is declared to be one of the Republic's defining characteristics in the preamble to its constitution. Its "fundamental rights" prohibit religious discrimination of any sort by the state and by anyone who controls access to public places, such as temples, wells and restaurants. Subject to the demands of public order and social reform, all Indian citizens are guaranteed the rights to "profess, practice and propagate" their religions and to maintain and manage their religious institutions. Constitutional secularism is intrinsic to the Republic's claim to legitimacy

Against this background, friends of Indian secularism have watched with concern, and some with horror, the coming to national power during the 90s of the BJP. It is the political wing of a *sangh pariwar* of Hindu revivalist organizations, led by the Hindu hardline RSS (Rashtriya Swayamsevak Samaj – National Volunteer Corps), and committed to some vague but nonetheless secularism-menacing *Hindutva* or "Hindu nationalism." The simple chronology of the BJP's meteoric rise is as follows: Its predecessor as the *pariwar's* party of Hindu *jagaram* (awakening), the Jan Sangh (the people's organization) won two Lok Sabha seats and less than 8 percent of the popular vote in the 1984 parliamentary elections. In 1989, the BJP won 88 Lok Sabha seats in the first parliamentary elections it contested, and 12 percent of the popular vote. In 1990, for the first time in the Indian Union's history, an avowedly Hindu communal party, the BJP, was elected to the government of an Indian state: and not one, but three, all in the Hindi-speaking north. From there, the BJP's call for *Hindutva* – undefined and ambiguous, but resonant nonetheless – brought voters to the party in Gujarat and Maharashtra. In the 1991 parliamentary elections, the BJP won 119 seats in the Lok Sabha. In 1996, it won 160 seats. In the 1998 parliamentary elections, the BJP won a plurality of Lok Sabha seats, 178, and formed a short-lived coalition government led by Atal Bihari Vajpayee. The party increased its tally of Lok Sabha seats to 182 in the 1999 elections and reclaimed government. It is there still, at the head of a National Democratic Alliance of twenty-odd parties:[7] the Centre's most long-lived coalition government.

There are at least three crucial events in this chronology: the Shah Bano–Muslim Women's Act affair of 1985–86, the BJP's defection in 1990 from the United Front government of V. P. Singh, and the ongoing Mandir-Masjid saga. These events are best understood in two related contexts, at least. First, of a political system in which Congress dominance had been abraded by Mrs Gandhi's attempts to centralize it, by corruption and by Congress having sat too long in power. And second, in the context of an Indian electorate coming into its own, feeling its oats, and with political and social values that are not always the same as those shared by the upper-caste, English-educated lawyers who framed India's constitution.

It was with those shared values, with article 44 of the Indian constitution, that the stage was set for the Shah Bano–Muslim Women's Act affair. As one of the constitution's "directive principles," article 44 commits the state to a key secular value: to the eventual legislation of a "uniform civil code throughout ... India," applicable to all its citizens without regard to their religions. Under the Raj, judicially recognized civil codes of Indian families were not uniform. They were derived from the injunctive scriptures of their separate religions, and modified by their separate caste and quasi caste customs and usage. So, the promise of a uniform civil code foreshadowed legislation that would distance India from its colonial past, and displace sacred rules from the regulation of Indian family life by rules that were secular. After 52 years, it is a promise that has yet to be kept. Most notably, the civil code for Indian Muslims is still derived from the *shar'iah*. And so it was for Shah Bano Begum, an elderly and indigent Muslim divorcee.

The Indian Supreme Court delivered its judgment in her case in 1985. Briefly, the court held that Shah Bano was entitled to maintenance payments from her husband's estate under the relevant provision of the Indian *criminal code*. However, under the relevant provision of the *shar'iah civil code*, a Muslim divorcee is entitled to maintenance from her former husband or his estate only for her three menstrual periods after divorce. A distant memory for Shah Bano. The court's judgment became a cause célèbre: strongly applauded by women's groups (including some Muslim women's groups), and hotly opposed by Muslim conservatives (including some other Muslim women's groups). The response of the Indian government was to push through Parliament the Muslim Women's (Protection of Rights on Divorce) Act of 1986. The act, in effect, overturned the Supreme Court's judgment in the Shah Bano Case. The *shar'iah*'s rule on maintenance payments was codified into Indian law. The prime minister of the day was Rajiv Gandhi, whose promise of a few years earlier was to bring India into the twenty-first century. The majority party in the Lok Sabha was Congress, forever and still the self-proclaimed guardian of Indian secularism. We might note that desertions from its Muslim vote bank contributed to Congress's loss of government in 1977.

Whatever it may have done for Congress (not much to judge from virtually every parliamentary election since 1990) the Muslim Women's Act was a godsend for the BJP. By overturning the Shah Bano decision in a widely publicized case, available and explicable to a nation-wide audience, the Rajiv Gandhi government gave apparent credence to the widespread and long-held charge against the Congress that the substance of its secularism was "pseudo-secularism," communally divisive "vote bank politics," "pampering" Muslims in order to get their votes. Why else, after all, and particularly when the Supreme Court had come down on the side of simple equity, should divorced Hindu men have to continue paying maintenance, and divorced Muslim men continue to go scot free? Why should ordinary Hindu women have some legal protection from the financial ravages of divorce, and ordinary Muslim women – one of India's poorest, most illiterate and generally vulnerable groups – remain unprotected?

Of the Shah Bano–Muslim Women's Act affair, the ironical legacy is that a hallmark of constitutional secularism and of the secular state elsewhere, one civil code applicable to all citizens, has become in India a symbol of communalism. Any move to legislate article 44 would be widely perceived by both conservative Muslims and liberal Hindus as a threat to secularism. In opposition, the BJP was the party of article 44. Now in government, it has made its peace with realpolitik. The legislation of a uniform civil code is not a part of the National Democratic Alliance's program. Indeed, nothing would wreck the alliance and bring down the Vajpayee government more surely than a move by the BJP to bring article 44 into law. Back home, any number of the provincial parties in the alliance have their own Muslim vote banks.

The BJP was the second party in the United Front government elected to office at the Centre in 1989. Less than a year after the election, the BJP defected from the Front and brought down the government. The BJP and the Front's prime minister, V. P. Singh, were at loggerheads over two related issues. The first was Singh's announcement that his government would implement the reservation policy for OBCs recommended in the Mandal Commission report. The second, was the prime minister's attempt to halt the *rath yatra* – the chariot ride – of the then president of the BJP, leading *Hindutva* ideologue, and now deputy prime minister at the Centre, L. K. Advani. In a Toyota van decorated to resemble the chariot used by the hero, Arjuna, in the televised serial presentation of the Hindu epic, *Mahabharata* – an Indian televison sensation of the 1980s – Advani set out to spread *Hindutva*'s good news. He was to travel more than a thousand kilometres, from village to village across northern India. His trip began at one Hindu temple that had been sacked by early Muslim invaders, Somnath in Gujarat, and was to end at another allegedly wrecked by later Muslim invaders, Ramjanmabhumi in Ayodhya.

By all accounts, the ride was a great success. The United Front was left behind and in shambles. The BJP set its course for New Delhi by way of Ayodhya. At the Centre it would lead a coalition and not be led by one. It would be the party of *Hindutva*: of Hindu *sangathanan*, not of V. P. Singh's Hindu-divisive *mandal*, but of Hindu-unifying *mandir*. It would keep its upper-caste constituency and augment it from the vast pool of those thousands who lined Advani's route and cherished the Lord Ram. Or so it all seemed a decade ago. The BJP's heyday began in the 90s and may now be drawing to a close. For a decade, things worked out well for the party. But not quite as its *pariwar*'s true believers thought that they would.

The Mandir-Masjid saga is, briefly, this: the Babri Masjid, ostensibly a mosque, was a prayer house used by both Hindu and Muslim worshippers in the Uttar Pradesh temple town of Ayodhya. Hindu revivalist organizations had argued since the 1940s that the Lord Ram's idol resided at the very center of the mosque, and beneath it were the ruins of a Hindu temple that marked nothing less than Ram's birthplace. The mosque was a Ram temple sitting on the ruins of a Ram temple. The Lord Ram is one of the two most popularly worshipped incarnations of God in the Hindu pantheon. His *mandir* was destroyed, so the story goes, on the orders of a Mughal emperor; and in an act typical of Muslim religious intolerance, iconoclasm and triumphalism, a mosque was built on the temple's ruins. But, to the committee of Muslim elders that was formed to vindicate the Islamic authenticity of the Babri Masjid, there was no story. The Babri Masjid was a mosque.

In the late 1940s, a prudent Indian court decided the matter by padlocking the structure. Decades later, in the 80s, another court ordered the opening of the Mandir-Masjid *to Hindu worshippers* on the plea of the VHP (Vishva Hindu Parishad – universal Hindu council), a leading member of the *sangh pariwar*. Muslim religious and communal organizations were outraged. The Parishad pressed on with elaborate plans to demolish the mosque and build on the spot a soaring cathedral to honor the Lord Ram. After it was demolished, the Babri Masjid might, or might not, be rebuilt elsewhere. A matter of indifference. But not to Muslims. Though unused as a mosque, Babri Masjid was still a mosque. A symbol of the Muslim right to be there: in Ayodhya, in Uttar Pradesh, in India. The Babri Masjid Action Committee of Muslim elders dug in.

For the *sangh pariwar*, including the BJP, "Ayodhya" became *Hindutva's* battle cry. Thousands and thousands of saffron-robed pilgrims flocked to the town. They brought tonnes of consecrated bricks to rebuild Ram's *mandir*. It would be a monument to His triumph over half a millennium of Muslim "foreign occupation" of *Bharat Mata*, over Muslim contempt for Hinduism and oppression of Hindus. The Uttar Pradesh and Union governments made some attempts to negotiate a settlement between the Babri Masjid committee and the *pariwar*, but they never got beyond deadlock. It was broken on December 6, 1992, when gangs of Hindu zealots demolished the Babri Masjid. Apparently well-prepared to do the job, well-trained and disciplined, cheered on by the *sangh pariwar*, and tacitly supported by the state's BJP government, the demolition crews did the job quickly and by hand. In the aftermath, through January, murderous communal violence erupted in several north Indian cities, spread to Pakistan and Bangladesh and, most ominously, in two terrifying episodes, to Mumbai.

The great electoral gains of the BJP were made in the years after Ayodhya, and for a while it seemed that Indian secularism would be swamped by the *Hindutva* wave. It no longer seems that way. It is certainly true that India has a "Hindu nationalist" party at the head of its central government. But what in political reality does that mean? Constitutionally, India is a "secular state." But what in political reality does that mean?

Those questions lead us back to our discussion of Hinduism. India is suffused by it. About 82 percent of India's population belongs to communities that identify themselves as Hindu. An even larger percentage of India's well-to-do, well-educated and well-placed population is Hindu. India is Hinduism's homeland and unlike the world's other major religions, it has never successfully migrated. Close to 100 percent of the world's Hindus either live on the subcontinent – the vast majority in India – or are of Indian ancestry. Virtually all of Hinduism's sacred sites are in modern India. Ayodhya is about 120 kilometers west of Lucknow, the capital city of Uttar Pradesh. Two hundred kilometers southwest of Ayodhya, on the banks of that great life-giving, sacred river, *Ganga Mata*, Mother Ganga, is Varanasi, known to Hindus as Kashi and sacred to the Lord Siva. It is from his hair that the river flows. A hundred and twenty-five kilometers east of Varanasi is Allahabad, known to Hindus as Prayag, a great pilgrimage site at the confluence of the Ganga, Yamuna and fabled Saraswati rivers. The great battle described in the *Mahabharata* and in its included scripture, one of Hinduism's holiest, *Bhagavad Gita*, was fought in the vicinity of Kurukshetra: a small city 150 kilometers north of Delhi. Then, 120 kilometers due east of Kurukshetra, on the Ganga, is Hardwar: sacred to the Lord Vishnu, a major pilgrimage center, and gateway to the holy places of the Lord Siva in the Himalayas. Vrindavan, on the train line between Delhi and Agra, is where the Lord Krishna (with Ram, the most worshiped incarnation of God) was born, dallied with the *gopis* (milk maids), and among them, with Radha, his divine companion. Three hundred and fifty kilometers west of Agra, in the footprint of Brahma, another of God's incarnations, is Pushkar Lake. All this within a radius of 750 kilometers from the capital city of secular India!

Far from New Delhi, everywhere in India, rivers, lakes, hills, trees, towns and cities, village festivals and rural fairs, urban concerts and dance recitals, movies, the dashboards of taxis, the decorations on trucks, the talismans of shopkeepers, the brand names of their merchandise, their names – all tell Hindu stories. The second televison sensation of the 1980s was the serial presentation of the Hindu epic, *Ramayana*. Like *Mahabharata*, it literally brought ordinary life to a halt during its viewing times. Both series were of a hundred or so episodes, done in popular Bollywood fashion, viewed as religious observances by many in their audiences and now preserved for the faithful on videotape.

The BJP did not invent "Hindu nationalism." Rather it is the ancestor of India's secular nationalism. Indian nationalism first appeared in the nineteenth century as Hindu nationalism: in the work of the Hindu revivalist Arya Samaj and in the writings of *bhadralok* litterateurs, particularly Bankim Chandra Chatterji (1838–94). Both excluded Muslims from their nationalism. Nationalism's first cause célèbre in India and its first triumph, the partition of Bengal in 1905 and its renunification six years later, was distinctly a Hindu *bhadralok* cause and triumph. In general, Bengali Muslims supported the partition and were aggrieved by reunification. The Lucknow Pact of 1916 and the alliance of 1920–22 between the Khilafat and the Non-Cooperation movements, were expressions not of secular but rather of inter-communal nationalism. To both, there was a Hindu partner and a Muslim partner. M. A. Jinnah's efforts to perpetuate this nationalism was defeated in 1928 at the All-Parties Conference by opposition from the Hindu Mahasabha – a BJP ancestor – no less than by opposition from secular nationalists. The Indian National Congress had a handful of Muslims at the top, but the overwhelming evidence of the 1937 and 1946 provincial elections is that it had no Muslim constituency. Muslims were first-class citizens in Mahatma Gandhi's notion of nationalism, but it was less secular than tolerantly multi-religious. He courted a Muslim constituency, but his appeal was to Hindus. Indeed, it would be difficult to invent a more authentic Hindu ascetic and *bhakti* than the "The Father of the Nation." In independent India, secular politicians – not least Indira Gandhi – have from time to time "saffronized" their public personas to meet the exigencies of politics.[8]

Take all this: the ubiquity of Hinduism and the Hindu ancestry of Indian nationalism, an adult suffrage-based parliamentary democracy in which the majority population is Hindu, and it is small wonder that the combination should intrude upon, press in on India's constitutional secularism. The intrusion, the pressure, has produced a *Hindu secularism*. By this I mean a political rather than a constitutional secularism. Hindu secularism is in the nature of a self-restraining injunction. It is an injunction to which the dominant group, at once, adheres and by its political majority reserves to itself the right to interpret and modify. Such a qualified political secularism is by no means unique to India. I have no difficulty in recognizing the United States' secularism-in-fact, its political secularism, as Christian.

To this Christian secularism, one comparison is apposite to the conclusion of our discussion of Hindu secularism. It enjoys less constitutional protection than does political secularism in the United States. Far more than the American constitution, the Indian constitution concentrates power in the national government, including the power to amend the constitution. The check on Hindu secularism comes from within Hindu society itself and is embedded in its politics. Again, Indian politics are largely the politics of caste factions: of *mandal* and not of *mandir*. Only when, as at Ayodhya, Muslims are made "them" do Hindus become "we." At the micro-level, the level of provincial politics in Uttar Pradesh, for example, India's Muslim population of 120 million breaks down into minorities among other minorities: Jats, Rajputs, Yadavs, Jatavs, Brahmans. In the 2002 elections in Uttar Pradesh, the two mutually hostile *mandal* parties, the Samajwadi and Bhujan Samaj – both provincial and with Muslim constituencies – won between them a majority of seats in the state's legislative assembly. About 25 seats, equal to the Congress's tally, and a disproportionate percentage of the votes went to an assortment of "one-caste" parties. In its election campaign, the BJP abandoned Ram in favor of *mandal*. But it is a newcomer to the game. To Muslims and *bhujan* (ordinary people) the BJP is still the party of *mandir* and *Manuvad*, and they turned its government out of office. In recent elections all over India the BJP has been losing out to provincial parties and to Congress. Of course, any number of things, from election to election and state to state, explain this.[9]

For one, *Hindutva* has probably ebbed, at least at the polls. Now, in post-*mandal* political time, *mandir* is bad politics, particularly for the middle classes. *India Today*, a journal whose insights into the middle classes are no less perceptive than its reportage, puts it this way:

> ... millions of perfectly middle class citizens – the sort who want good governance, a better economy and limit their religiosity to private practice – ... may or may not want a temple or a mosque in Ayodhya but they certainly don't want a return to Golgotha ... [Ayodhya] is no longer the number one issue on [their] minds. Rather, it is the number one cause of fear.[10]

But there are elections every few years. The public mood changes, *Hindutva* will doubtlessly come and go – as it has under various names and at various times and places for more than a century. Communalism is an underlying reality in Indian politics. Since the 1920s, communal riots in north Indian towns have become commonplace. Their trigger is usually some apparently trivial local incident – an argument between neighbors, a quarrel over a right of way, an insult, a Muslim peddlar moved on by a Hindu constable, a Hindu child chastised by a Muslim shopkeeper. And then, days and sometimes weeks of localized arson, pillage, rape and murder follow. Partition nationalized communalism. North Indian towns, particularly Delhi, accumulated large populations of Sikh and Hindu refugee families and their remnants who had experienced the horror and bequeathed the hatred to their children and grandchildren. And lest they forget, Pakistan is there to remind them.

For the past decade and a half, Ayodhya re-nationalized communalism. Ram tumbled *Hindutva* out of its closet. Leaders of *pariwar* organizations such as the RSS and the VHP (Vishva Hindu Parishad – world Hindu council) are unrelenting in their hostility to Muslims. As never before, *pariwar* rabble-rousers give regular and unbridled public expression to their hatred and contempt of Muslims and of Islam. Sparked by Ayodhya, communal carnage between 1989 and 1992 did its worst in three decades. To make good its threat of some years' standing, the VHP made its first moves to begin building its temple in March 2002. It moved in the face of cautions from the BJP, government orders, court injunctions, Muslim sentiments. The most destructive communal rampage since 1992 followed. In February 2002, an exchange of insults and missiles on a train station in Gujarat between local Muslims and Hindu *kar sevaks* (volunteer construction workers-cum-pilgrims) returning from Ayodhya led, first, to 57 of them being burnt alive, and then, to the murder of hundreds of Muslims and the wholesale destruction of their property by Hindu mobs in towns and cities across Gujarat. At this writing, communal tensions continue to simmer in Gujarat and occasionally come to a bloody boil. In March, the BJP government in New Delhi ordered the cordoning-off of Ayodhya and the stationing of 15,000 police in the town of fewer than 100,000 residents to enforce its injunction against the VHP's plan to begin building its monument to Ram.

To hold its National Democratic Alliance together, the Atal Bihari Vajpayee government has had to distance itself from the more extreme actions and pronouncements, at least, of the *pariwar*. And it has done so. But however strained the ties of ideology, the ties of politics remain. The BJP counts on the *pariwar's* footsoldiers to turn out the vote, and the *pariwar* has no other political party. Its party is the BJP. And as such, Muslims are apparently unrelenting in their mistrust of it. The BJP has tried, but without success, to recruit a Muslim constituency. It is unlikely to recruit one for its embrace of an American "war on terrorism," whose usual suspects are Muslim. The Union Minister for Human Resource Development is unlikely to help recruit a Muslim constituency for the BJP by his strenuous efforts to introduce a Hindu spin into the textbooks used by Indian schoolchildren. A Muslim constituency for the BJP is unlikely to be recruited by the prime minister's unwavering support for his party's chief minister of Gujarat, widely regarded by Muslims as a Hindu sympathizer in the state's communal carnage of 2002.

The frequently reiterated statements by the BJP's leading politicians – by the prime minister, certainly – of their commitment to constitutional secularism are taken with a pinch of salt. However, I think that there is a realization among them, as among politicians in general, that India's vast diversities of faith, not only across communal lines, but as well within the Hindu majority, make untenable any political arrangement other than secularism. But it will be a *Hindu secularism*, whoever sits on the Delhi *gaddi*.[11]

Finally and briefly, with regard to coalition governments: it may be that as all parties, central and provincial, reconcile themselves to having partners in government, gain experience as coalition partners and in negotiating partnership agreements, their coalitions will be more likely to hold together. The BJP-led National Democratic Alliance has been in power at the Centre since 1998, twice as long as the longest serving coalition government that preceded it. We know from India's experience of coalition governments that the balance in seats held between the central party in a coalition and its partners has some effect on coalition longevity. The coalition is more likely to survive, it would seem, if the balance is tipped in favor of the central party, and less likely to survive if it is tipped in favor of its provincial partners.

Survival, of course, is not all there is to it. If not the expectation, there is at least the hope that Indian governments will justify their survival by their accomplishments. Here again the balance of seats may be important. A central party cannot push through parliament legislation that is abhorrent to many or most of its coalition partners: for one uniform civil code, for example. But a central party is unlikely to be able to lead its partners in any legislation, much less a legislative program, if its coalition survives on the sufferance of one or two of its provincial parties. The era of one-party dominance has passed. The era of provincial parties has arrived. But without the lead of a central party – only Congress and the BJP, as of now – a coalition of provincial parties is unlikely to cobble together a central government that will last for long, much less accomplish anything.

Industrial development and the educated and modern business middle classes

Of the world's major industrial economies, and second only to those of the Soviet Union and its eastern European client states, the industrial economy of India until the 1990s was probably the most closed and government-dominated and directed. It was characterized by central planning, controls on the activities of privately owned industries through a regime of licenses and permits, an import-substitution strategy of industrialization, public sector occupation of the industrial economy's "commanding heights" and, below these, a "mixed economy" in which private and public sector enterprises competed. This was India's "socialism." It is no more, except as a drag on economic reform in the twenty-first century.

From 1951–52, the industrialization that began under the Raj was pursued within the framework of comprehensive, officially planned economic development. The basic planning documents were the occasionally interrupted, sequential five-year plans issued by the Indian government's Planning Commission. Driven by Nehru, planned industrialization was begun in earnest in the second plan, from 1956 to 1961. For their periods of operation, the plans established objectives and priorities for national economic development, specified targets within these in terms of particular goals and/or physical achievements, and recommended requisite public expenditure, private investment and fiscal and regulatory controls to achieve these targets. Under Nehru's chairmanship, the Planning Commission was probably the most powerful decision-making body in India. But not the most successful. Not until the sixth plan of 1980 to 1986 did planning meet its major objectives.

In the mid-1980s, some half-measures to liberalize the Indian economy and disempower its presiding "license-permit *raj*" were taken by the Rajiv Gandhi government. Under this late and unlamented regime, Indian businessmen, other than those of a protected small-scale sector, were required to seek government approval, and often from more than one ministry, for virtually anything relating to their businesses: importing and exporting; expanding, contracting and relocating; establishing new and different product lines; restructuring, merging, amalgamating or inviting foreign investment or participation; appointing directors to their boards.

Import-substitution was the basic strategy for industrialization. Its goals were to make India industrially self-reliant and, ultimately, a major industrial power. In general, and applicable to heavy basic no less than to light consumer industries, India's policy was to import only those manufactured goods that enhanced India's capacity itself to manufacture them. Behind this comprehensive barrier to imports, with little regard to social and economic costs and "comparative advantage," and in spite of a relatively low rate of industrial growth, India industrialized. Its industries developed to manufacture virtually everything that was manufactured anywhere: from tinned fruit to nuclear energy. The social costs of this were high, however. Much of the manufacture was of shoddy and overpriced goods. Corruption flourished in the nexuses of businessmen who had to apply for licenses and permits, bureaucrats who approved or rejected their applications and politicians who made themselves beholden to licensees and licensors. Because the strategy was driven by the government's plans to develop capital goods industries – steel, for example – which are generally capital-intensive, employment opportunities in industry were notably underdeveloped.

In accordance with the landmark Industrial Policy Resolution, which Nehru presented to parliament in 1956, the commanding heights of the Indian economy were placed in the public sector. The government became the dominant or monopolistic producer and/or supplier of military ordnance, basic iron and steel, ships, heavy engineering and foundry goods, energy from all sources, telecommunications and broadcasting, rail and air transport. India's largest corporations were in the public sector and run by bureaucrats. Its major financial institutions were also brought under bureaucratic command. The life insurance business was nationalized in 1956, as was India's largest bank, the State Bank of India. Driven by the need of Green Revolution farmers for credit and of Indira Gandhi for some creditable act to accompany her *garibi hatao* (abolish poverty) sloganeering, her government in 1969 and 1980 nationalized 20 of India's largest commercial banks.

Below these commanding heights, there was a mixed economy in which private industry operated, subject to the government's fiscal and regulatory controls and to competition from public sector corporations. These were engaged in a wide variety of manufacturing enterprises – automobiles, cement, engineering goods, for example – the operations of hotel chains, warehousing, wholesaling and even retailing. In 2000, after a decade of economic liberalization, 37 percent of the fixed capital in India's factories was still in the public sector. Most of it is owned and managed by the states, and much of it is unproductive and unprofitable.

The architects of this comprehensive policy for industrialization considered themselves, as Philip Mason, following Plato, called their British predecessors, "guardians."[12] They were the Indian professional elite of British India. In profile they were upper middle class and upper caste, urban, educated in English and trained in the law. They were inclined to the view that educated men know what is best for their society. In establishing a policy for industrializing India, they were not ostensibly concerned to articulate and accommodate the interests of the producers or consumers who would be affected by such a policy. Rather, they were themselves deciding what was best for India. Its industrial revolution was to be engineered from the top. But definitely not from the business top, not by the families of "merchant princes"-cum-industrial magnates of British India.

For the professional elite, industrialization was simply too important a matter to be entrusted to Indian industrialists. First, they lacked the resources necessary to initiate an industrial revolution. Second, they lacked the proper motivation. Not the good of society, but profit would be their spur. Finally and *sotto voce*, Indian industrialists were at heart still *baniyas*, traders who buy cheap and sell dear. Only the state – the preserve of the professional middle classes – could industrialize India. Only the state could accumulate the necessary resources and allocate them productively and in the interests of society. Those interests, according to Nehru's Industrial Policy Resolution, would be best served in a "socialist pattern of society." In accordance with the preamble and directive principles of India's constitution, it would be a society whose government's commitment was to provide all its citizens with social, economic and political justice, to reduce inequalities in income and wealth and to prevent the "concentration of wealth and means of production to the common detriment."

By nominating themselves to be the planners, regulators and adjudicators, technical experts and managers of an industrializing India, the professional middle classes retained the primacy that they had enjoyed under the bureaucratic Raj. Their real interests were never served in a "socialist pattern of society." It was a pattern that existed only on paper. The real interests of the English-educated middle classes were served in a pattern of industrialization that established them as its directors.

But they could not do it alone. They needed British India's "merchant princes" as their junior partners. In 1956, these were still a handful of families – Tatas, Birlas, Dalmias, Singhanias, Goenkas, Thapars – that ruled India's great industrial houses: conglomerates, in modern terms. They were mostly Marwaris from Rajasthan and Gujarati-speaking Hindus, Jains and Parsis. Their operations were concentrated in Bombay and Calcutta. Discounted in the ideology which underlay the "socialist pattern of society" and relegated by it to second place in India's industrial future, the patresfamilias of India's great business families were by no means opposed to the general substance of

Nehru's Industrial Policy Resolution. Indeed, in their Bombay Plan of 1944, they suggested active roles for the government of independent India in planning, financing and managing industrial development. In an India that was overwhelmingly rural, agricultural and poor, only government could husband and economically allocate the resources necessary to the development of an industrial infrastructure. It was certainly beyond the capacities of Indian industrialists, and it was clearly unprofitable.

An import-substitution strategy of industrial development suited the great business houses. The Raj had protected British interests primarily and not theirs. They wanted an Indian government to protect them. However tardily, they had voted with their purses for the protective shield of a Congress *raj*, not for its prod to use their "comparative advantages" in competition with the Japanese on world markets. They had already gone to the British to shield them from the Japanese! No, they wanted the vast Indian market for themselves and for whatever they manufactured and without competition from abroad. And they got it. Perhaps the most ubiquitous symbol of their triumph was Hindustan Motor's venerable Ambassador: a Birla enterprise version of a 1950s Morris sedan and manufactured in India virtually unchanged for half a century.

The captains of Indian industry would certainly have preferred fewer government regulations on their activities and less government operation and control of industrial enterprises. In the 1960s, a few industrialists even funded and flirted with a short-lived "free enterprise" party, the Swatantra (freedom). As it turned out, however, it was they who profited most from the "license-permit *raj*" that they berated. In spite of government policies to prevent the monopolizing of manufacturing by established big business houses, they were advantaged vis-à-vis smaller and newer businesses in competing for permits to expand their operations and licenses to import. They were advantaged not only by their superior resources, but by the privileged access these provided to decision-making bureaucrats and politicians. By the mid-1970s, economic power and wealth in the large-scale private sector of Indian industry was probably no less concentrated in its 20 largest business houses than it had been two decades earlier.

The most notable growth in manufacturing from the mid-1970s, however, was not in big business, but in small-scale modern industries. Protected by government reservations to it of any number of product lines – more than 800 of them by 1990 – and by various tax incentives, the small-scale sector boomed. It produced such simple manufactures as food and clothing, and such complex ones as precision tools and electronic goods. In a decade and a half, the number of small-scale industrial firms quadrupled and the value of their manufactures increased sevenfold. Small industry employed about 80 percent of India's factory workers, accounted for more than 50 percent of the value added in India's manufacturing industries and about one-third of its exports. Textiles and jewelry, India's two major exports, were manufactured almost entirely by small businesses.

With what success did this regime of "Nehruvian socialism" effect the industrialization of India? It was least successful in realizing the social goals of the Industrial Policy Resolution. It had mixed success in itself, but less than other regimes in the industrialization of other third world economies. At once, it fostered bourgeois revolution and created an impasse to its progress.

A "socialist pattern of society" was the officially declared "objective of social and economic policy," including industrialization. That objective was never reached. Indeed, it was never seriously approached, unless government-orchestrated capitalism is taken to mean "socialism." "The economic foundations for increasing opportunities for gainful employment and improving living standards and working conditions for the mass of the people" were not laid. By 1992 fewer than one-fifth of Indian workers were employed in industry. Ironically, the limited opportunities for industrial employment were a consequence of the strategy of industrialization endorsed by Nehru's Industrial Policy Resolution. The capital and intermediate goods industries that were meant to develop behind the protective wall of import-substitution, and did, are inherently capital-intensive rather than labor-intensive. Small businesses were protected to be *the* mass employers, but they did not employ masses large enough to ameliorate India's chronic unemployment and underemployment. There was not an increase in employment by small businesses commensurate with their boom in productivity. After four decades of "Nehruvian socialism," the largest national populations of poor and illiterate people were still in India.

Once again, the achievements of Indian industrialization qua industrialization have been considerable. During three decades of economic planning, India's industrial economy grew in size. The number of public sector companies trebled from about 6,000 in 1961, and their paid-up capital grew from about Rs10 million to about Rs150 million. Large- and medium-size firms in the private sector grew in number from about 20,000 to more than 120,000, and their paid-up capital increased from less than Rs10 million to almost Rs300 million. Starting from a very low base, India's annual growth rate of GDP from manufacturing was about 7 percent until the drought years of the mid-1960s. But then for various reasons of supply and demand, over which economists contend, industrial growth declined to the very low rate of about 4.5 percent annually for almost two decades until the mid-1980s. From then, briefly, industrial production grew at an Indian record rate of about 8 percent annually. It was slowed by drought in 1986–87 and finally brought to a halt in 1991 by fiscal crisis. Save for Bangladesh, Sri Lanka,

Myanmar (Burma) and the Vietnam War-torn and strife-ridden countries of Southeast Asia, India had over the decades from 1960 the slowest industrial growth rate in Asia.

In general, public sector industries were disappointing and expensive industrializers. They used more capital to produce a smaller output than comparable firms in the Indian private sector. Private-sector firms, sheltered by import-substitution, were less efficient producers than many comparable firms abroad. To reduce these inefficiencies was one of the goals of the economic liberalization that was hesitantly begun by the Rajiv Gandhi government, particularly after its 1985 budget. Another goal was to open the Indian economy, if only by a crack, to the world: to give guarded encouragement to the export of Indian goods, to foreign direct investment, collaborative arrangements and joint-ventures with foreign firms. But while these liberalizing reforms reduced some of the worst excesses of "license-permit *raj*" – confiscatory tax rates which invited evasion and labyrinthine licensing procedures which inhibited enterprise and invited corruption – they left its bureaucratic structure largely intact. Buttressed by the interests that were vested in it, the structure impeded the reforms.[13]

Indian industry grew in its diversities. When the Nehru government announced its Industrial Policy Resolution, about 70 percent of India's manufacturing was in food and textile industries. By 1990, these were less than one-third of India's industrial output which had grown to include a complete range of capital, intermediate and consumer goods. The growth in size and manufacturing diversity of Indian industry, in both public and private sectors, was paralleled by a growth in size and diversity of its entrepreneurial and salaried workforce. There was certainly a diversification in the social backgrounds of successful entrepreneurs as a consequence of small business's exponential growth in manufacturing and the provision of services. Self-made and university-trained people of other than traditional business castes and families became small businessmen, and some of them were notably and exemplarily successful. The great business houses, even their newest and most spectacular rags-to-riches member, the Ambanis, were still largely from traditional business communities, and employed their sons and nephews – and occasionally daughters and nieces – in top management positions. However, as Indian industry from the mid-1980s edged toward international commerce, its demands for professionally trained managers and skilled technicians increased. They, like the technologically and scientifically trained personnel who made the diversification of Indian industry both possible and Indian, were from an increasingly wide variety of social backgrounds: including, particularly in the public sector, employees from Dalit castes and Other Backward Classes.

Indian industry became increasingly diversified in its sources of capital and technology. Indian share markets boomed during the 1980s. The number of stock exchanges doubled to 15. From fewer than 2 million investors in 1980, there were more than 10 million a decade later, and the value of all shares in the market increased from about Rs65 million in 1980 to about Rs600 million in 1990. Indian governments succeeded in tapping the resources of non-resident Indians (NRIs) for investment in India. Under investment schemes tailored for them, NRIs held deposits in India, in both rupee and foreign currency accounts, which increased from a value of about Rs13 billion in 1981 to about Rs110 billion a decade later.

From the mid-1980s, following India's first steps away from a closed economy, foreign firms increased their stake in India's industrialization. Through various collaborative arrangements between Indian and foreign firms, including the limited import of technology, foreign investment in India grew from about Rs32 million in 1973 to more than Rs1 billion in 1990. Companies owned by non-resident Indians became major collaborators with Indian firms. Non-resident Indians who returned to India brought with them technological skills and consumer goods expectations that they had learned abroad.

Government programs to disperse and encourage the dispersal of manufacturing to non-industrialized, "backward areas" and away from overcrowded cities were not notably successful. Still, in contrast to the all-but-complete concentration in 1947 of manufacturing in the "presidency" towns of British India – particularly Calcutta and Bombay – the geographical spread of Indian industry in 1990 was almost as remarkable as its growth in size and diversity. About 15 percent of India's national product was produced by manufacturing. Seven states and territories out of 32 did better than this, and in only seven small states and territories did manufacturing contribute less than 10 percent to their domestic products. The Indian industrial landscape of 1990 was dotted with large provincial cities: Bangalore in Karnataka, Ludhiana in Punjab, Saharanpur in Uttar Pradesh, Bhilwara and Kotah in Rajasthan, Vadodara (Baroda) and Bhavnagar in Gujarat. India's town and city dwellers, who were about 17 percent of its population at the time of independence, were in 1990 about 25 percent. The major growth was in large and medium-size cities, and it was driven largely by industrial development. An urban population emerged in independent India which reproduces itself, rather than depending on rural immigration for its reproduction.

India may look back on its decades of "Nehruvian socialism" as the state-orchestratrated, post-Independence establishment of bourgeois revolution: the more or less coincident development of capitalism and parliamentary democracy. This is, perhaps, obvious. But it will do no harm to bring its bits and pieces together here. As a group, the "merchant princes" of British India had no particular interest in parliamentary democracy. They were, however, committed in their own interests to planned industrialization as the junior partners of a government that was committed to parliamentary democracy and allied with landed farmers to whom government had gifted a stake in parliamentary democracy. The stake was soon integrated into provincial politics. Following land reform and the establishment of parliamentary democracy at the provincial level, landed farmers came quickly to dominate state politics. Government-sponsored and subsidized commercialization of agriculture and the participation of farmers in local industry and the white collar professions, brought them into the mainstream of capitalism's and parliamentary democracy's coincident development. The social spread of industrialization was furthered by a government-promoted and protected small-business sector. A bureaucracy subject to the direction of its demo-cratically elected political masters presided over the economy. Congress's one-party dominance kept bourgeois revolution in place. There was no "marriage of iron and rye" in India.

But, as bourgeois revolution proceded, it produced its vested interests. By and large, these were middle-class. Once again, though generally insufficient, the benefits of India's economic growth over four decades of a closed and controlled economy accrued particularly and with relative sufficiency to the middle classes. This is hardly surprising given that economic growth in India was (and is) an integral part of the more comprehensive growth of capitalism and parliamentary democracy in more or less tandem. Hardly surprising, too, but a cause for concern was that middle-class interests and the webs of inter-connections among them had become so vested in an inefficient, corrupt and inequitable economic system as to threaten the further development of industrial capitalism and, perhaps, parliamentary democracy.

Big business was protected from foreign competition, and small business was protected from big business. Farmers were protected in their enjoyment of direct and indirect government subsidies and of freedom from the burden of tax on their incomes. Thanks to labor union pressure, factory workers in the public and large-scale private sectors were guaranteed employ-ment, however "sick"-even-unto-death their factories.[14] Bureaucrats enjoyed their protected public sector employment and their private sector "rents." Politicians enjoyed their "rents" from both sectors, and the perks afforded to them by inefficient and unprofitable government-owned hotels and airlines.

Vested interests were inter-connected. The protection afforded by an import-substitution policy to Indian manufacturers raised the price of their goods. To compensate farmers for the high price of manufactured goods, government subsidized the supply of fertilizer, irrigation waters, electricity. The tariffs that kept the price of domestically manufactured goods high, were also a major source of government revenue. If tariffs were reduced, from which vested interest's pockets would the revenues come? The argument that revenues can be better used by efficient administration of the economy collided with the reality of an entrenched bureaucracy's interests in inefficient and circumambulatory administration. The black money earning of Indian industrialists was grease for the bureaucratic and political wheels within wheels on whose turnings the fortunes of almost every Indian enterprise depended. Less clear and immediate than its threat to capitalist development was the challenge posed to parliamentary democracy by this regime of vested interests. It takes no great predictive powers, however, to foresee a problematic future for a developing parliamentary democractic regime immobilized by vested interests and more responsive to them than to the popular expectations that have been aroused by limited development and *garibi hatao* propaganda.

The final break with "Nehruvian socialism" began in 1991. Exports increased during the 1980s. But imports increased more rapidly and substantially. India's balance of payments deficit trebled over the decade, as did its external debt. By the end of 1990, India had become one of the third world's major international debtors. It was desperately short of hard currency reserves to pay its debts and buy its necessary imports, particularly petroleum. Its credit rating was downgraded. For the first time in its history, India came close to defaulting on the repayments of its foreign debts. It was denied access to foreign commercial credit markets. It could borrow only against the security of its gold reserves. There was a net outflow of NRI deposits. India's internal debt, too, grew exponentially: largely as a result of excessive government borrowings to prop up an economy that was closed, inefficient, regulated and subsidized. Coincidently and exacerbated by the "oil shock" of the Gulf War, inflation climbed to 12 percent: in a country where half the population lived in relative to dire poverty. Prominent among those items whose prices rose most dramatically were "wage goods": items of ordinary consumption, mostly foodstuffs, the consumables of the poor. In January 1991, hat in hand, the government in Delhi asked the International Monetary Fund (IMF) for an emergency loan to rescue the Indian economy.

The shock of India's 1991 fiscal crisis, its depth and the fear of its adverse consequences for further economic growth and bourgeois well-being; the IMF's stringent loan conditions to "deflate, devalue, denationalize and deregulate";[15] the growing realization among Indian businessmen and bureaucrats that liberalization of its economy was Hobson's Choice for India – all this made certain that the issue would be seriously addressed by P. V. Narasimha Rao's Congress government, rather than being fiddled with or finessed. Initially led in its drive by a highly competent and determined finance minister, Manmohan Singh, and subsequently pursued by the finance ministers of Congress's successors at the Centre, India set off on an occasionally tortuous and politically roadblocked, but nonetheless irreversible, course toward economic liberalization.

The Indian economy in 2002 bears little resemblance to the Indian economy of a decade ago.[16] From the Union Budget of 1992–93 to today, and in contrast to what preceded the crisis of 1991, India's industrial economy and the wider economy that encompasses it have been subject to nothing short of radical liberalization. A rupee that was valued officially and overvalued was officially devalued in 1991 and its value nowadays is determined in the international foreign exchange market. The banking sector has been opened, cautiously, to privately owned Indian banks and branches of foreign-owned banks. Its monopoly of the insurance industry was ended by the Centre. The infamous regime of licenses and permits has been overthrown. But for intruding on the small sector's reservations, big business in India is as free as counterparts elsewhere to alter its product lines, merge, amalgamate, relocate, and so forth. The barriers that protected Indian big business from international competition and barred Indian consumers from purchasing foreign manufactures – tariffs, quantitative restrictions and exchange controls – have been brought down. Except in the manufacture of defense equipment and atomic energy and the provision of rail transport, the public sector has been opened to competition from private enterprise. The economy has been opened to foreign direct investment, not only in joint ventures with Indian firms but in the setting-up by foreign firms of their subsidiaries. Restrictions on the import of technologies have been scrapped.

Virtually from the dawn of liberalization and for a few years afterward, India's industrial economy boomed, and between 1994 and 1997 its national income grew at an unprecedented average annual rate of more than 7.5 percent. Then it stalled, and it remains stalled. The economist Kirit S. Parikh of the Indira Gandhi Institute of Development Research sums up "the proximate determinants" of its stalling: "deceleration in exports, industrial investment and consumer demand (due to low growth of rural incomes), coupled with moderate growth in money supply and credit and infrastructure bottlenecks."[17]

Of course, we cannot yet say whether the slowdown is merely a "decelaration" in an onward course, or whether it is the beginning of a reversion to a long-term, slightly elevated and slightly less dismal, "Hindu rate of growth." If it is not to be this, if the Indian industrial economy, the Indian economy as a whole and India and its citizens are to prosper into the decades ahead, Indian governments, of whatever composition, will have to pursue a number of "second generation reforms." There is a growing consensus across party lines, central and provincial, that this must be done; although, of course, there are differences among parties as to how and when and who should pick up the tab. "Pro-poor" posturing is an opposition prerogative. But what parties rail against in opposition, they are most likely to support or let pass in government. In government, the BJP abandoned the *"swadeshi"* – protectionist, under a good name – program of its *pariwar*; and, to its intense annoyance and frustration, the Atal Bihari Vajpayee government has followed in the reforming footsteps of the Congress government that preceded it. The vested interests of the old regime seem reconciled to reform, and have turned their attention to making the best of it.

In 2002, the government of India took some notable second generation steps away from its control of the economy. There were a handful of privatizations, most notably of hotels in a public-sector chain. Most restrictions were lifted on the storage and movement of food grains and other agricultural products. Price controls were ended on most pharmaceutical and petroleum products. Aiming to reduce its annual wage bill by the equivalent of approximately US$6.5 million, the Centre announced a new voluntary retirement scheme for government employees.[18] But much more remains to be done. And unlike some reforms of the first generation, they cannot be done by government fiat but only through some hard bargaining with vested interests.

As it was before 1991, so now the Government of India is chronically in debt. Its interest payments account for more than 70 percent of its tax revenues and 50 percent of all its revenues. Left to their own devices, many, if not most, state governments would be bankrupt. To do anything other than service its debts, New Delhi must borrow. By its excessive borrowing, the government reduces its capacity for public investment and inhibits private investment in industrial development by reducing the supply of money, increasing interest rates and putting a brake on further liberalization of the financial sector. For most of its revenue, the Centre relies on various indirect taxes such as customs and excise duties. Income tax evasion is widespread. From a population of almost a billion, only 8 million income tax returns were filed in 1995–96.[19] A broadening of the tax base – to include tax on agricultural income, for example – and determined tax-collection are likely to add to government revenues.

Savings on subsidies will reduce the demand for government revenues. Many of today's subsidies go neither to enhance productivity, nor to the poor, nor to the general good, but to middle-class welfare. For example, with no proportionate increase in agricultural production, government subsidization of fertilizer, which is of disproportionate benefit to the agricultural middle classes, increased tenfold in the decade to 1991 – twice the rate at which total government expenditure increased. Money spent on subsidies for the middle classes would be better used to provide reliable and adequate services for which they would be expected to pay. Money is needed to encourage invest-ment in new industries, such as power and information technology, and to provide infrastructure to further industrial growth: pipelines which carry petroleum at a substantially smaller cost than railways, urban transport for the county's rapidly growing big city population, roads to ameliorate the nightmare traffic, phone lines and cables to make the most of India's development as a major information technology producer. Subsidies to the poor ought to be closely targeted to the poor, aimed to relieve them of poverty and protected against "leakages." India's infrastructure for human resource development is woefully inadequate. It needs to save more on other things in order to spend more on rural schools and health services. It needs the will to ensure that teachers in public employment teach and doctors in public employment tend to their patients.

Privatization of some public sector enterprises and selling off shares of others – "disinvesting" – are ways of sourcing capital to retire public debt, broaden the government's tax base, and increase industry's productivity. But like "globalization," privatization and disinvestment ought to be approached selectively, intelligently and as a matter of public interest rather than ideologically as a "free trade" *mantra* or disingenuously to serve some private interests. Except when they serve the public good, businesses that remain in the public sector ought to be run as businesses, and neither as "rent" payers to politicians, nor sinecures for bureaucrats, nor featherbeds for labor, nor vote bank-nurturing milch cows. Since the abolition in 2001 of tariffs on consumer goods, the small business sector has been faced with competition from foreign big business. It cannot for long continue to be sheltered, by government policy, from the competition of Indian big business. What, then, for Indian small businesses? And there are other questions that need addressing: the "exit" from business of sick companies, the issues of labor productivity and job creation, the restructuring of the banking industry, and the further reduction of the government's wage bill. From these and other reforms, there will inevitably be those who lose out. Both for humane concerns and for the future course of bourgeois revolution, the losers will have to be provided with social security safety nets – pensions, super-annuation schemes, job-retraining.

International politics

There is a persistence in India's international politics. It is the persistance of mutual hostility with Pakistan over the issue of Kashmir. In 1948, the republics of India and Pakistan made their entrance onto the world's stage with a war in Kashmir. They fought a "short-sharp," inconclusive war over Kashmir in 1965. In 1971, they fought their war in what a victorious India helped to become Bangladesh. But for New Delhi, a major aim of the war was the fortification of its military and diplomatic position in Kashmir. India's victory in the east ended the possibility of its having to defend its claim to Kashmir on two fronts in future wars with Pakistan, increased the improbability of Pakistan's Chinese ally intervening in them, and facilitated the negotiation of a victor's peace in Kashmir – or so it seemed at the time. From 1989 to the present, an armed secessionist movement in Kashmir has gradually and tragically dragged ordinary Kashmiris, Hindu and Muslim, into the crossfire between an Indian army of occupation and militias of local and Pakistan-sponsored *mujahidin*.

When, in 1998, India tested a nuclear weapon, Pakistan soon followed with its test. Both New Delhi and Islamabad began to develop their missile capabilities: not to fight a nuclear war, however, but to deter the other from reinforcing by nuclear blackmail its position on Kashmir. In the "Kargil War" of 1999, Indian troops fought a series of pitched and bloody battles against a Pakistani corps of *mujahidin* and regular soldiers in disguise. Stealthily and in numbers, they had infiltrated across the de facto border – the "line of control" – that separates Pakistani from Indian Kashmir, threatened to interdict India's east-west route through Jammu and Kashmir and, more generally, to loosen New Delhi's hold on its restive state.

Both Islamabad and New Delhi have made the most of the United States' "war on terrorism." Pakistan has been rescued from bankruptcy by Washington's largesse in return for its services, once again, as a front-line state in an American war in Afghanistan. In the 1980s, the war, fought with Taliban soldiers, was against Soviet occupation. India has been the the beneficiary of on and off American pressure on Islamabad to curb the activities of its sponsored *mujahidin* in Kashmir and Washington's discovery of a need "... to strengthen military-to-military and defense ties ..." between it and New Delhi.[20]

On December 13, 2001, a suicide attack on the Indian parliament by *jihadis* based in Pakistan brought relations between the two countries to a boil and thrust into the headlines of the Western press the issue of Kashmir and the specter of a nuclear war on the subcontinent. Since then, war clouds have gathered and dispersed, gathered and dispersed. A million troops in battle gear line both sides of the India–Pakistan border. Across Kashmir's mountains, exchanges of artillery fire between Indian and Pakistani batteries intensify and subside, intensify and subside. *Mujahidin* detained by Pakistan on American orders are rebranded and gradually released. Indian politicians threaten. Pakistani polititicians are defiant. There is a set-piece quality to it all. Certainly, there is the possibility of it exploding into a nuclear disaster. But the probability, for now, is that the subcontinent's "balance of terror" is a deterrent to the big war that neither India nor Pakistan want. Meanwhile, Kashmiris in their thousands continue to suffer the "collateral damage" in the little war that engulfs them, and the issue of Kashmir is no closer to resolution than it was in 1948.

What story lies behind these dismal events? The Indian state of Jammu and Kashmir and the Pakistani dependency of Azad (free) Kashmir, were, before 1947, one of the Raj's premier princely states. Bordering India to the south and Pakistan to the west, the principality was ruled by a Hindu dynasty, but most of its subjects, concentrated in Kashmir, were Muslim and its surface connections were to what was to become Pakistan. Kashmir's maharaja might have acceded to either India or Pakistan. But he hesitated. In desperation, perhaps, or folly, he toyed with the idea of independence.[21] Pakistan joined the efforts of armed Muslim tribesmen to force the issue and depose the maharaja. Frightened, he acceded to India. Indian soldiers were airlifted to Kashmir where they fought a year's war with Pakistani soldiers, only yesterday members of the same army. The fighting ended with a cease-fire signed in January 1949 and negotiated through the United Nations.

The agreement left both sides in temporary control of those portions of Jammu and Kashmir that were occupied by their troops. About two-thirds of the area was held by India, including its core, the Vale of Kashmir. The Pakistanis held a corner in the northwest. Both parties agreed that the issue would be permanently resolved and the future of Jammu and Kashmir decided by a plebiscite of its people. But subsequently, time and again, and always to Pakistan's infuriation, India found grounds to renege on its agreement. A plebiscite has never been held in Jammu and Kashmir. Had it been, it is most unlikely that Jammu and Kashmir would now be a state in the Indian Union. Whenever taken, the votes of its Muslim majority would almost certainly have been either to join their coreligionists in Pakistan or, if given the option, to become an independent country. Either way, in New Delhi's estimation, the consequences would probably have been disastrous for India. A hostile Pakistani government in Kashmir would hold hostage the Himalayan headwaters of the Indus River's tributaries which irrigate Punjab's agriculture. The southern borders of a hostile Jammu and Kashmir, well below the Himalaya's sheltering peaks, would be dangerously close to the Gangetic Plain, northern India's heartland.

But, the direst consequences anticipated by New Delhi of a Muslim electorate voting to separate itself from India would be its shock to the secular legitimacy of the Indian Union, and following dangerously from that, to communal relations – already bad enough – between India's Hindus and Muslims. Would a vote by Kashmiri Muslims to quit India not affirm the argument of Muslim middle-class nationalists from Sir Saiyid Ahmad Khan to Mohammad Ali Jinnah to Islamabad's propagandists that the subcontinent is really home to "two nations"? Would it not give credence to Pakistan's contention, inherited from the Muslim League of British India and broadcast throughout the subcontinent and to the world, thus: if ordinary Muslims are given the choice, would they choose to live in a Muslim country and not in some Indian "secular" sham that was really a Hindu *raj*? And if Kashmiri

Muslims made this choice, would it not give credence to the accusation of Hindu revivalists that India's Muslims – and not only in Kashmir – were, at best, reluctant residents in the Republic and, at worst, a Pakistani fifth-column: not merely a religious minority but a subversive presence? And if such an accusation were widely accepted by Hindus, and they denied the reality of equal citizenship to their Muslim neighbors, what would be the consequences for India's survival as a secular state? For India's survival as a state?

In Ayodhya's shadow, now more than ever, the fear of a plebiscite going wrong in Kashmir is that it would release both spontaneous and instigated, widespread and murderously destructive spates of anti-Muslim pogroms across northern Indian. The fear that underlies that fear is that these pogroms would turn into communal warfare, and that it would tear India apart: on the one side, embolden *Hindutva*'s violent, lunatic fringe and, on the other, breed and let loose a generation of home-grown *jidahis*. Secessionist movements in other parts of India would be encouraged, the Union and its parliamentary democracy would face destruction, the middle classes' newly revived hopes for economic development would be dashed, India would be reduced to the shameful status of some failed third world state.

Given the current state of communal relations in India – the slaughter of innocents in Gujarat is only the worst case currently – these fears are not unfounded. They cannot be dismissed as a mere pretext to avoid holding (and losing) a plebiscite in Kashmir. Kashmir is a tinderbox not only in relations between India and Pakistan but in communal relations in India. The *pariwar* is implacably opposed to a plebiscite in Kashmir. The custodians of *Hindu Rashtra* (the Hindu nation) will never surrender, no matter the number of Muslim votes, the Himalayan homeland of the Kashmiri Pandits,[22] the abode of the Lord Siva and the sacred sites and pilgrimage places associated with Him. The *pariwar* is the strange bedfellow of the champions of secularism among their fellow Hindus. One affirming the legitimacy of sectarian nationalism, the other denying it. So, nowadays, the suggestion of a plebiscite confronts a militantly aggressive Hinduism as well as an unmovably defensive secularism. A handful of Kashmiri Muslims – now about 6.5 million – will not be permitted to determine the Indian Union's fate. There has not been and there will be no plebiscite in Kashmir.

Neither is there likely to be a negotiated settlement of the Kashmir issue between India and Pakistan, nor – except through accident or miscalculation – a large-scale war between them, nuclear or otherwise. New Delhi's entrenched position is that there is nothing to negotiate, except perhaps a de jure border between India's Jammu and Kashmir and Pakistan's Azad Kashmir. New Delhi will talk about Kashmir, but it will always say the same thing. Jammu and Kashmir is a state of the Indian Union. Its status as such is not negotiable: not with Pakistan, not with Kashmiris and not with the "international community." Before September 11, 2001, and since,

Pakistan's plea after plea for international mediation of the Kashmir issue have invariably fallen on deaf ears. The United States is not interested. Nor is the United Nations, among whose sovereign states, secessionism – negotiated or otherwise – has never been a popular cause.

By a vote of its constituent assembly, Jammu and Kashmir became an Indian state in 1957, and its statehood has been popularly affirmed in the regular exercise by Kashmiris of the same democratic rights enjoyed by all Indians. Or so the argument from New Delhi goes. In reality, Kashmir has been under Indian paramilitary occupation for most of its history in the Union, and its parliamentary democracy has been managed from New Delhi. It has not lost a square centimeter of India to secessionism. It oppposes secessionist movements – in Punjab, the northeast, Kashmir – with repressive force. The right to secede is not a democratic right in India.

As for war: India is the industrial and military power on the subcontinent. It is far less dependent on foreign suppliers for its military hardware than is Pakistan. India spends four times as much on defense as Pakistan, its army is twice as large, as is its air force and its navy. Between these and their Pakistani counterparts, there are no significant qualitative differences, either in materiel or personnel. Pakistan is unlikely to start a war that it is likely to lose. The costs of defeat would be high, if not catastrophic. Even in peacetime, Pakistan barely manages. India is unlikely to start a war that it need not fight. Its only quarrel with Pakistan is over Kashmir, and India's hold on Kashmir is secure. Pakistan's *mujahidin* can worry it, but cannot pry it loose. The worry is bothersome, but tolerable. India would like to be rid of it, of course. But the worry is more tolerable – less costly and more predictable – than going to war with a politically unstable, nuclear-armed Pakistan. India will try, as it has in the past, with money and politics but little success, to reconcile Kashmiri Muslims to living in India. But I have no doubt, that if need be, and into the indefinite future, India will continue to occupy Kashmir, ignore the wishes of Kashmiris not to live in India, kill *mujahidin*, and suffer the loss of paramilitary policemen.

For the first four decades of India's and Pakistan's independence, their ongoing quarrel over Kashmir conflated with the Cold War. Nehru positioned India. It was "non-aligned." It would have no Cold War alliances with either of the antagonists, the United States or the Soviet Union. In general, non-alignment may be understood as a moral and rational position for third parties in a Cold War between nuclear armed superpowers. Or it might be understood in the spirit of George Washington's farewell address as a general prescription for serving one's own interests by remaining aloof from the quarrels of others and profiting from their distress. And, of course, it may be understood as both. They are not mutually exclusive. Nehru understood them as both. And certainly, specifically, he understood that the position he wanted for India on the subcontinent, its dominant power, was contingent on the Cold War's superpowers being kept aloof from the subcontinent's quarrels.

Doubtless, Pakistan's politicians understood this as well. But the conclusions that they drew from it were diametrically opposed to Nehru's. Their fear was that India would become the subcontinent's dominant power. The Congress politicians who had agreed to Pakistan's birth seemed intent on strangling it in its cradle. New Delhi withheld Pakistan's fair share of the empire's cash assets and government and military supplies. Mahatma Gandhi, who grieved at Pakistan's birth, went on his final penitential fast to pressure the Indian government into treating Pakistan fairly, into sticking to its agreement. The Congress government was suspected by Pakistan's founders, and not without reason, of regarding their new republic as "nothing but a temporary secession of territories from India that were soon to be reabsorbed."[23] Only let the British quit.

The Cold War was Pakistan's opportunity. Faced with a hostile India, Pakistan could not compete in the non-alignment game of negotiating its interests at equidistance from the Cold War's superpowers. To keep from being dominated and even reabsorbed by India, Pakistan would have to be aligned. It would have to bring the Cold War into the subcontinent's quarrels: into the balance that otherwise tipped so decisively in favor of India. In the 1950s, Washington was focused on "containing international communism." America wanted allies on the periphery of the great, mythic Sino-Soviet land mass and it paid handsomely for their services with diplomatic, economic and military assistance. In 1954 and 1955, Pakistan joined the United States' SEATO and CENTO alliances. It signed a mutual defense treaty with Washington in 1959. It made available to the American Central Intelligence Agency a Pakistani airbase from which CIA pilots took off on reconnaisance missions over the Soviet Union. From 1954 to 1965, Pakistan received from Washington more than a billion dollars worth of military hardware.[24] "The only guarantee of our survival," wrote one Pakistani scholar, "was military aid from the United States."[25]

To the generals and bureaucrats who ruled Pakistan, their fear of India and their claim to Kashmir were closely related. In a sense, Pakistan's insistence on a plebiscite in Kashmir, its claim to an irredenta in the Himalayas, was the offensive thrust of a defensive strategy. New Delhi understood correctly that Pakistan had become an American ally to support this thrust, for whatever ostensible Cold War reasons the alliance had been offered. Pakistan's alignment imposed a qualification on India's non-alignment. India moved closer to the Soviet Union. It became India's major supplier of arms and its champion in the United Nations and elsewhere on the issue of Kashmir. India reciprocated with its reluctance to censure Soviet military ventures:

from its suppression of the Hungarian revolution in 1956 to its invasion of Afghanistan in 1979. Thus was the issue of Kashmir incorporated into the Cold War and the Cold War incorporated into the issue of Kashmir.

Cold War lines were never as clear as its ideologues and propagandists proclaimed them to be. In spite of its non-alignment, and fulminations against it by American politicians – at Armageddon, who is not with us is against us – India was always recognized in Washington as the subcontinent's most important country. By the 1960s, Cold War lines, on the subcontinent as elsewhere, were being blurred by open hostility between the Soviet Union and China. India's non-alignment seemed vindicated, at least for the moment. In spite of its quarrel with the Soviet Union, the United States joined it in providing India with diplomatic and military assistance during and after its disastrous border war with China in 1962. Islamabad was outraged. That, on top of Washington's unwillingness to give its clear support to its loyal ally's position on Kashmir!

Without abandoning its ties to the United States, Pakistan turned to the communist government in Beijing for its help against India. An enemy's enemy is a friend. Presumably, China shared India's understanding of Pakistan's primary motivation for becoming an American ally. After its war with China, India's two most threatening foreign policy concerns merged into one: a Sino–Pakistani axis on the subcontinent. It troubled India's defeated and demoralized army with the specter of a future war on two fronts. One, across the borders of West Pakistan and China into Rajasthan, Punjab and Kashmir; the other, across the borders of East Pakistan and China into the short and narrow corridor that connects India's northeastern wing with the rest of the Union.

When, in 1965, war finally came, however, it was a much less dramatic, more modest affair: a limited conflict between India's and Pakistan's armies that began in the Rann of Kach and ended, predictably, in Kashmir. China supported Pakistan with arms and anti-Indian invective, but did not join the battle directly. A truce between the belligerents, which more or less restored the status quo ante, was mediated by the Soviet Union at Tashkent in 1966. Afterwards, Islamabad resumed its ties to the United States which had been more or less neutral in favor of Pakistan during its second war with India and regarded Pakistan still as useful in the Cold War. At the same time, Washington made some heavy-handed use of its intelligence agencies and the levers of its aid programs to intrude into India's domestic affairs and influence its foreign policy. The issue of "neocolonialism" raised its head in New Delhi. The complementarity of Soviet and Indian interests vis-à-vis the Sino–Pakistani entente was undisturbed by the 1965 war, and New Delhi renewed its special relationship with its most steadfast and unobtrusive supporter.

Moscow had long accepted and encouraged India's claim to being the dominant power in South Asia. As a consequence of the Bangladesh War in 1971, India seemed to have achieved its dominance. The Indian army had mobilized and trained a *mukti bahini*, an irregular "liberation army," of former East Pakistani soldiers, and finally led them in a successful, lightning war of secession. Under India's aegis, East Pakistan became the independent republic of Bangladesh in 1971. Pakistan lost its entire eastern wing and more than half its population. While this was happening, US president Richard Nixon and secretary of state Henry Kissinger were busily engaged in arranging the United States' rapprochement with China. Pakistan's military government was their intermediary. Nixon "tilted" American foreign policy toward the support of Pakistan, and presumably as an appropriate gesture, dispatched a naval task force led by the *USS Enterprise* to the Bay of Bengal. China, too, made the appropriate gestures in support of Pakistan, but no more. If the objective of these gestures was to intimidate Prime Minister Indira Gandhi, they failed. "Madam" was not easily intimidated. Presumably, her courage in this instance was fortified, in part, by the Indo-Soviet treaty of friendship and cooperation, signed in 1971 before India invaded East Pakistan. It was not quite a mutual security pact, but close enough. It is an irony of India's non-alignment that it should have produced for it one of the most durable and unwavering alignments in post-Second World War international politics.

After the Bangladesh War, the subcontinent's politics seemed to tilt decisively in India's direction. A hostile Pakistan had disappeared from India's eastern flank to be replaced by a poor, war-ravished neighbor which owed its independence to New Delhi. Only Pakistan's western province re-mained, its total population no larger than India's Muslim minority, its economy in tatters, its army defeated, deserted by its great friends in Washington and Beijing. In defeat, Pakistan turned for assistance and acceptance to the Muslim west: to the Shah of Iran and friendly Arab countries. It seemed to turn away from the subcontinent and the futility of trying to redeem Kashmir. Kashmir seemed irredeemably India's. In 1975, Mrs Gandhi offered the chief ministership of Jammu and Kashmir to India's long-serving and most famous political prisoner, head of the proscribed Kashmiri Plebiscite Front, champion of self-determination for Kashmiris, the Lion of Kashmir, Sheikh Mohammad Abdullah. He accepted the offer. Implicitly, he accepted that there would be no plebiscite. The issue of Kashmir seemed closed.

Pakistan hoped to reopen it from 1979. For its services as Washington's front-line state in its proxy war with the Soviet Union in Afghanistan, Pakistan was rewarded with an arsenal of some of America's best military hardware. China also contributed, particularly in helping Pakistan to develop its "Islamic [nuclear] Bomb." If not redressed, the South Asian military balance of power that tipped so decidedly to India's advantage after the Bangladesh War was readjusted. Once again, Islamabad accomplished this by adding to its large and competent military establishment the military resources of countries outside the region, but with interests in it that can be served by Pakistan. But neither Washington nor Beijing offered Islamabad any real diplomatic support or encouragement on the issue of Kashmir.

In the decade or so after its easy defeat by China in 1962, India made costly and strenuous efforts to improve its army. Its performances in Kashmir in 1965 and in East Pakistan in 1971 were creditable. The reinforcement of its defenses on China's borders was formidable. In its next war with the Chinese, the Indian Army would be a well-matched opponent. To strengthen its defenses, India annexed its Himalayan protectorate, Sikkim, in 1975. The year before, as a message to China particularly, India exploded a nuclear "device" in the Rajasthan desert. An uneasy peace prevailed between the two countries. The borders over which they fought have never been settled de jure by treaty, but they seem to have been settled de facto by inaction, time, an exchange of prime ministerial visits and a return to diplomatic business as usual. There is still the occasional exchange of angry words. But neither side is willing to fight for territory that it does not have, and both sides have under their control the territory that they most want.

The Indians have the area south of the Tibetan-Chinese border in Arunachal Pradesh, formerly the North East Frontier Agency. That territory, like Sikkim, is incorporated in India's defenses of its politically restive and militarily vulnerable northeastern wing. The Chinese have the Aksai Chin plateau in northern Kashmir, more than 30,000 square kilometers of barren waste, through which they have built a military highway connecting their two restive provinces of Xinjiang and Tibet. The plateau is of no particular interest to India, except that it is in Kashmir. And for that reason, primarily, India will not negotiate a border settlement based on lines of control, in spite of China's willingness to do so. To every government of the Indian Union, the territorial integrity of the state of Jammu and Kashmir is non-negotiable. New Delhi wants no precedent set for negotiations over the division of Kashmir. Not because China holds a corner of it, but because Pakistan insists that all of it is negotiable.

The recent incursions of the Chinese navy into the Bay of Bengal from its bases in Burma attracts wary watching from New Delhi. But, in general, China is less a source of worry to India nowadays than the yardstick against which India measures its international ambitions. Initially, not Pakistan but China inspired India's nuclear testing in 1998 and its subsequent development of its missile capability. To be a great power of the second division, a predominant regional power, India must measure up to China, particularly in its military capabilities. The standard of measurement is costly and depletive of resources that might be better used domestically. But, however regretably, in this best of all possible worlds it is still a standard, and not only in Asia. So, most of the competition between India and China these days is not so much with one another but against a common measure.

Like China, India has been developing its blue-water navy. In spite of Pakistan's unwillingness to acknowledge it, India has been assuming a "managerial role"[26] in South Asian affairs. The Indian army's "peace keeping" enterprise in Sri Lanka from 1987 to 1989 produced a debacle, but it delivered New Delhi's message: If there is to be foreign intervention into the domestic affairs of South Asian countries, it will not be by Pakistan or its friends or anyone else, but by India. India intervened to frustrate a coup d'état in the small Indian Ocean state of Maldives in 1988. It maintains a presence in Nepal's domestic and international politics with regard to its "Maoist" guerrillas and its relations with China. Since September 11, 2001, Washington has taken a new interest in India. Once again, Pakistan has been rewarded by the Americans for its services as its front-line state in a war in Afghanistan. But it has received no encouragement from Washington on the issue of Kashmir, only pressure to pull out its *mujahidin*. It has been forgiven for its nuclear testing of 1998, as has India; and General Pervez Musharraf has been honored for his contributions to Washington's "war on terrorism," forgiven for his coup of 1999 and his military dictatorship. But Washington's perception of a linked relationship between India and Pakistan has been de-linked. Pakistan has been a friend in need, and suitably rewarded for its friendship. India is a major power in Asia. Its new link in Washington's, no less than in New Delhi's, calculations is to China.

Epilogue

In May 2002, *jihadis* patronized by Pakistan executed a murderous attack on an Indian military camp in Jammu. My discussion, above, of India's international politics was written before the attack and is unchanged afterward. Afterward, throughout the northern hemisphere's spring, tensions on the border between India and Pakistan escalated. India appeared ready to attack *jihadi* base camps in Pakistan's Azad Kashmir. The subcontinent's unfriendly neighbors appeared ready for a war that threatened to culminate in a nuclear cataclysm. But in this, as in other things, we distinguish between appearances and reality.

Except through inadvertence, the reality, I think, was that war on the subcontinent was no more likely after May than it had been before. The initiative was always with India, and I do not believe that India wanted another war with Pakistan. What did India want? We gain little insight from the ominous and repeated reminders of our politcians and media commentators that India and Pakistan had thrice since 1948 fought wars. We understand more by recalling that the United States had twice since 1948 frustrated India's ambition for subcontinental dominance and closure on the issue of Kashmir. Again, Pakistan was Washington's front-line state in the Cold War: in the "containment" alliances of the 1950s and 1960s and against the Soviet Union in Afghanistan in the 1980s. For these services to the "free world," Pakistan's military establishment was generously rewarded, and the American alliance became for Pakistan its make-weight in the balance of subcontinental politics. From 2001, now in another American war, the complementarity of Pakistani and American interests seemed once again destined to disserve Indian interests. Once again, the fortunes of war had brought the alliance of a great friend to Pakistan's defiance of India's hold on Kashmir. And a decade of guerilla warfare there had given some credence and moral standing to Pakistan's contentions that Kashmir was a disputed territory and only international mediation could resolve the dispute.

India's sabre-rattling, familiar enough to the Pakistanis, was tuned up in 2002 in order to be heard in Washington. It carried these messages, at least. First, if, as President Bush proclaims (or proclaimed), the United States' "war against terrorism" is unambiguous – everywhere against not only "terrorists" but countries that sponsor them – then Pakistan must be held to account by its great friend for Islamabad's well-known sponsorship of "cross border terrorism" into Kashmir. Second, if Washington makes no serious effort to halt this "terrorism," then India would have to look to its own interests. At the very least, this would involve diverting Pakistani troops from serving the American pursuit of al-Qaeda and Taliban remnants in Afghanistan to reinforcing the line against a threatened Indian advance into Azad Kashmir. At most, if war ensued between India and Pakistan – even with conventional weapons – it could scuttle the whole American "war against terrorism" in Afghanistan. Finally, and in sum, Pakistan may from time to time be useful to the United States and be suitably compensated for its usefulness. But not to India's detriment. Not to the detriment of Jammu and Kashmir's status as a state in the Indian Union.

In its own interests, no less than in the interest of the subcontinent's return to its uneasy peace, it was important for Washington to hear these messages from New Delhi. It was more important than for New Delhi to listen to gratuitous warnings from American officials about the perils of nuclear warfare, or to listen again to new variations on old proposals that India has repeatedly rejected over half a century for third-party mediation on the issue of Kashmir, or even to be welcomed by Washington as a superpower of the second division and its ally against "terrorism" on America's South and Central Asian fronts. Washington relayed New Delhi's messages to General Musharraf and apparently insisted that they be heard by him and attended to. In reply, India's sabre-rattling has been tuned down, but not off.

Sabre-rattling serves domestic as well as international politics, and not only in India. Facing inward, the BJP government in New Delhi hopes that its aggressive reassertion of India's sovreignty in Jammu and Kashmir will re-endorse its *Hindutva* credentials with a stamp of patriotism. Facing outward, the BJP government is heir to a half-century of government policy. It has not changed. India will never surrender Kashmir. It knows that Musharraf's control over the *jihadis* is limited. He cannot end their activies in Kashmir, but he can to some degree limit them; and may do so: not at New Delhi's insistence, certainly, but at Washington's. New Delhi is willing to accept a reduction in "cross border terrorism." It does not expect a cessation. After more than half a century, India is used to holding Kashmir by paramilitary and military force. Only, it would prefer to reduce that force. It is biding time. A half-century is no great stretch of time on the subcontinent. It may be that in time, Kashmiri Muslims, so wearied and wounded by war, may chose – if not in the next election then in the ones after or after that – to live in India rather than on a battlefield. It may be that in time, General Musharraf will be succeeded in office by a civilian government. Unlike the *jihadis* and the generals, the civilian members of Pakistan's dominant-class coalition have no particular interest in Kashmir. Their inclination is to park the issue, and get on with the business of business. Many of them understand the wastefulness and futility, the disservice to domestic order in Lahore and Karachi, of the army's use of *jihadis* to bleed India into surrender in Kashmir. India has not and will not be bled into surrender. Over half a century India has prospered, built a viable nation-state and held its grip on Kashmir. Pakistan has neither prospered nor built a viable nation-state, nor gained in any way from keeping the Kashmir issue alive. Ironically, it is Pakistan as a nation-state, not India, that has been bled the most by Kashmir.

Appendix One

Major political events in the related histories of British imperialism and Indian nationalism, 1858–1947

1858 The Mutiny defeated, imperial rule is directly assumed by the British government. Queen Victoria's proclamation promises Indians impartial admittance to the empire's governing bureaucracies.

1869 The opening of the Suez Canal facilitates British rule in India and commerce between the subcontinent and Britain.

1875 Two portentous events in Hindu–Muslim relations: the foundation of the major Hindu revivalist organization in northern India, the Arya Samaj; and Saiyid Ahmad Khan's establishment of his Muhammadan Anglo-Oriental College.

1883 The Indian government's withdrawal of the Ilbert Bill is widely interpreted by the educated middle classes as a concession to Anglo-Indian racism.

1885 The first meeting of the Indian National Congress: initially an interest group of the, primarily Hindu, professional middle classes.

1892 The Indian Council Act begins the history of participation in central and provincial assemblies of wise, wealthy and well-born Indians.

1900 The Punjab Alienation of Land Act favors Muslims, in general, and disfavors urban Hindus, in particular, in an important British Indian province.

1905 The viceroy, Lord Curzon, partitions Bengal into separate Hindu- and Muslim-majority provinces, thus providing Congress with its first nationalist cause célèbre and provoking the first major trauma in Hindu–Muslim relations under the Raj.

1906 The All-India Muslim League is founded in Dhaka by landlords and haut bourgeois.

1907 The Tata Iron and Steel Company is established at Jamshedpur, in what is now Jharkhand state.

1909 The Morley–Minto Reforms expand considerably the representation of Indians in provincial assemblies, and establish the precedent for separate communal representation by reserving a "weighted" number of constituencies for Muslims.

1911 The partition of Bengal is annulled.

1916 The Lucknow Pact between the Congress and the Muslim League recognizes Hindus and Muslims as separate communities in an inter-communal nationalism.

1919 Under its scheme of "dyarchy," the Montagu–Chelmsford Reforms enable elected Indians to hold minor ministries in provincial governments. A Chamber of Princes is created by the reforms to "balance" the growing political assertiveness of the professional middle classes by encouraging the princes to represent their corporate interests.
   The Jallianwallahbagh Massacre takes place in Amritsar.

1920–22 Mahatma Gandhi becomes the Congress supremo. A troubled and short-lived alliance between the Muslim Khilafat and the Congress/Hindu Non-cooperation movements begins and ends.

1923 The Government of India sets tariffs to protect selected Indian industries – too little, too late.

1927–28 The British government in London sends the Simon Commission to India to recommend further constitutional reforms. In protest against it having no Indian member, an All-Parties Conference drafts a constitution for India. It rejects the efforts of the All-India Muslim League's representative, M. A. Jinnah, to provide special representation for Muslims.

1930 Gandhi initiates civil disobedience with his Salt Satyagraha.

1932 In protest against the British government's "communal award," which provided "Harijans" with separate representation in provincial assemblies, Gandhi begins a "fast unto death" and ends it when B. R. Ambedkar reluctantly agrees to the "Poona Pact" compromise.

1937 After elections held under the India Act of 1935, Congress forms ministries in 8 of 11 provinces. The Muslim League polls poorly in Muslim constituencies. Congress does even worse.

1939 Congress's provincial ministries resign in protest against the viceroy's declaring India at war without consulting any Indian politicians. Jinnah declares it a "Day of Deliverance."

1940 "Pakistan Resolution" passed by the All-India Muslim League.

1942–44 Congress rejects the Cripps Mission's formula for post-war Indian government and calls for a mass civil disobedience campaign to force Britain to "quit India." All of Congress's "high command," including Gandhi and Nehru, are jailed. During the Second World War there is considerable anti-British violence in India. The Bengali firebrand and former Congress president, Subhas Chandra Bose, organizes the Indian *National* Army among Indian POWs held by the Japanese to fight against the British Indian Army.

1944 The patresfamilias of India's leading business houses agree in their "Bombay Plan" to an independent Indian government-led plan for post-War industrialization.

1946–47 In provincial elections, "Pakistan" sweeps the field in Muslim constituencies for the Muslim League. The Muslim League and Jinnah sit as negotiators, apparently equal to Congress and the British, in determining the subcontinent's future.

The London government's Cabinet Mission formula for an Indian confederation is accepted by Jinnah but rejected by the Congress.

Communal violence engulfs northern India.

There is a mutiny in the Indian navy and popular demonstrations against the treason trials of Indian National Army soldiers.

The newly elected Labour Party government in Britain, led by Clement Attlee, sends Lord Louis Mountbatten as viceroy to negotiate an end to the Raj.

Independence for India and Pakistan and a violent beginning of their separate careers as independent states.

Appendix Two

Major political events in the history of the Indian Union, 1947–2002

1947 Indian independence. Congress led by Jawaharlal Nehru becomes India's ruling party. The subcontinent is partitioned. An independent Pakistan, of two wings on India's east and northwest borders, comes into being.

1948 War in Kashmir. Mahatma Gandhi is assassinated by a Hindu militant.

1950 The secular, quasi-federal constitition of the Republic of India is promulgated.

After the death of Sardar Vallabhbhai Patel, Nehru becomes head of the Congress Party organization as well as prime minister.

1952 First general elections for parliament and state legislative assemblies establish the pattern of Congress's "one-party dominance."

States begin to pass and enforce land reform legislation

1953 The formation of "linguistic states" begins with the creation of a Telegu-speaking Andhra Pradesh.

1955 The first of the major Hindu Code bills becomes law. The Marriage Act.

1957 India's planned industrialization begins in earnest under the Second Five Year Plan.

In the second general elections, a Communist Party government is elected in Kerala.

1959 Nehru uses constitutional provision of "President's Rule" to dismiss Kerala's elected government.

Panchayati raj institutions make their first appearance.

1961 The Indian Army "liberates" Goa from Portuguese rule.

1962 The third general elections confirm Congress's dominance.

War with China.

1964 Jawaharlal Nehru dies; he is succeeded by Congress stalwart, Lal Bahadur Shastri.

1965 "Short-sharp" war with Pakistan. A truce mediated by the Soviet Union in 1966.

1966 Lal Bahadur Shastri dies. To succeed him, the Congress "syndicate" chooses Nehru's daughter, Indira Gandhi.

A Sikh-majority state, Punjab, carved from northern districts of existing Hindu-majorty Punjab.

1967 Congress's majority in Parliament reduced in fourth general election, and its one-party dominance begins to disappear from the states.

Short-lived rural insurgencies begun in West Bengal, Andhra Pradesh and Kerala by Naxalite communists.

Green Revolution begun.

1969 Major commercial banks nationalized.

1971 Bangladesh War. With Indian military assistance, East Pakistan secedes to become Bangladesh.

Indira Gandhi finally routs the "syndicate" and wins decisive control over the Congress Party with her resounding victory in the fifth parliamentary elections.

1972 In the state legislative assembly elections, Congress polls well but fails to re-establish its one-party dominance in the states.

1975 India annexes Sikkim. It becomes a state in the Union.

In response to a threat to her regime, Indira Gandhi proclaims an "emergency" which effectively suspends parliamentary democracy.

1977 In the sixth parliamentary elections, India elects its first non-Congress government at the Centre. Morarji Desai, a former member of the

Congress's "syndicate," becomes prime minister at the head of a patchwork of factions called the Janata Party.

1980 The Janata Party disintegrates and Indira Gandhi leads the Congress back to power at the Centre.

1981 Indira Gandhi's younger son and political heir, Sanjay, is killed in an airplane accident and is succeeded at his mother's side by elder brother Rajiv.

1984 In response to its use as an armory and sanctuary by Sikh secessionists, the Golden Temple in Amritsar – the Sikhs' holiest of holy places – is stormed and damaged by Indian troops.

Mrs Gandhi is assassinated by Sikh members of her bodyguard. A brief but murderous anti-Sikh pogrom follows in Delhi.

Rajiv Gandhi leads the Congress to election victory at the Centre in the eighth parliamentary elections.

1985–86 The Rajiv Gandhi Congress government makes some tentative moves toward liberalizing the Indian economy.

Parliament passes the Muslim Women's Act which overturns the Supreme Court's decision in the Shah Bano case and, in effect, passes the Muslim *shar'iah* rules on divorce into Indian statute law.

1987 The Bofors scandal surfaces, casting allegations of corruption against the Rajiv Gandhi family and government, and bringing to prominence the dissident in the Rajiv cabinet, V. P. Singh.

1989–90 A National Front of non-Congress parties wins the ninth parliamentary elections. V. P. Singh becomes prime minister. He courts controversy and defeat by leading parliament to enact the 1980 Mandal Commission's recommendations that positions in central government services be reserved for OBCs.

The BJP's leader, A. K. Advani, brings the Ramjanmabhumi Mandir-Babri Masjid controversy and his party into national prominence with his *rath yatra* – chariot ride – across northern India.

The BJP quits the National Front and brings down the V. P. Singh government.

1991 Rajiv Gandhi is assassinated by a Sri Lankan Tamil suicide bomber. Congress forms a government at the Centre under P. V. Narasimha Rao. In response to India's near-bankruptcy and pressure from the IMF, the government begins in earnest to liberalize the Indian economy.

1992–93 Ayodhya's Babri Masjid is demolished by Hindu militants. Communal rioting follows across towns of northern India and in Mumbai.

1996–98 The Narasimha Rao Congress government is defeated in the eleventh parliamentary elections. BJP's Atal Behari Vajpayee becomes prime minister briefly. After a vote of no confidence in his government, it is succeded by a short-lived United Front coalition. It falls when Congress withdraws its support.

Vajpayee forms a BJP-led coalition government at the Centre after the twelfth parliamentary elections in 1998.

India conducts underground nuclear tests.

1999 The Vajpayee government is returned to power in the thirteenth parliamentary elections.

"Kargil War" with Pakistan.

2001 An attack on the Indian parliament by Pakistan-connected *jihadis*. An armed stand-off between Pakistan and India follows.

2002 The BJP loses and Congress and provincial parties gain in state elections. A government headed by Mayawati of the Dalit-based BSP comes to power in Uttar Pradesh.

Months of communal rioting sweeps through the towns of Gujarat.

Notes

Introduction

1 For this and all subsequent references to bourgeois revolution, see Barrington Moore, Jr., *Social Origins of Dictatorship and Democracy*, (Boston: Beacon Press, 1966).

2 Tata Services Limited, Department of Economics and Statistics, *Statistical Outline of India 1999–2000* (Mumbai 1999), table 241.

3 World Bank, *World Development Indicators 2000* (Washington, DC, 2001), pp. 66–69. The relevant survey was held in 1997.

4 Tata, *Statistical Outline 1999–2000*, tables 18–20, 73, 79–80.

5 "The New Economy," *India Today*, February 19, 2001, pp. 32–35.

6 *The Times of India Online*, February 23, 2001.

7 For example see, World Bank, *India: Reducing Poverty, Accelerating Development* (New Delhi: Oxford University Press, 2000).

8 Ibid., p. 23.

9 Not a novel, but Mira Nair's delightful film of 2001, *Monsoon Wedding*, comes to mind. The story of romance and marriage in the film's urban, upper-middle-class family is entirely plausible. The romance and marriage between the lower-middle-class wedding arranger – apparently a Brahmin – and a Christian maidservant from Bihar – apparently a Dalit – is certainly possible, but improbable. Less improbable are most of the stories in at least two comprehensive series of English translations of Indian-language novels, published by Penguin Books India and Macmillan India Limited. They include stories from the bottom of Indian rural society, written by people who have lived there. As literature, some of these novels suffer from their translations. But most are written with more intimate knowledge of ordinary Indian life and cut closer to its bone than their English-language counterparts. They are not, however, readily available in the West.

10 Basically, the application of plentiful water, and chemical fertilizers and pesticides to high yielding varieties (HYV) of seed; and the development of an infrastructure conducive to commercial agriculture: access to credit for farmers, transport for their goods, price information, local markets, farm-to-market roads and so forth.

11 Kirit S. Parikh, "Overview," *India Development Report 1999–2000*, ed. Karit S. Parikh (New Delhi: Oxford University Press for the Indira Gandhi Institute of Development Research, 1999), p. 1.

12 "Sharing the spoils: group equity, development and democracy," *The Success of India's Democracy*, ed. Atul Kohli (Cambridge: Cambridge University Press, 2001), pp. 226–241.

13 Rajesh Chada et al.: "Introduction," *Economic and Policy Reform in India* (New Delhi: National Council of Applied Economic Research, 2001), pp. 1–5.

14 *The Times of India Online*, April 20, 2001.

15 So named for the central sector of the de facto border, the "Line of Control," between Indian and Pakistani Kashmir. The Kargil sector was the scene of pitched battles between units of the Indian armed forces and Pakistani-sponsored *mujahidin* and regular troops in disguise.

16 Alexis de Tocqueville, *Democracy in America*, trans. Henry Reeves, revised by Francis Bowen and further edited by Phillip Bradley (New York: Vintage Books, 1956), p. 452.

17 For the concept of imagined communities, see Benedict Anderson, *Imagined Communities* (London: Verso, 1991).

18 "A Pagan Sacrifice," *India Today*, October 15, 1987, pp. 58–61 and Jaishree et al., "Charan Shah's Immolation: Countering Earlier Reports," *Manushi*, no. 115, Internet edition.

19 *India Today*, April 16, 2001, pp. 44–45.

20 From Rabindranath Tagore's *Songs of Kabir*, quoted in *Sources of Indian Tradition*, compiled by Wm. Theodore de Bary et al. (New York: Columbia University Press, 1958), pp. 360–61. Situated within the precincts of the Great Mosque at Mecca, the Kaaba is the most sacred site in Islam. Kailash is the abode of the Lord Siva, one of Hinduism's most worshipped manifestations of God.

21 "Sikh" is derived from *"shishaya"* – disciple.

1 Families and villages

1 Robert Frost, "Death of the Hired Man."

2 "Introduction" and "Is the Joint Household Disintegrating?" A. M. Shah, *The Family in India* (New Delhi: Orient Longman, 1998), pp. 1–13 and 64–80.

3 Ibid.

4 Marc Bloch argues that "the duality of descent by male and female lines" attenuated family ties in Europe's early Middle Ages and led to the development of feudalism, *Feudal Society*, vol. 1, trans. L. A. Manyon (London: Routledge and Kegan Paul Ltd, 1975), ch. 10.

5 Robert W. Stern, *The Cat and the Lion: Jaipur State in the British Raj* (Leiden: E. J. Brill, 1988).

6 *Toward Equality*, Report of the Committee on the Status of Women in India, Government of India, Ministry of Education and Social Welfare, 1974, p. 301.

7 Sarbani Banerjee, "Sex Disparity in Infant and Child Mortality: India and Major States," *www.unfpa.org.in*

8 Government of India, Ministry of Human Resource Development, *Selected Educational Statistics, 1999–2000*, 2001.

9 Robert W. Stern, *Democracy and Dictatorship in South Asia* (Westport, Connecticut, Praeger, 2000), p. 109.

10 "The Changing Woman," *India Today*, July 15, 1992, p. 42.

11 Poornima and Vinod Vyasulu, "Women in Panchayati Raj: Grassroots Democracy in India – Experience from Malgudi," a paper delivered to the Meeting on Women and Political Participation, New Delhi, March 24–26, 1999.

12 Bishakha Datta, ed., *And Who Will Make the Chapattis?* (New Delhi: Vedams eBooks, 1998), p. 113.

13 Nirmala Buch, *"Panchayats* and Women," George Mathew and Nirmala Buch, eds, *Status of Panchayati Raj in the States and Union Territories of India 2000* (New Delhi: Concept Publishing Company for the Institute of Social Sciences, 2000), pp. 34–41.

14 Louis Dumont, *Homo Hierarchicus*, trans. Mark Sainsbury (Chicago: University of Chicago Press, 1970).

15 A term used by anthropologists to describe economically and politically powerful castes, eg. Jats in western Uttar Pradesh. I keep the term in quotation marks because nowadays some of these castes are no longer as dominant as they once were.

2 Caste

1 Anderson, *Imagined Communities*.

2 It was for this reason that I abandoned the use of "caste" in the first edition of *Changing India*. It was a good reason for a bad decision: particularly for someone who writes about politics.

3 From de Bary, *Sources of Indian Tradition*, pp. 16–17.

4 Mahatma Gandhi, *An Autobiography* (Ahmedabad: Navajivan Publishing House, 1966), p. 183.

5 *The Bhagavad Gita*, trans. from the Sanskrit by Swami Nikhilananda (New York: Ramakrishna-Vivekananda Center, 1952).

6 Premchand, *Godan or the Gift of a Cow*, trans. Jai Ratan and P. Lal (Bombay: Jaico Publishing House, 1979).

7 M. N. Srinivas, *Social Change in Modern India* (Berkeley: University of California Press, 1966).

8 For this and other insights into caste, I am particularly indebted to Dipankar Gupta, *Interrogating Caste: Understanding hierarchy & difference in Indian society* (New Delhi: Penguin Books, 2000).

9 M. Mujeeb, *Indian Muslims*, 1st Indian ed. (Delhi: Munshiram Manoharlal, 1985), p. 13.

10 Quoted in Sekh Rahim Mondal and Rokiya Begum, "Do the Muslims Have Caste? A Critical Appraisal," ed. Noor Mohammad, *Indian Muslims: Precepts & Practices*, (Jaipur: Rawat Publications, 1999), pp. 214–236.

11 Valerie Kozel and Stephen Howes, "Poverty Reduction: Progress and Challenges," World Bank, *India: Reducing Poverty, Accelerating Development*, ch. 1.

12 Ibid.

13 Anil Sharma, "The Agricultural Sector," *Economic and Policy Reform in India* (New Delhi: National Council of Applied Economic Research, 2001), pp. 185–231.

14 Quoted in Zoya Hasan, *Quest for Power: Oppositional Movements and Post-Congress Politics in Uttar Pradesh* (Delhi: Oxford University Press, 1998), p. 160.

15 For a brief survey of these complaints, see National Campaign on Dalit Human Rights, *www.dalits.org*.

16 Gilbert Etienne, *India's Changing Rural Scene 1963–1979* (Delhi: Oxford University Press, 1982), p. 130.

17 S. P. Singh, "Agricultural Labourers," *Alternative Economic Survey 2000–2001, Second Generation Reforms: Delusion of Development* (New Delhi: Published for the Alternative Survey Group by Rainbow Publishers, 2001), pp. 69–71.

3 Class

1 "Class, Status and Party," *From Max Weber, Essays in Sociology*, ed., trans. and with an introduction by H. H. Gerth and C. Wright Mills (New York: Oxford University Press, 1946).

2 "A New Calculation in Uttar Pradesh," *Frontline*, Internet ed., September 15–28, 2001.

3 Derived from table 53, Operational Holdings, *Statistical Outline of India 1995–96* (Bombay: Tata Services Limited, 1995), p. 58.

4 "Class, Status, and Party."

5 "Farmers for Freedom," Shetkari Sangathana, *www.swatantrabharat.org/sangathana.htm/*

6 Ibid.

7 Planning Commission, Government of India, *The Report of the Balwant Rai Mehta Committee on Community Development and National Extension Services*.

8 West Bengal is the major exception. There the Left Front government has found it in its interests to patronize and use its *panchayati raj* institutions. Buddhadeb Ghosh, "West Bengal," Mathew and Buch eds, *Status of Panchayati Raj*, pp. 306–319.

4 Homelands and states

1 A neology of c.1918 and not in general use until after WWII.

2 The literal meaning of "babu" is father. It is also used as a title for "white-collar" workers. In Anglo-Indian English it was a contemptuous reference to "*mere* clerks," and Bengalis in particular. In contemporary Indian English the term survives as a contemptuous reference to bureaucrats in general.

3 For a fuller discussion of the reorganization of Indian states in the 1950s, readers might consult Robert W. Stern, *The Process of Opposition in India* (Chicago: University of Chicago Press, 1970).

4 This includes Pondicherry, a former French possession, and nowadays a Union territory.

5 *India Today*, October 15, 1981, p. 89.
6 A centrally appointed "head of state" at the state level with formal powers similar to those of the president at the Centre.
7 Paul R. Brass, "The Punjab Crisis and the Unity of India," in *India's Democracy: An Analysis of State-Society Relations*, ed. Atul Kohli (Princeton: Princeton University Press, 1988), p. 212.
8 English was Rajiv Gandhi's first language. An election joke in the 80s was that Rajiv was not exactly a foreigner but, rather, a resident NRI (non-resident Indian).
9 A reasonably comprehensive study of these reexaminations may be pieced together from the relevant sections of Parikh, ed., *India Development Report 1999–2000*; NCAER, *Economic and Policy Reforms in India, 2001*; World Bank, *India: Reducing Poverty, Accelerating Development*; Alternative Study Group, *Alternative Economic Survey 2000–2001*.
10 A reliable and readily available source of information about Indian universities is the annual *Commonwealth Universities Handbook*.

Part II Change from above

1 I pursue this argument at length in *Democracy and Dictatorship in South Asia* (Westport Connecticut: Praeger, 2000).

5 British imperialism, Indian nationalism and Muslim separatism

2 B. R. Tomlinson, *The Political Economy of the Raj: 1914–47* (London: The Macmillan Press Ltd, 1979), pp. 157, 6.
3 Morris D. Morris, "The Growth of Large Scale Industry to 1947," *The Cambridge Economic History of India*, vol. II (Cambridge: Cambridge University Press, 1983) pp. 668–76.
4 Ibid., pp. 588–92.
5 Neil Charlesworth, *British Rule and the Indian Economy: 1880–1914* (London: The Macmillan Press Ltd, 1982), pp. 51–55.
6 Ibid.
7 Peter Hardy, *The Muslims of British India* (Cambridge: Cambridge University Press, 1972).
8 Quoted in P. E. Roberts, *History of British India under the Company and the Crown*, 3rd ed., completed by T. G. P. Spear (Oxford: Oxford University Press), pp. 383–84.
9 Quoted in Burton Stein, *A History of India* (Oxford: Blackwell Publishers, 1998), pp. 265–66.
10 Edward Said, *Orientalism* (New York: Random House, 1979).
11 "The Rajput States of India," *Asiatic Studies: Religious and Social*, a collection of essays by Alfred C. Lyall (London: John Murray, 1882).
12 M. V. Pylee, *Constitutional Government In India* (London: Asia Publishing House, 1960), p. 114.
13 Judith M. Brown, *Modern India: The Origin of an Asian Democracy* (Delhi: Oxford University Press, 1985), p. 297.

14 Quoted in Damodar P. Singal, *Pakistan* (Englewood Cliffs, New Jersey: Prentice-Hall, 1972), pp. 58–59.

15 Except in East Pakistan, where the Bengali provincial League's alliance was similar to the Congress's in the rest of India – professional middle classes and landed peasants – and at odds with Jinnah. Secession eventually followed.

16 Through a program of naval expansion that catered to the interests of aspiring industrialists, coupled with tariff protection and a reassertion of militarism that catered to the interests of established titled landlords, a "marriage of iron and rye" was contracted and consummated in turn-of-the-nineteenth-century Germany between two powerful partners both opposed to political democracy. Hans-Ulrich Wehler, *The German Empire*, trans. Kim Traynor (Leamington Spa: Berg Publishers, 1985). p. 168.

17 Claude Markovits, *Indian Business and National Politics, 1931–1939* (Cambridge: Cambridge University Press, 1985), pp. 165 and 3.

18 Robert W. Stern, *The Cat and the Lion: Jaipur State in the British Raj* (Leiden: E. J. Brill, 1988), chs. 6 and 7.

19 Markovits, *Indian Business*.

20 Literally, our own government, but in what sense "our own" – inside or outside the empire, and on what terms – was left undefined by the Mahatma, and open to negotiation.

21 Markovits, *Indian Business*, p. 30.

22 In Punjab, however, when land was being lost by landlords – who were mostly Muslim and "loyal" to moneylenders who were mostly Hindu and "seditious" – the government legislated the Punjab Alienation of Land Act of 1900, which effectively barred the latter from acquiring agricultural land. Stern, *Democracy and Dictatorship*.

23 The official name in Hindi for the Republic of India is *Bharatavarsha*.

24 A collection of their histories appears in the multiple volumes published since 1982 of *Subaltern Studies: Writings on South Asia*, ed. Ranajit Guha (Delhi: Oxford University Press).

25 E. Wolfe, *Peasant Wars of the Twentieth Century* (New York: Harper and Row, 1969).

26 Quoted in K. M. Prasad, *Sarvodaya of Gandhi*, ed. Ramjee Singh (New Delhi: Raj Hans Publications, 1984), p. 90.

27 A. R. Desai, *Social Background of Indian Nationalism*, 4th ed. (Bombay: Popular Prakashan, 1966), p. 371.

28 Ishtiaq Husain Qureshi, *The Muslim Community of the Indo-Pakistan Subcontinent 610–1947* ('Gravenhage: Mouton and Co., 1962) pp. 84, 270.

29 Quoted in Mujeeb, *Indian Muslims*, p. 477.

30 W. W. Hunter, *Indian Musalmans* (1871; reprint, Delhi: Indological Book House, 1969).

31 Quoted in Ram Gopal, *Indian Muslims: A Political History, 1858–1947* (London: Asia Publishing House, 1959), pp. 329–35.

32 Hardy, *Muslims of British India*, p. 151.

33 Quoted in Ibid., p. 231.

34 Ayesha Jalal, *The Sole Spokesman: Jinnah, the Muslim League and the Demand for Pakistan* (Cambridge: Cambridge University Press, 1985).

6   The Indian Union in a changing India

1   Dietrich Rueschemeyer, Evelyne Huber Stephens and John D. Stephens, *Capitalist Development and Democracy* (Cambridge: Polity Press, 1992), p. 9.

2   Ravinder Kumar, "The Past and Present: An Indian Dialogue," *Daedalus*, 118:4, Fall 1989, pp. 27–49.

3   For recent tabulations see *Times of India Online*, "Indian Democracy: Of, For and By Dynasties," April 20, 2001 and "Punjab Parties Depend on Sons and Relatives," January 31, 2002.

4   Gunnar Myrdal, *Asian Drama: An Inquiry into the Poverty of Nations*, abridged by Seth S. King, (New York: Vintage Books, 1972), pp. 202–10.

5   N. Vittal, "Applying Zero Tolerance to Corruption," *www.expage.com/gascompass4/* and Confederation of Indian Industry, CII News, November 2000, *www.ciionline.org*

6   Transparency International's home page is *www.transparency.org*

7   Over the years some parties have left the alliance, and some have joined or rejoined it.

8   That is, to take on, chameleon-like, the color of Hinduism.

9   In a brief article, Ashutosh Varshney cites some evidence to suggest, in effect, that *mandal* politics drive *mandir* politics out of the political market. "Democracy and Ethnic Assertion in India," *www.isp.msu.edu/asianstudies/outreach/oio919.html*

10   "Primal Fear," *India Today*, March 18, 2002.

11   For some indication of this, see "Congress Turns to Lord Ram," *Times of India Online*, April 23, 2002.

12   Philip Mason, *The Men Who Ruled India*, 2 vols. (London: Jonathan Cape, 1953–54), endnote 4 in ch. 6, CII.

13   The chairman of Infosys, one of India's major information technology producers, reports that at some unspecified time before the economic reforms of 1991, he had to make 25 visits over a period of 18 months to obtain bureaucratic approval to import one $15,000 computer. "What Enabled the Software Revolution in India," *Times of India Online*, April 28, 2002.

14   A company or a part thereof is "sick" in India if its accumulated losses are greater than its net worth.

15   *Far Eastern Economic Review*, October 31, 1991, pp. 61–62.

16   For much of the information on economic reform, I am particularly indebted to the authors of various articles in: NCAER, *Economic and Policy Reforms in India*; K. S. Parikh, ed., *India Development Report 1999–2000*; Alternative Study Group, *Alternative Economic Survey 2000–2001*.

17   "Overview," K. S. Parikh, ed., *India Development Report*, p.3.

18   "The Economy: Will it Fly," *India Today*, pp. 30–32.

19   "Government Finances," NCAER, *Economic and Policy Reforms*, p. 27.

20   "Falling Back on India," *India Today*, November 19, 2001, p. 12.

21   V. P. Menon, *The Story of the Integration of the Indian States* (Bombay: Orient Longmans, 1969), p. 377.

22   A notable Brahmin caste. The Nehru family were Pandits.

23 Chaudhri Muhammad Ali, *The Emergence of Pakistan* (Lahore: Research Society of Pakistan, 1973), p. 175.

24 Talukder Maniruzzaman, *The Bangladesh Revolution and its Aftermath* (Dhaka: University Press, 1994), p. 119.

25 Mushtaq Ahmad, *The United Nations and Pakistan* (Karachi: Pakistan Institute of International Affairs, 1955), p. 140.

26 Mohammad Ayoob, "India in South Asia: The Quest for Regional Predominance," *World Policy Journal*, 7:1, Winter 1989–90.

Guide to further reading

There is a rough parallel between *Changing India*'s chapters or their parts and the categories in this section. Inevitably, there is a measure of arbitrariness in my placement of works in particular categories. For example: **Family, *jati*, caste and village** tend to be written about together, but not always; and works so categorized may differ only from those listed under **Class** more or less according to their emphasis or the ideological persuasions of their authors. I have listed books about contemporary Hinduism either under **Major religions and religious communities** or under **Politics**. It's six of one or half-dozen of another nowadays. And so forth. Readers in search of anything in particular will have to fossick: here, in the bibliographies of the works cited, and in the comprehensive *Bibliography of Asian Studies*, published as a delayed annual by the Asian Studies Association, Ann Arbor, Michigan.

In the works cited below, I have, in general, preferred more to less recent publications, ones that are more accessible to those that are less accessible, books to journal articles (useful periodicals are cited in the next section), edited collections to their separate pieces, more to less comprehensive studies, variety to consistency in theoretical underpinning and methodology. Only if they suit these preferences are endnote citations repeated below.

Works of general reference and relevance

Anderson, Benedict, *Imagined Communities*. London: Verso, 1991.
The Cambridge Economic History of India. 2 vols. vol. I, c.1200–1750 AD, edited by Tapan Raychaudhuri and Irfan Habib; vol. II, c.1757–1970,

edited by Dharma Kumar with Megnad Desai. Cambridge: Cambridge University Press, 1981–82.

Cohn, Bernard S. *India: The Social Anthropology of a Civilization*. Englewood Cliffs, New Jersey: Prentice-Hall, 1971.

de Bary, Wm. Theodore, Stephan N. Hay, Royal Weiler and Andrew Yarrow, eds and compilers. *Sources of Indian Tradition*. New York: Columbia University Press, 1958.

Douglas, Mary. *Purity and Danger: An Analysis of the Concepts of Pollution and Taboo*. London: Routledge and Kegan Paul, 1966.

Heesterman, J. C. *The Inner Conflict of Tradition: Essays in Indian Ritual, Kingship and Society*. Chicago: University of Chicago Press, 1985.

Inden, Ronald. *Imagining India*. Oxford: Basil Blackwell, 1990.

India. Ministry of Information and Broadcasting. Publications Division. *India*. New Delhi, an annual publication.

Lannoy, Richard. *The Speaking Tree: A Study of Indian Culture and Society*. Oxford: Oxford University Press, 1971.

Moore, Barrington, Jr. *Social Origins of Dictatorship and Democracy*. Boston: Beacon Press, 1966.

Naipaul, V. S. *India: A Million Mutinies Now*. London: Heinemann, 1990.

Robinson, Francis, ed. *The Cambridge Encyclopedia of India, Pakistan, Bangladesh, Sri Lanka, Nepal, Bhutan and the Maldives*. Cambridge: Cambridge University Press, 1989.

Rueschemeyer, Dietrich, Evelyne Huber and John D. Stephens. *Capitalist Development and Democracy*. Cambridge: Polity Press, 1992.

Said, Edward. *Orientalism*. New York: Random House, 1979.

Schwartzberg, Joseph E. *A Historical Atlas of South Asia*. Chicago: University of Chicago Press, 1978.

Sen, S. P., ed. *Dictionary of National Biography*. 4 vols. Calcutta: Institute of Historical Studies, 1972–74.

Major religions and religious communities

Ahmad, Imtiaz, ed. *Modernization and Social Change among Muslims in India*. Delhi: Manohar, 1983.

Andersen, Walter K. and Shridhar Damle. *The Brotherhood in Saffron: The Rashtriya Swayamsevak Sangh and Hindu Revivalism*. New Delhi: Sage Publications, 1987.

Appadurai, Arjun. *Worship and Conflict Under Colonial Rule*. New York: Cambridge University Press, 1981.

Basham, A. L. *The Wonder that was India*. New York: Grove Press, 1954.

Bayly, Susan. *Saints, Goddesses and Kings: Muslims and Christians and South Asian Society 1700–1900*. New York: Cambridge University Press, 1990.

Bhagavad Gita. Translated by Swami Nikhilananda. New York: Rama-krishna-Vivekananda Center, 1952.

Bjorkman, James Warner, ed. *Fundamentalism, Revivalists and Violence in South Asia*. Riverdale, Maryland: The Riverdale Company, 1988.

Dumont, Louis. *Homo Hierarchicus*. Translated by Mark Sainsbury. Chicago: University of Chicago Press, 1970.

Freitag, Sandra B. *Collective Action and Community: Public Arena and the Emergence of Communalism in North India*. Berkeley: University of California Press, 1989.

Fuller, C. J. *The Camphor Flame: Popular Hinduism and Society in India*. Princeton: Princeton University Press, 1992.

Hardy, Peter. *The Muslims of British India*. Cambridge: Cambridge University Press, 1972.

Hasan, Mushirul. *Legacy of a Divided Nation: India's Muslims since Independence*. Boulder, Colo.: Westview Press, 1997.

Keyes, Charles F. and E. Valentine Daniel, *Karma: An Anthropological Inquiry*. Berkeley: University of California Press, 1983.

Khalidi, Omar. *Indian Muslims since Independence*. New Delhi: Vikas, 1995.

McLeod, W. H. *Who is a Sikh? The Problem of Sikh Identity*. Oxford: Oxford University Press, 1989.

Mujeeb, Mohammad. *Indian Muslims*. 1st Indian ed. Delhi: Munshiram Manoharlal, 1985.

Neill, Stephen. *A History of Christianity in India*. 2 vols. Cambridge: Cambridge University Press, 1984–85.

Qureshi, Ishtiaq Husain. *The Muslim Community of the Indo-Pakistan Subcontinent: 610–1947*. 'S-Gravenhage: Mouton, 1962.

Radhakrishnan, Sarvepalli and Charles A. Moore. *A Sourcebook in Indian Philosophy*. Princeton: Princeton University Press, 1957.

Singh, Khushwant. *A History of the Sikhs*. 2nd ed., 2 vols. Delhi: Oxford University Press, 1977.

Zimmer, Heinrich. *Philosophies of India*. Edited by Joseph Campbell. New York: Meridian Books, 1959.

Family, *jati*, caste and village

Ahmad, Imtiaz, ed. *Family, Kinship and Marriage among Muslims in India*. Delhi: Manohar, 1976.

——, ed. *Caste and Social Stratification among Muslims in India*. Delhi: Manohar, 1978.

Bayly, Susan. *Caste, Society and Politics in India*. Cambridge: Cambridge University Press, 1999.

Béteille, André. *Society and Politics in India: Essays in Comparative Perspective*. Delhi: Oxford University Press, 1991.

Gould, Harold A. *The Hindu Caste System: The Sacralization of a Social Order*. New Delhi: Chanakya Publications, 1987.

Gray, John N. and David J. Mearns, eds. *Society from the Inside Out: Anthropological Perspectives on the South Asian Household*. New Delhi: Sage Publications, 1989.

Gupta, Dipankar. *Interrogating Caste: Understanding Hierarchy and Difference in Indian Society*. New Delhi: Penguin Books, 2000.

Joshi, Barbara R. *Untouchable! Voices of the Dalit Liberation Movement*. London: Zed Books, 1986.

Kolenda, Pauline. *Caste, Cult and Hierarchy: Essays on the Culture of India*. Meerut: Folklore Institute, 1981.

Ludden, David. *Peasant History in South India*. Princeton: Princeton University Press, 1985.

Mandlebaum, David G. *Society in India*. 2 vols. Berkeley: University of California Press, 1970 and 1972.

Mendelsohn, Oliver and Marika Vicziany. *The Untouchables: Subordination, Poverty and the State in Modern India*. Cambridge: Cambridge University Press, 1998.

Michael, S. M. ed. *Untouchable: Dalits in Modern India*. Boulder, Colo.: Lynne Rienner Publishers, 1999.

Östör, Åkos, Lina Fruzzetti and Steve Barnett, eds. *Concepts of Person: Kinship, Caste and Marriage in India*. Cambridge: Harvard University Press, 1982.

Premchand. *Godan*. Translated by Jai Ratan and P. Lal. Bombay: Jaico Publishing House, 1979.

Raheja, Gloria Goodwin. *The Poison in the Gift: Ritual Prestation and the Dominant Caste in a North Indian Village*. Chicago: University of Chicago Press, 1988.

Shah, A. M. *The Family in India: Critical Essays*. New Delhi: Orient Longman, 1998.

Srinivas, M. N. *Social Change in Modern India*. Berkeley: University of California Press, 1966.

——. *On Living in a Revolution and Other Essays*. Delhi: Oxford University Press, 1992.

Zelliot, Eleanor. *From Untouchable to Dalit: Essays on the Ambedkar Movement*. 2nd ed. New Delhi: Manohar, 1996.

Class

Alavi, Hamza and John Harriss. *Sociology of 'Developing Societies': South Asia*. London: Macmillan Education, 1989.

Bardhan, Pranab. *The Political Economy of Development in India*. London: Basil Blackwell, 1984.

Breman, Jan. *Of Peasants, Migrants and Paupers: Rural Labour Circulation and Capitalist Production in West India.* Delhi: Oxford University Press, 1985.

Hasan, Zoya. *Dominance and Mobilization: Rural Politics in Western Uttar Pradesh.* New Delhi: Sage Publications, 1989.

India. Ministry of Home Affairs. High Power Panel on Minorities, Scheduled Castes, Scheduled Tribes and Other Weaker Sections. *Report on Scheduled Castes.* 1983.

Weber, Max. "Class, Status, Party." From *Max Weber, Essays in Sociology.* Translated, edited and with an introduction by H. H. Gerth and C. Wright Mills. New York: Oxford University Press, 1946.

Wolfe, Eric. *Peasant Wars of the Twentieth Century.* New York: Harper and Row, 1969.

Women

Agarwal, Bina. *A Field of One's Own: Gender and Land Rights in South Asia.* Cambridge: Cambridge University Press, 1994.

Basu, Amrita. *Two Faces of Protest: Contrasting Modes of Women's Activism in India.* Berkeley: University of California Press, 1992.

Chatterji, Shoma A. *The Indian Woman's Search for an Identity.* New Delhi: Vikas, 1988.

Forbes, Geraldine. *Women in Modern India.* Cambridge: Cambridge University Press, 1996.

Ghadially, Rehana. *Women in Indian Society, A Reader.* New Delhi: Sage Publications, 1988.

India. Ministry of Education and Social Welfare, Committee of the Status of Women in India. *Toward Equality,* 1974.

Jain, Devaki. *Women's Quest for Power. Five Indian Case Studies.* Assisted by Nalini Singh and Malini Chand. Delhi: Vikas, 1980.

Karlekar, Malavika. *Poverty and Women's Work: A Study of Sweeper Women in Delhi.* Delhi: Vikas, 1982.

Kishwar, Madhu and, Ruth Vanita, eds. *In Search of Answers: Indian Women's Voices from Manushi.* London: Zed Books, 1984.

Liddle, Joanna and Rama Joshi. *Daughters of Independence: Gender, Caste and Class in India.* New Brunswick, New Jersey: Rutgers University Press, 1989.

Mandelbaum, David G. *Women's Seclusion and Men's Honor: Sex Roles in North India, Bangladesh and Pakistan.* Tucson: University of Arizona Press, 1988.

Palriwala, Rajni and Lila Dube, eds. *Structures and Strategies: Women, Work and Family.* Newbury Park, California: Sage Publications, 1990.

Papanek, Hanna and Gail Minault. *Separate Worlds: Studies of Purdah in South Asia*. Columbia, Missouri: South Asia Books, 1982.

Ram, Kalpana. *Mukkuvar Women: Sexual Contradictions in a Southeast Indian Fishing Community*. Sydney: Allen and Unwin, 1991.

Ramu, G. N. *Women, Work and Marriage in Urban India: A Study of Dual- and Single-Earner Couples*. Newbury Park: Sage Publications, 1989.

Sarker, Tanika and Urvashi Butalia, eds. *Women and Right Wing Movements: Indian Experiences*. London: Zed Books, 1995.

Wignaraja, Poona. *Women, Poverty and Resources*. New Delhi: Sage Publications, 1990.

Ethnicity and ethnic movements

Brass, Paul R. *Ethnicity and Nationalism: Theory and Comparison*. New Delhi: Sage Publications, 1991.

Das Gupta, Jyotirindra. *Language, Conflict and National Development: Group Politics and National Language Policy in India*. Bombay: Oxford University Press, 1970.

Duyker, Edward. *Tribal Guerrillas: The Santals of West Bengal and the Naxalite Movement*. Delhi: Oxford University Press, 1987.

Furer-Haimendorf, C. von. *Tribal Populations and Cultures of the Indian Subcontinent*. Leiden: E. J. Brill, 1985.

Gupta, S. K. *The Scheduled Castes in Modern Indian Politics: Their Emergence as a Political Power*. New Delhi: Munshiram Manoharlal, 1985.

Hardiman, David. *The Coming of the Devi: Adivasi Assertion in Western India*. Delhi: Oxford University Press, 1987.

Irschick, Eugene F. *Politics and Social Conflict in South India: The Non-Brahman Movement and Tamil Separatism, 1916–1939*. Berkeley: University of California Press, 1969.

Jeffrey, Robin. *What's Happening to India? Punjab, Ethnic Conflict and the Test for Federalism*. 2nd ed. Houndmills: Macmillan, 1994.

Katzenstein, Mary Fainsod. *Ethnicity and Equality: The Shiv Sena Party and Preferential Politics in Bombay*. Ithaca: Cornell University Press, 1979.

O'Hanlon, Rosalind. *Caste, Conflict and Ideology: Mahatma Jotirao Phule and Low-Caste Protest in Nineteenth Century Western India*. Cambridge: Cambridge University Press, 1985.

Phadnis, Urmilla. *Ethnicity and Nation-building in South Asia*. New Delhi: Sage Publications, 1989.

Stern, Robert W. *The Process of Opposition in India: Two Case Studies of How Policy Shapes Politics*. Chicago: University of Chicago Press, 1970.

Weiner, Myron. *Sons of the Soil: Migration and Ethnic Conflict in India*. Princeton: Princeton University Press, 1978.

British imperialism and Indian nationalism

Ballhatchet, Kenneth. *Race, Sex and Class Under the Raj: Imperial Attitudes and Policies and their Critics, 1793–1905.* London: Weidenfeld and Nicolson, 1980.

Bayly, C. A. *Empire and Information: Intelligence Gathering and Social Communication in India, 1780–1870.* Cambridge: Cambridge University Press, 1996

Borman, William. *Gandhi and Non-Violence.* Albany: State University of New York Press, 1986.

Bridge, Carl. *Holding India to the Empire: The British Conservative Party and the 1935 Constitution.* Asian Studies Association of Australia, South Asian Publications series 1. New York: Envoy Press, 1986.

Brown, Judith M. *Modern India: The Origins of an Asian Democracy.* Delhi: Oxford University Press, 1985.

Chakrabarty, Dipesh. *Rethinking Working Class History: Bengal 1890–1940.* Princeton: Princeton University Press, 1989.

Chandra, Bipan and others. *India's Struggle for Independence 1857–1947.* New Delhi: Penguin Books, 1989.

Charlesworth, Neil. *British Rule and the Indian Economy: 1880–1914.* London: Macmillan, 1982.

Chaturvedi, Vinayak, ed. *Mapping Subaltern Studies and the Postcolonial.* London: Verso, 2000.

Chaudhuri, K. N. and, Clive J. Dewey. *Economy and Society: Essays in Indian Economic and Social History.* New York: Oxford University Press, 1979.

Copland, Ian. *The Princes of India in the Endgame of Empire, 1917–1947.* Cambridge: Cambridge University Press, 1997.

Dewey, Clive J. *Arrested Development in India: The Historical Dimension.* Riverdale: The Riverdale Co., 1988.

Fisher, Michael H. *Indirect Rule in India: Residents and the Residency System.* Delhi: Oxford University Press, 1991.

Fox, Richard G. *Gandhian Utopia: Experiments with Culture.* Boston: Beacon Press, 1989.

Gallagher, John, Gordon Johnson, and Anil Seal, eds. *Locality, Province and Nation: Essays on Indian Politics, 1870 to 1940.* Cambridge: Cambridge University Press, 1973.

Gandhi, Mohandas Karamchand. *An Autobiography.* Ahmedabad: Navajivan Publishing House, 1966.

Gilmartin, David. *Empire and Islam, Punjab and the Making of Pakistan.* Berkeley: University of California Press, 1988.

Guha, Ranajit, ed. *Subaltern Studies: Writings on South Asian History and Society.* Delhi: Oxford University Press, multiple volumes from 1982.

Hirschmann, Edwin. *"White Mutiny": The Ilbert Bill Crisis in India and the Genesis of the Indian National Congress*. Columbia, Missouri: South Asia Books, 1980.

Hutchens, Francis G. *The Illusion of Permanence: British Imperialism in India*. Princeton: Princeton University Press, 1967.

Jalal, Ayesha. *The Sole Spokesman: Jinnah, the Muslim League and the Demand for Pakistan*. Cambridge: Cambridge University Press, 1985.

Jeffrey, Robin, ed. *People, Princes and Paramount Power: Society and Politics in the Indian Princely States*. Delhi: Oxford University Press, 1978.

Kumar, Ravinder, ed. *Essays on Gandhian Politics: The Rowlatt Satyagraha of 1919*. Oxford: Clarendon Press, 1971.

Low, D. A. *Britain and Indian Nationalism: The Impact of Ambiguity, 1919–1942*. Cambridge: Cambridge University Press, 1997.

——, ed., *Congress and the Raj: Facets of the Indian Struggle, 1917–1949*, London: Heinemann, 1977.

McGuire, John. *The Making of a Colonial Mind: A Quantitative Study of the Bhadralok in Calcutta, 1857–1885*. Canberra: Australian National University Press, 1983.

Markovits, Claude. *Indian Business and National Politics, 1931–1939*. Cambridge: Cambridge University Press, 1985.

Masselos, Jim, ed. *India: Creating a Modern Nation*. Delhi: Sterling Publishers, 1990.

Menon, V. P. *The Story of the Integration of the Indian States*. Bombay: Orient Longmans, 1969.

Minault, Gail. *The Khilafat Movement: Religious Symbolism and Political Mobilization in India*. New York: Columbia University Press, 1982.

Moon, Penderel. *The British Conquest and Dominion of India*. London: Duckworth, 1989.

Nehru, Jawaharlal. *The Discovery of India*. London: Meridian, 1947.

Parekh, Bhiku. *Colonialism, Tradition and Reform: An Analysis of Gandhi's Political Discourse*. New Delhi: Sage Publications, 1989.

Prasad, K. M. *Sarvodaya of Gandhi*. Edited by Ramjee Singh. New Delhi: Raj Hans Publications, 1984.

Raj, Rajat K. *Industrialization in India: Growth and Conflict in the Private Corporate Sector, 1914–1947*. New York: Oxford University Press, 1979.

Rothermund, Dietmar. *Government, Landlord and Peasant in India: Agrarian Relations under British Rule, 1865–1935*. Wiesbaden: Franz Steiner Verlag GmbH, 1978.

Sarkar, Sumit. *Modern India, 1885–1947*. Madras: Macmillan India, 1983.

Seal, Anil. *The Emergence of Indian Nationalism: Competition and Collaboration in the Late Nineteenth Century*. Cambridge: Cambridge University Press, 1988.

Sisson, Richard and Stanley Wolpert, eds. *Congress and Indian Nationalism: The Pre-Independence Phase.* Berkeley: University of California Press, 1971.

Stein, Burton. *A History of India.* Oxford: Blackwell Publishers, 1998.

Stern, Robert W. *The Cat and the Lion: Jaipur State in the British Raj.* Leiden: E. J. Brill, 1988.

Stokes, Eric. *The Peasant and the Raj.* Cambridge: Cambridge University Press, 1978.

Tomlinson, B. R. *The Political Economy of the Raj: 1914–1947.* London: Macmillan, 1979.

Wurgaft, Lewis D. *The Imperial Imagination: Magic and Myth in Kipling's India.* Middletown, Connecticut: Wesleyan University Press, 1983.

Yang, Anand A. *The Limited Raj: Agrarian Relations in Colonial India, Saran District, 1793–1920.* Berkeley: University of California Press, 1990.

Economic development

Ahluwalia, I. *Industrial Growth in India: Stagnation since the Mid-Sixties.* Delhi: Oxford University Press, 1985.

Alternative Study Group. *Alternative Economic Survey 2000–2001.* New Delhi: Rainbow Publishers, 2001.

Bala, Raj. *Trends in Urbanization in India.* Jaipur: Rawat Publications, 1986.

Balasubramanyam, V. *The Indian Economy.* London: Weidenfeld and Nicolson, 1984.

Basu, Kaushak, ed. *Agrarian Questions.* Delhi: Oxford University Press, 1994.

Bhagwati, Jagdish. *India in Transition: Freeing the Economy.* Oxford: Clarendon Press, 1993.

Chaudhri, D. P. and Ajit K. Das Gupta. *Agriculture and the Development Process: A Study of Punjab.* London: Croom Helm, 1985.

Chugh, Ram L. and J. S. Uppal. *Black Economy in India.* New Delhi: Tata McGraw Hill, 1986.

Crook, Clive. "India." *Economist*, May 5, 1991, survey pp. 3–18.

Dreze, Jean and Amartya Sen, eds. *Indian Development: Selected Regional Perspectives.* Delhi: Oxford University Press, 1997.

Etienne, Gilbert. *Food and Poverty: India's Half Won Battle.* New Delhi: Sage Publications, 1988.

Gupta, Akhil. *Postcolonial Developments: Agriculture in the Making of Modern India,* Durham, NC: Duke University Press, 1997.

Inoue, Kyoko. *Industrial Development Policy of India.* Tokyo: Institute of Developing Economies, 1992.

Myrdal, Gunnar. *Asian Drama: An Inquiry into the Poverty of Nations.* Abridged by Seth S. King. New York: Vintage Books, 1972.

National Council of Applied Economic Research. *Economic and Policy Reform in India*. New Delhi, 2001.

Nayar, Baldev Raj. *India's Mixed Economy: The Role of Ideology and Interest in its Development*. Bombay: Popular Prakashan, 1989.

Parikh, Kirit S., ed. *India Development Report 1999–2000*. Delhi: Oxford University Press for the Indira Gandhi Institute of Development Research, 1999.

Raj, K. N. and others. *Essays in the Commercialization of Indian Agriculture*. Delhi: Oxford University Press, 1985.

Rao, C. H. Hanumantha. *Agricultural Growth, Rural Poverty and Environmental Degradation in India*. Delhi: Oxford University Press, 1994.

Rodgers, Gerry. *Population Growth and Poverty in Rural South Asia*. New Delhi: Sage Publications, 1989.

Rosen, George. *Contrasting Styles of Industrial Reform: China and India in the 1980s*. Chicago: University of Chicago Press, 1992.

Sharma, Rita and Thomas T. Poleman. *The New Economics of India's Green Revolution: Income and Employment Diffusion in Uttar Pradesh*. Ithaca, NY: Cornell University Press, 1993.

Sims, Holly. *Political Regimes, Public Policy and Economic Development: Agricultural Performance and Rural Change in the Two Punjabs*. New Delhi: Sage Publications, 1988.

Sundrum, R. M. *Growth and Income Distribution in India: Policy and Performance since Independence*. New Delhi: Sage Publications, 1987.

Suri, K. B., ed. *Small Scale Enterprises in Industrial Development: The Indian Experience*. New Delhi: Sage Publications, 1988.

Tata Services Limited, Department of Economics and Statistics, *Statistical Outline of India*. Mumbai, an annual publication.

Toye, John. *Public Expenditure and Indian Development Policy: 1960–1970*. Cambridge: Cambridge University Press, 1981.

World Bank. *India: Reducing Poverty Accelerating Development*. Delhi: Oxford University Press, 2000.

——. *World Development Indicators*. Washington, DC, an annual publication.

Politics

Brass, Paul R. *The Politics of India since Independence*. New York: Cambridge University Press, 1990.

Calman, Leslie J. *Protest in Democratic India: Authority's Response to Challenge*. Boulder, Colorado: Westview Press, 1985.

Desai, I. P. and others. *Caste, Caste Conflict and Reservations*. Delhi: Ajanta Publications for the Centre for Social Studies, Surat, 1985.

Galanter, Marc. *Competing Equalities: Law and the Backward Classes in India*. Berkeley: University of California Press, 1984.

Gopal, Sarvepalli, ed. *Anatomy of a Confrontation: Ayodhya and the Rise of Communal Politics in India*. London: Zed Books, 1993.

Hasan Zoya, ed. *Politics and the State in India*. New Delhi: Sage Publications, 2000.

———. *Quest for Power: Oppositional Movements and Post-Congress Politics in Uttar Pradesh*. Delhi: Oxford University Press, 1998.

Haynes, Douglas and Gyan Prakash. *Contesting Power: Resistance and Everyday Social Relations in South Asia*. Berkeley: University of California Press, 1993.

India. Planning Commission. Committee on Plan Projects. *Report of the Team for the Study of Community Projects and National Extension Service*, Balvantray Mehta Study Team Report, 1958.

Jaffrelot, Christophe. *The Hindu Nationalist Movement in India*. New York: Columbia University Press, 1996.

Jeffrey, Robin. *What's Happening in India? Punjab, Ethnic Conflict, Mrs. Gandhi's Death and the Test for Federalism*. Basingstoke, Hampshire: Macmillan, 1986.

Kakir, Sudhir. *The Colors of Violence: Cultural Identities, Religion and Conflict*. Chicago: University of Chicago Press, 1996.

Kohli, Atul, ed. *India's Democracy: An Analysis of Changing State–Society Relations*. Princeton: Princeton University Press, 1988.

———, ed. *The Success of India's Democracy*. Cambridge: Cambridge University Press, 2001.

Kothari, Rajni. *Human Consciousness and the Amnesia of Development*. London: Zed Books, 1995.

Ludden, David, ed. *Contesting the Nation: Religion, Community and the Politics of Democracy in India*. Philadelphia: University of Pennsylvania Press, 1996.

McKean, Lise. *Divine Enterprise: Gurus and the Hindu Nationalist Movement*. Chicago: University of Chicago Press, 1996.

Malik, Yogendra K. and Jesse F. Marquette. *Political Mercenaries and Citizen Soldiers: A Profile of North Indian Party Activists*. Delhi: Chanakya Publications, 1990.

Mathew, George and Nirmala Buch, eds. *Status of Panchayati Raj in the States and Union Territories of India 2000*. New Delhi: Concept Publishing Company for the Institute of Social Science, 2000.

Mitra, Subrata and Dieter Rothermund, eds. *Legitimacy and Conflict in South Asia*. New Delhi: Manohar Publishers, 1997.

Nandi, Ashis. *At the Edge of Psychology: Essays in Politics and Culture*. Delhi: Oxford University Press, 1980.

Omvedt, Gail. *Reinventing Revolution: New Social Movements and the Socialist Tradition in India*, New York: M. E. Sharpe, 1993.

Oommen, T. K. *State and Society in India: Studies in Nation-Building*. New Delhi: Sage Publications, 1990.

Radhakrishnan, P. *Peasant Struggles, Land Reforms and Social Change: Malabar, 1836–1982*. New Delhi: Sage Publications, 1989.

Rudolph, Susanne H. and Lloyd, I. *In Pursuit of Lakshmi: The Political Economy of the Indian State*. Chicago: University of Chicago Press, 1987.

Singh, V. B. and Shanker Bose. *Elections in India: Data Handbook on Lok Sabha Elections, 1952–1985*. 2nd ed. New Delhi: Sage Publications, 1986 and *State Elections in India: Data Handbook on Vidhan Sabha Elections, 1952–1985*. 5 vols. New Delhi: Sage Publications, 1988.

Stern, Robert W. *Democracy and Dictatorship in South Asia: Dominant Classes and Political Outcomes in India, Pakistan and Bangladesh*. Westport, Conn.: Praeger, 2000.

Vanaik, Achin. *The Painful Transition: Bourgeois Democracy in India*. London: Verso, 1990.

Varshney, Ashutosh. *Democracy, Development and the Countryside: Urban-Rural Struggles in India*. Cambridge: Cambridge University Press, 1995.

Weiner, Myron and Mary Fainsod Katzenstein. *India's Preferential Politics: Migrants, the Middle Classes and Ethnic Equality*. Chicago: University of Chicago Press, 1982.

Wood, John R., ed. *State Politics in Contemporary India: Crisis or Continuity*. Boulder, Colo.: Westview Press, 1984.

Foreign relations

Abraham, Itty. *The Making of the Indian Atomic Bomb: Science, Secrecy and the Postcolonial State*. London: Zed Books, 1998.

Ayoob, Mohammad. "Dateline India: The Deepening Crisis." *Foreign Policy*, Winter 1991–92, no. 85. and "India in South Asia: The Quest for Regional Predominance." *World Policy Journal*, Winter 1989–90, vol. 12, no. 1.

Babbage, Ross and A. D. Gordon, eds. *India's Strategic Future: Regional State or Global Power*. New York: St. Martin's Press, 1992.

Behora, Navnita Chadha. *State Identity and Violence: Jammu, Kashmir and Ladakh*. New Delhi: Manohar, 2000.

Bose, Sumanta. *The Challenge in Kashmir: Democracy, Self-Determination and a Just Peace*. New Delhi: Sage Publications, 1997.

Cohen, Stephen P., ed. *The Security of South Asia: American and Asian Perspectives*. Urbana: University of Illinois Press, 1987.

Engineer, Asghar Ali. *Secular Crown on Fire: The Kashmir Problem*. Delhi: Ajanta Press, 1991.

Gordon, Sandy. *India's Rise to Power: In the Twentieth Century and Beyond*. New York: St. Martin's Press, 1995.

Kapur, Ashok with A. Jeyaratnam Wilson. *The Foreign Policy of India and Her Neighbors*. New York: St. Martin's Press, 1996.

Malik, Hafeez, ed. *Dilemmas of National Security and Cooperation in India and Pakistan*. New York: St. Martin's Press, 1993.

Mansingh, Surjit. *India's Search for Power: Indira Gandhi's Foreign Policy, 1966–1982*. New Delhi: Sage Publications, 1984.

Strategic and Defence Studies Centre, Research School of Pacific Affairs, Australian National University, "India's Strategic Future." Conference papers. Canberra, 1990.

Thomas, Raju G. C. *Democracy, Security and Development in India*. New York: St. Martin's Press, 1996.

Periodicals

These have been particularly useful: *Asian Survey* (Berkeley, California), *Contributions to Indian Sociology* (Delhi), *Economic and Political Weekly* (Mumbai), *Far Eastern Economic Review* (Hongkong), *India Today* (Delhi), *Journal of Asian Studies* (Ann Arbor, Michigan), *Journal of Commonwealth and Comparative Politics* (London), *Keesings Contemporary Archives* (London), *Modern Asian Studies* (Cambridge), *Pacific Affairs* (Vancouver, British Columbia), *Seminar* (Delhi), *South Asia* (Armidale, New South Wales), *South Asia Research* (London). Online national and provincial Indian dailies can be accessed at *http://newsdirectory.com/news/press/as/in/*

16 - diversities of a continent
unities of a civilization
20 - diversity of Europe in India alone
24 - " mind universes
29 - religion cohesion / conflict
44 - dowries female infanticide
47 - superordinate female
49 - panchayati raj + female
51 - urban → slowly to 1 mil
55 - villages arenas not communities
59/60 - origin of caste
61 - anatomical / zoological metaphors
dharma - order / duty. Created unequal
62 - purity / pollution + contagion (water / food)
64 - varnadharma - Hindu, caste / jati - India - "breed"
66 - new world of Dalit presidents + CMs.
69 - sanskritization / upward mobility
71 - wealth + power rule
72 - Indian society - particles tapestry? mosaic
73 - caste / jati colonization of govt. institutions
74 - Muslim caste / jatis
77 - ↑ movement
80 - Gandhi / Ambedkar re: Dalits
90 ff - political groupings
92 - OBCs 5000 castes / 52% of population
93 - 2001 divisions - incroyable
impacts for S. Asia

103/104 - panchayati - raj
105 - 1992 ... 73rd amend
108 - multi-nation state of nation - provinces
- homelands → states
110 - Dravidinadu
111 - linguistic states 1953 - 55 - 60 - 66
113 - 400 STs - 80 million
issues confronted à la monsoon / over + over again
125 - university education
132 - Princely states 1/3 of India - parallel imperium
500
153 - satyagraha / dharna
truth / insistence
156 - Jallianwallah bagh massacre 1919
160 - Saiyid Ahmad Bareilly - à la Wahhabi
161 - izzat
162 - Muslim backwardness Saiyid Ahmad Khan
Aligarh
166 - 1906 Muslims / Brits
169 - Partition
175 - political dynasties
181 ff. - corruption
190 - Hindu secularism
191 - partition nationalized communalism -
207 - if Kashmir goes to Pakistan
213 - nuclear cataclysm
215 - Pakistan businessmen re: Kashmir

Index